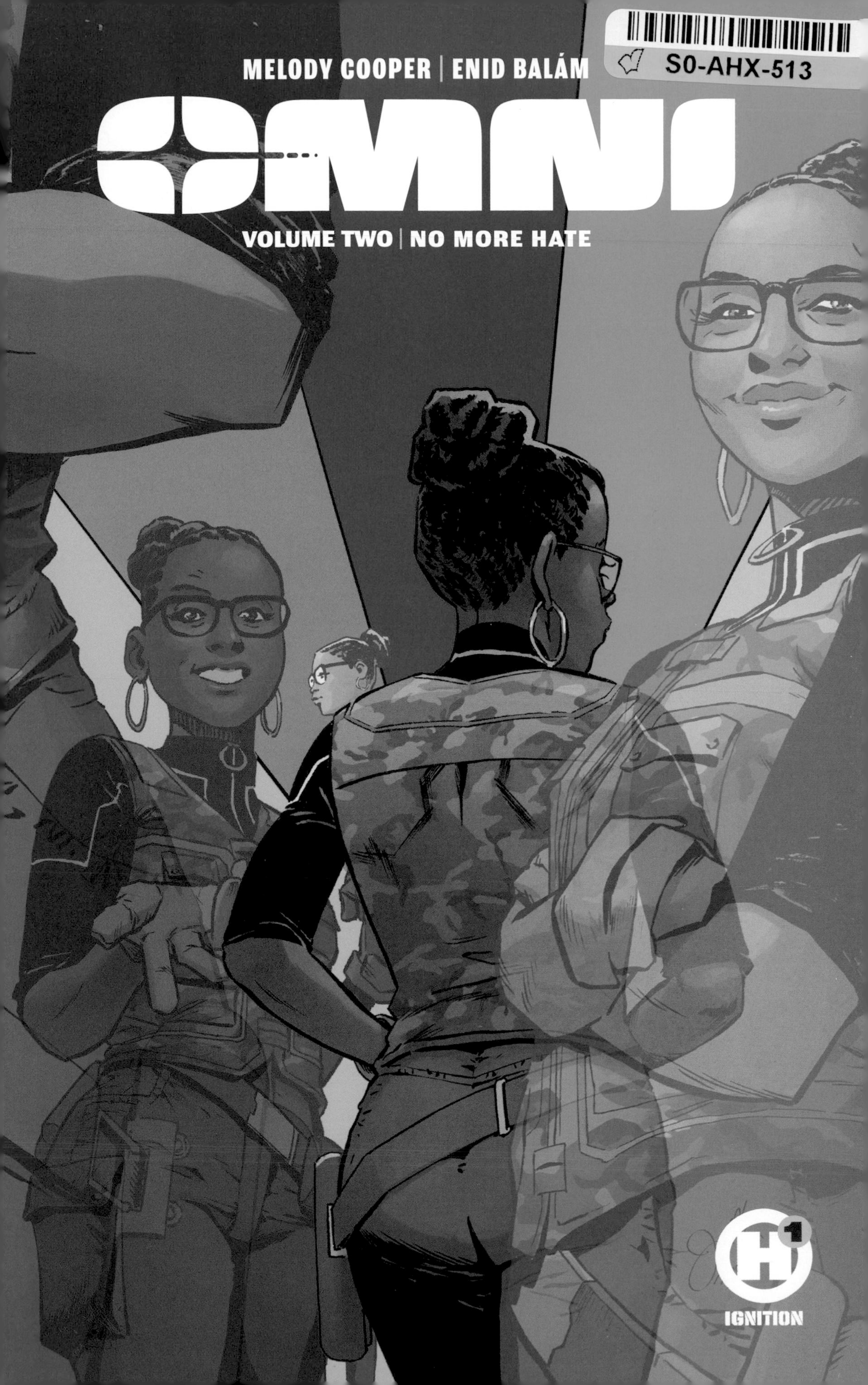
MELODY COOPER | ENID BALÁM
OMNI
VOLUME TWO | NO MORE HATE
IGNITION

OMNI

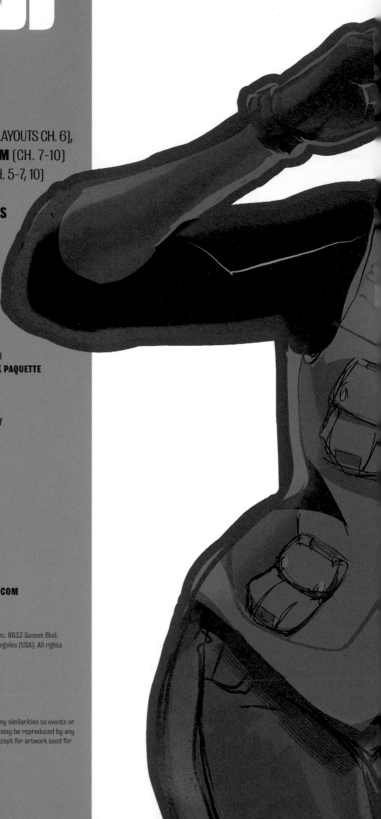

WRITER | **MELODY COOPER**
ARTISTS | **GIOVANNI VALLETTA** (CH. 5, LAYOUTS CH. 6),
CRIS BOLSON (CH. 6) AND **ENID BALÁM** (CH. 7-10)
COLOR ARTISTS | **BRYAN VALENZA** (CH. 5-7, 10)
AND **ROB SCHWAGER** (CH. 8-9)
LETTERS | **A LARGER WORLD STUDIOS**
COVER | **DAVE JOHNSON**

STORY CONSULTANT (CH. 5) | **DEVIN GRAYSON**
TITLE PAGE ILLUSTRATION | **JOHNNIE CHRISTMAS** AND
TAMRA BONVILLAIN
PAGES 2-3 ILLUSTRATION | **AFUA RICHARDSON**
PAGE 4 ILLUSTRATION | **YANICK PAQUETTE** AND
LEONARDO PACIAROTTI

SHARED UNIVERSE BASED ON CONCEPTS CREATED WITH
KWANZA OSAJYEFO, CARLA SPEED MCNEIL, YANICK PAQUETTE

PUBLISHER | **MARK WAID**
CHIEF CREATIVE OFFICER | **JOHN CASSADAY**
SENIOR EDITORS | **ROB LEVIN** AND **FABRICE SAPOLSKY**
ASSISTANT EDITOR | **AMANDA LUCIDO**
LOGO DESIGN | **RIAN HUGHES**
SENIOR ART DIRECTOR | **JERRY FRISSEN**
JUNIOR DESIGNER | **RYAN LEWIS**

CEO | **FABRICE GIGER**
COO | **ALEX DONOGHUE**
CFO | **GUILLAUME NOUGARET**
SALES MANAGER | **PEDRO HERNANDEZ**
SALES REPRESENTATIVE | **HARLEY SALBACKA**
DIRECTOR, LICENSING | **EDMOND LEE**
CTO | **BRUNO BARBERI**
RIGHTS AND LICENSING | **LICENSING@HUMANOIDS.COM**
PRESS AND SOCIAL MEDIA | **PR@HUMANOIDS.COM**

OMNI VOL 2: NO MORE HATE This title is a publication of Humanoids, Inc. 8033 Sunset Blvd.
#628, Los Angeles, CA 90046. Copyright © 2021 Humanoids, Inc., Los Angeles (USA). All rights
reserved. Humanoids and its logos are ® and © 2021 Humanoids, Inc.
Library of Congress Control Number: 2019910050

This volume collects OMNI issues 5-10.

H1 is an imprint of Humanoids, Inc.

HUMANOIDS

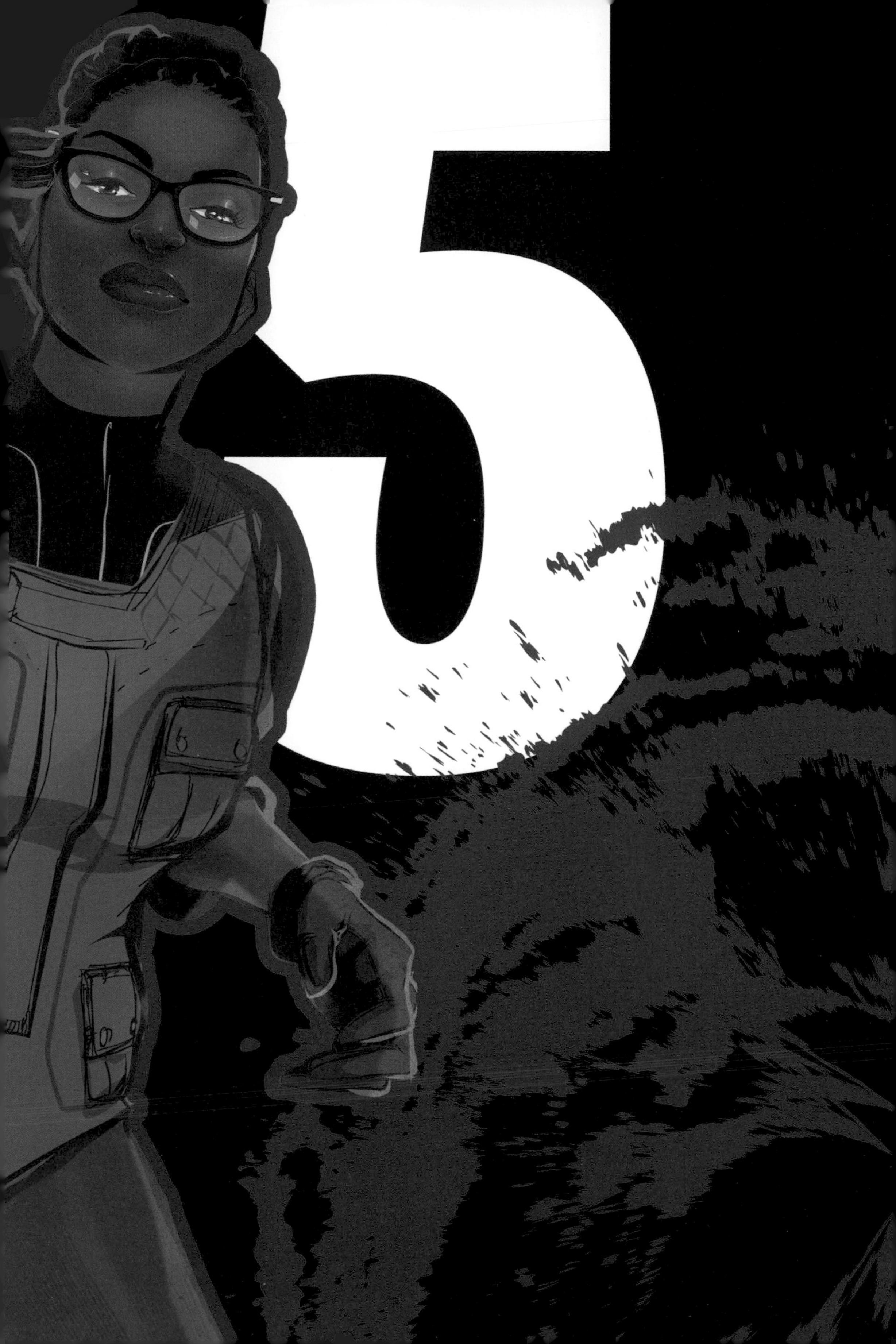

OUR WORLD'S DNA IS CHANGING.

UNPRECEDENTED TECTONIC SHIFTS.
SPONTANEOUS, RADICAL CHANGES IN THE ECO SYSTEMS.

IN MOMENTS OF UNIMAGINABLE AGITATION,
THE HUMAN RACE ACTS OUT IN UNIMAGINABLE WAYS.

AND THOSE ARE JUST INDIVIDUAL SPECIES. NOW EARTH ITSELF IS PUSHING BACK.

CERTAIN PEOPLE WORLDWIDE ARE ... CHANGING. ***TRANSFORMING***.

IGNITING WITH ***POWER***.

H1 IGNITION

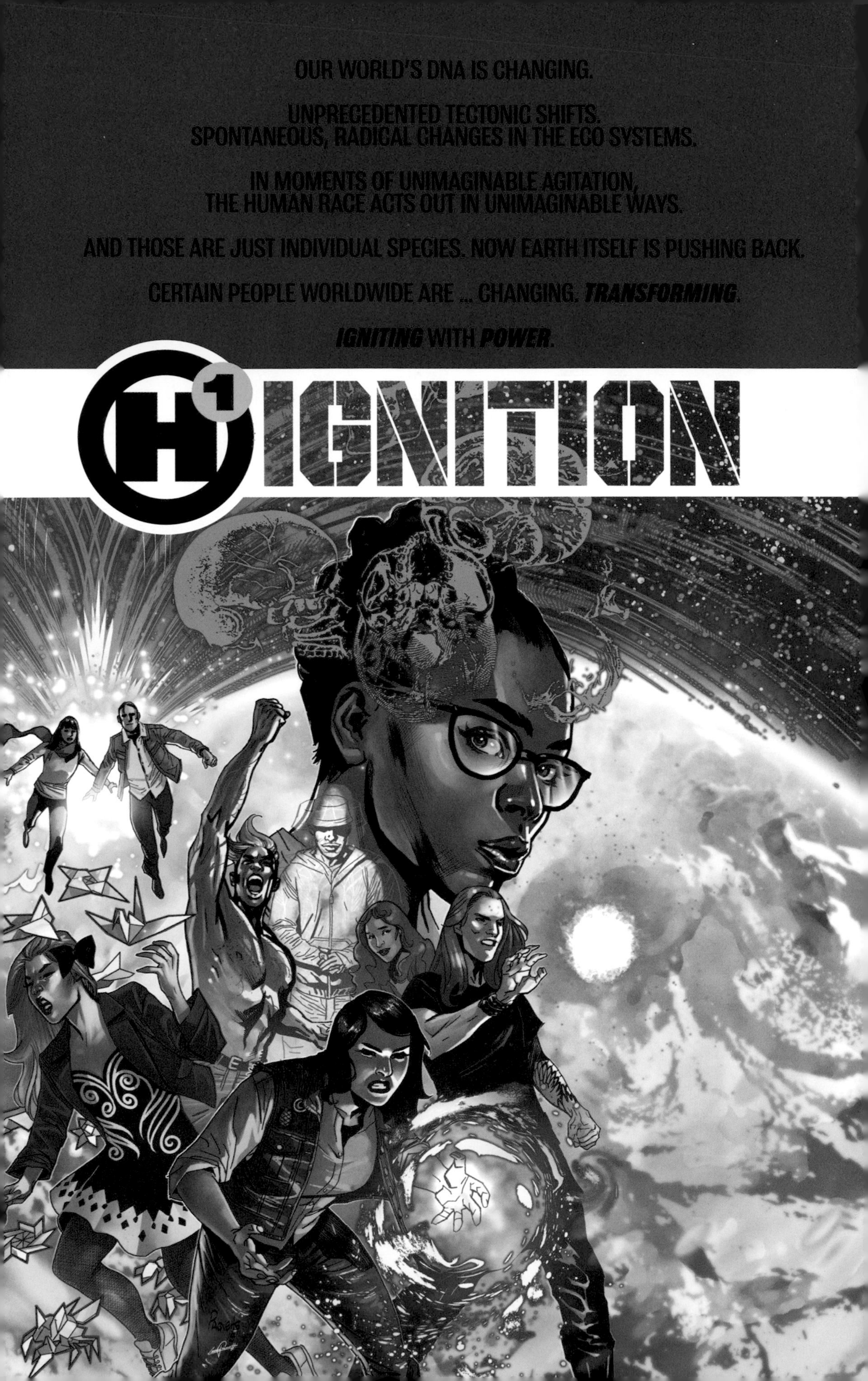

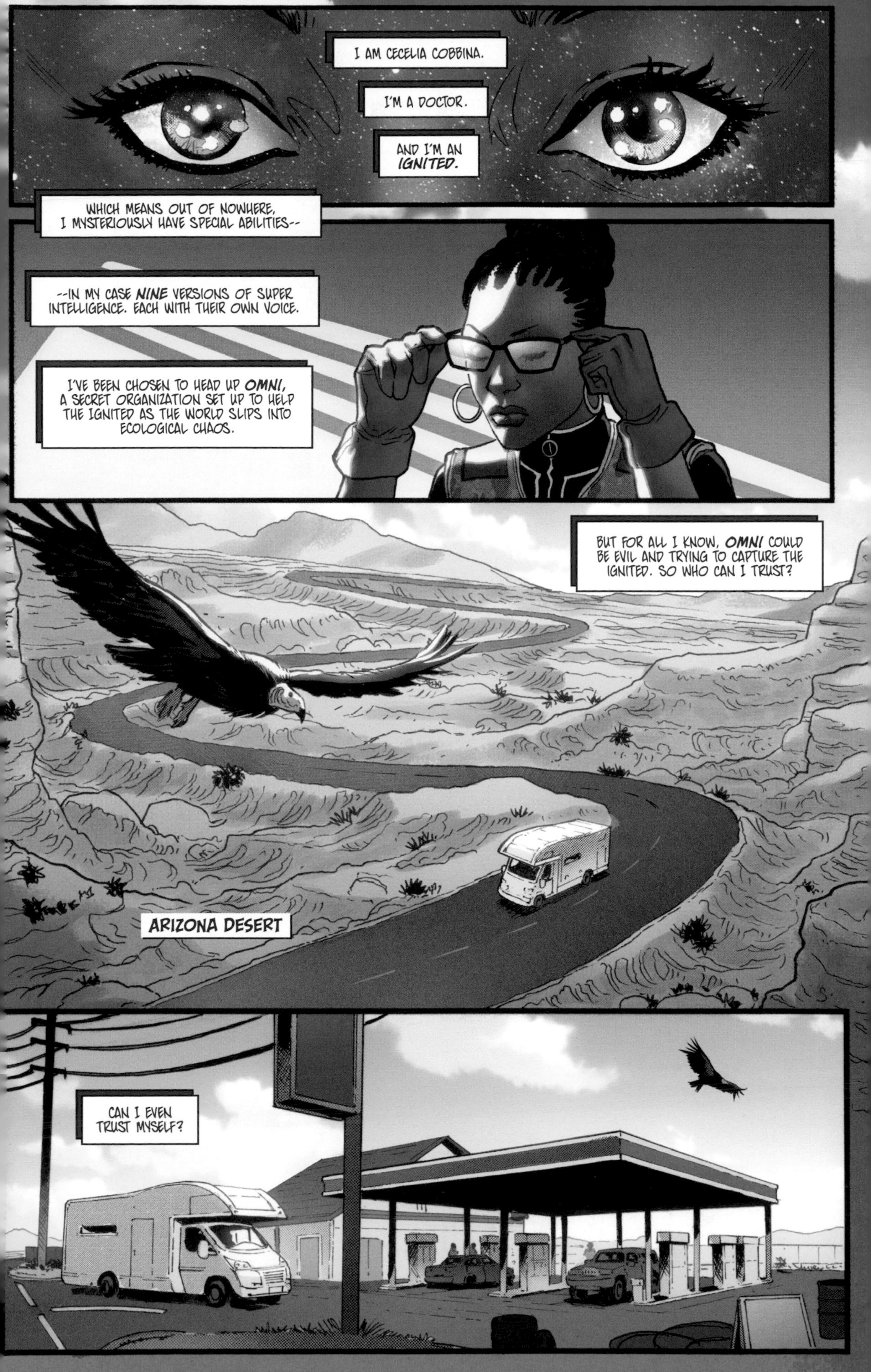
I AM CECELIA COBBINA.
I'M A DOCTOR.
AND I'M AN IGNITED.
WHICH MEANS OUT OF NOWHERE, I MYSTERIOUSLY HAVE SPECIAL ABILITIES--
--IN MY CASE NINE VERSIONS OF SUPER INTELLIGENCE. EACH WITH THEIR OWN VOICE.
I'VE BEEN CHOSEN TO HEAD UP OMNI, A SECRET ORGANIZATION SET UP TO HELP THE IGNITED AS THE WORLD SLIPS INTO ECOLOGICAL CHAOS.
BUT FOR ALL I KNOW, OMNI COULD BE EVIL AND TRYING TO CAPTURE THE IGNITED. SO WHO CAN I TRUST?
ARIZONA DESERT
CAN I EVEN TRUST MYSELF?

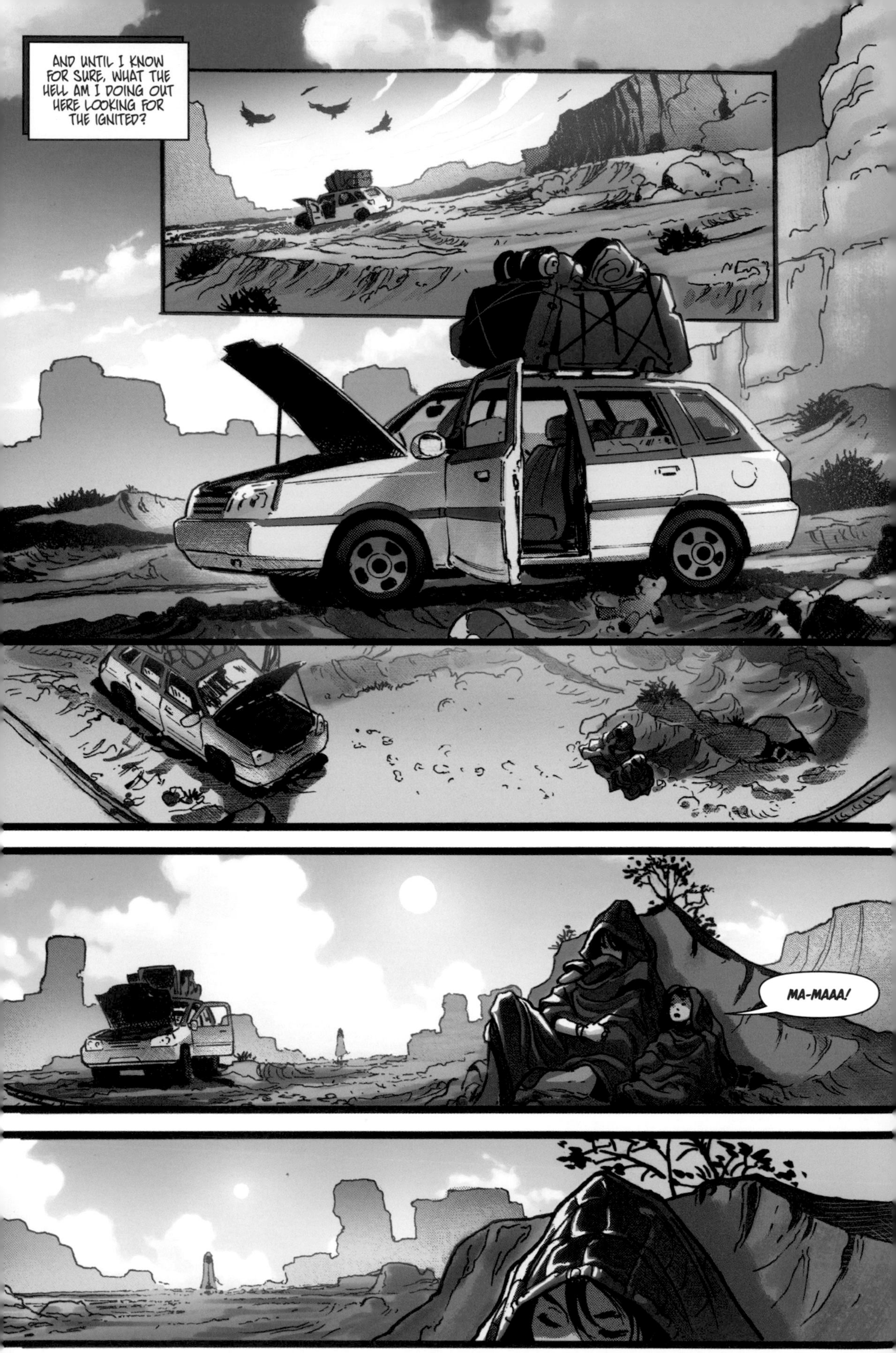
AND UNTIL I KNOW FOR SURE, WHAT THE HELL AM I DOING OUT HERE LOOKING FOR THE IGNITED?
MA-MAAA!

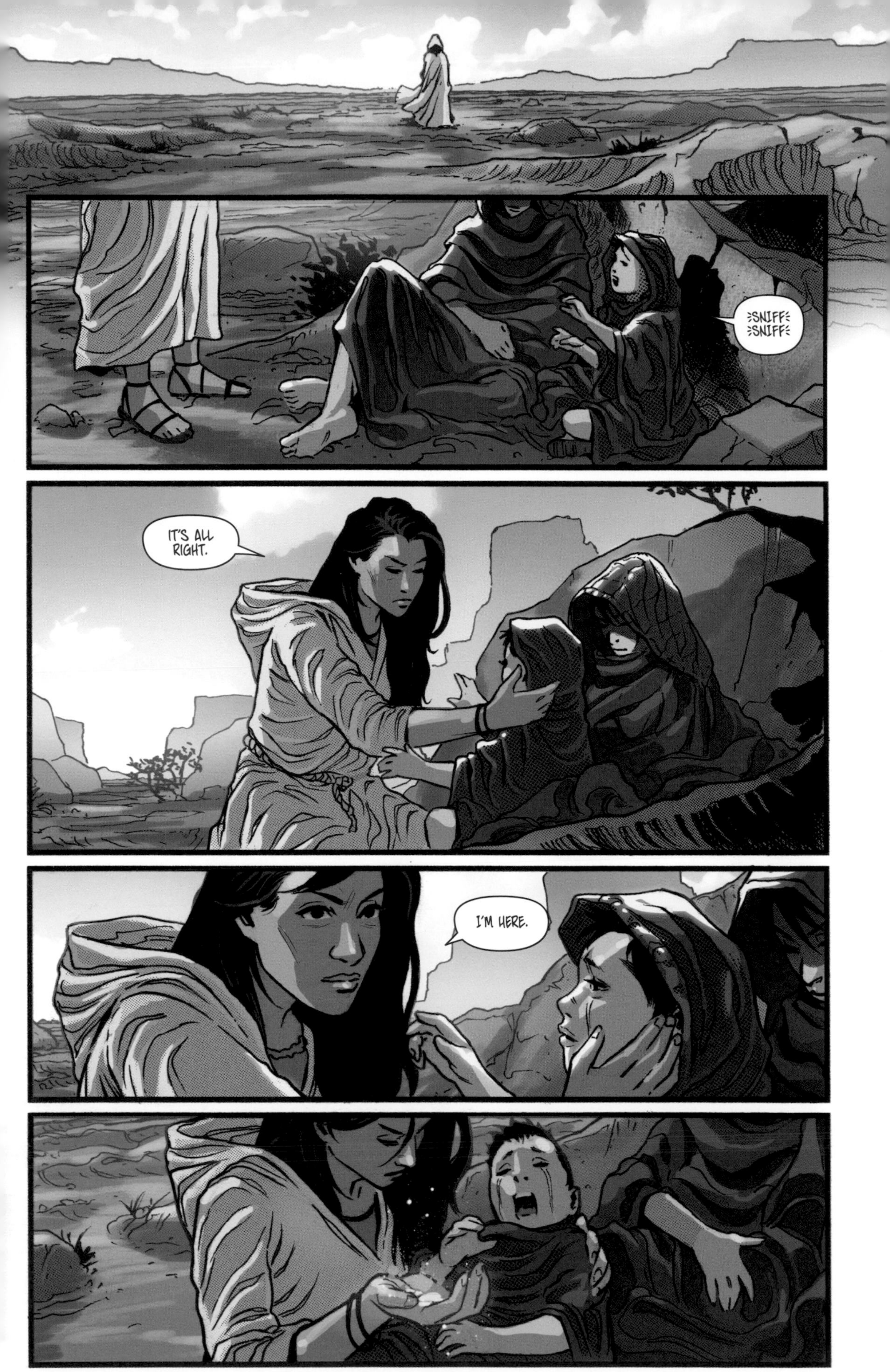
SNIFF
SNIFF
IT'S ALL RIGHT.
I'M HERE.

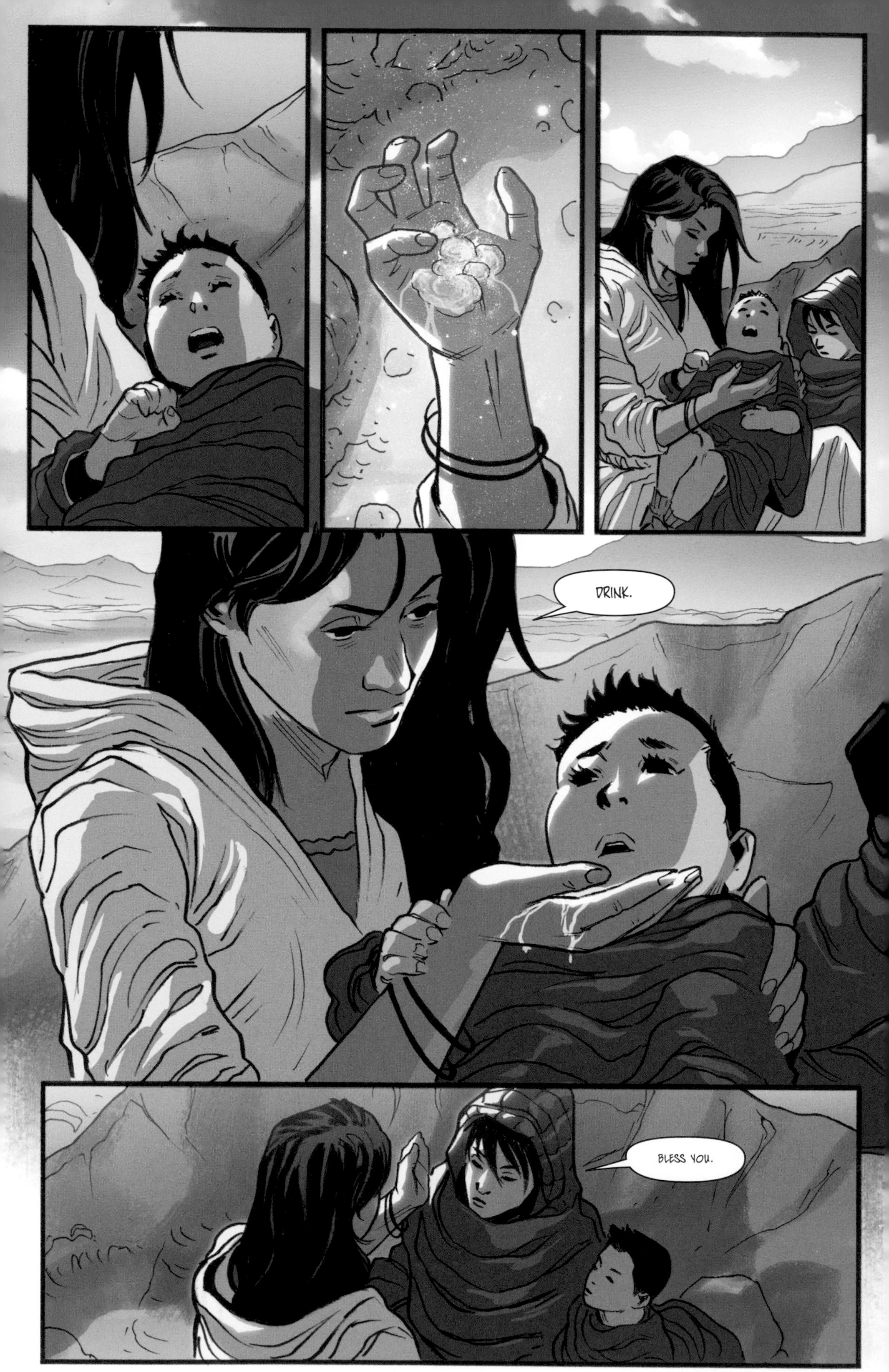
DRINK.
BLESS YOU.

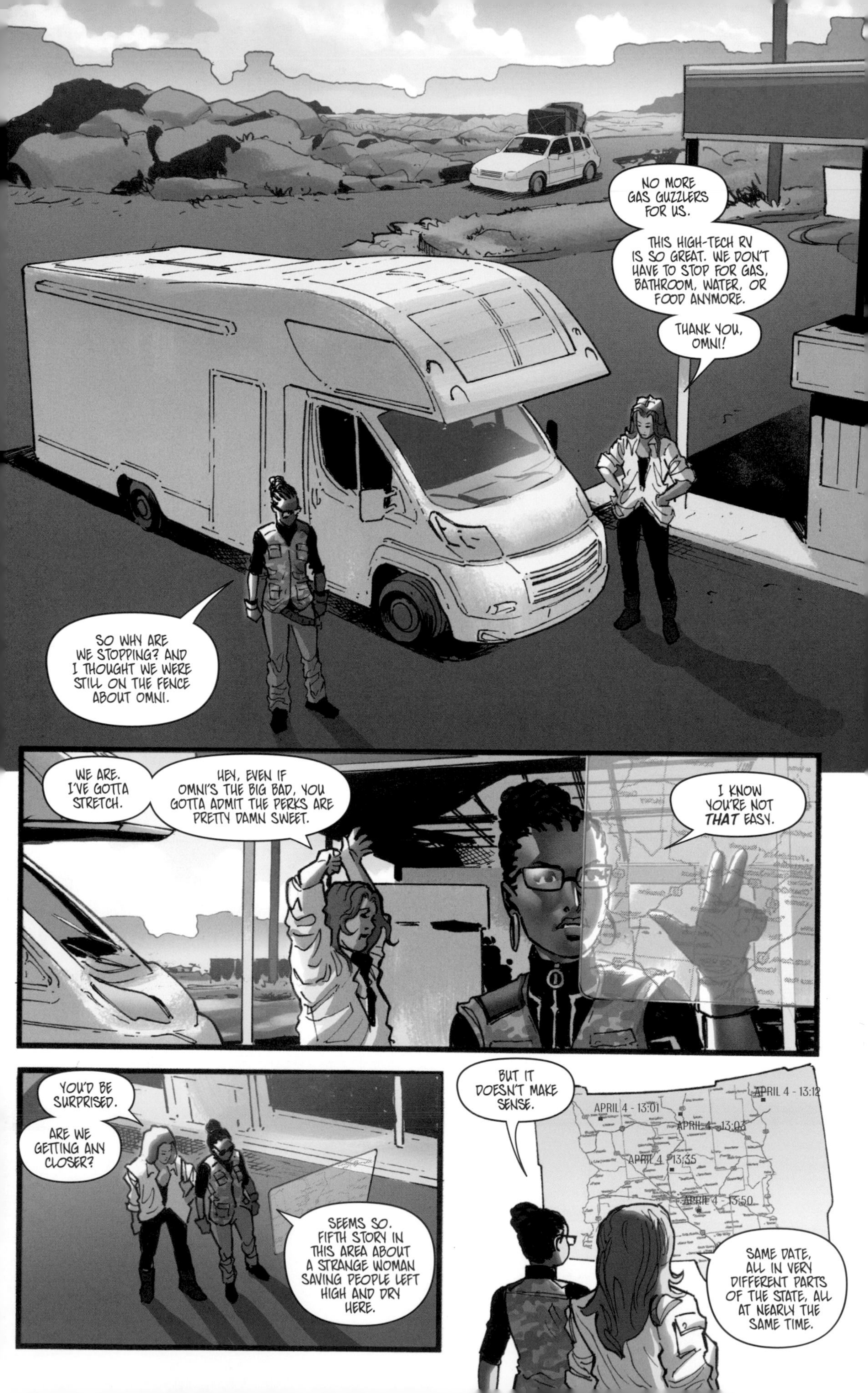
NO MORE GAS GUZZLERS FOR US.
THIS HIGH-TECH RV IS SO GREAT. WE DON'T HAVE TO STOP FOR GAS, BATHROOM, WATER, OR FOOD ANYMORE.
THANK YOU, OMNI!
SO WHY ARE WE STOPPING? AND I THOUGHT WE WERE STILL ON THE FENCE ABOUT OMNI.
WE ARE. I'VE GOTTA STRETCH.
HEY, EVEN IF OMNI'S THE BIG BAD, YOU GOTTA ADMIT THE PERKS ARE PRETTY DAMN SWEET.
I KNOW YOU'RE NOT ***THAT*** EASY.
YOU'D BE SURPRISED.
ARE WE GETTING ANY CLOSER?
SEEMS SO. FIFTH STORY IN THIS AREA ABOUT A STRANGE WOMAN SAVING PEOPLE LEFT HIGH AND DRY HERE.
BUT IT DOESN'T MAKE SENSE.
APRIL 4 - 13:01
APRIL 4 - 13:12
APRIL 4 - 13:03
APRIL 4 - 13:35
APRIL 4 - 13:50
SAME DATE, ALL IN VERY DIFFERENT PARTS OF THE STATE, ALL AT NEARLY THE SAME TIME.

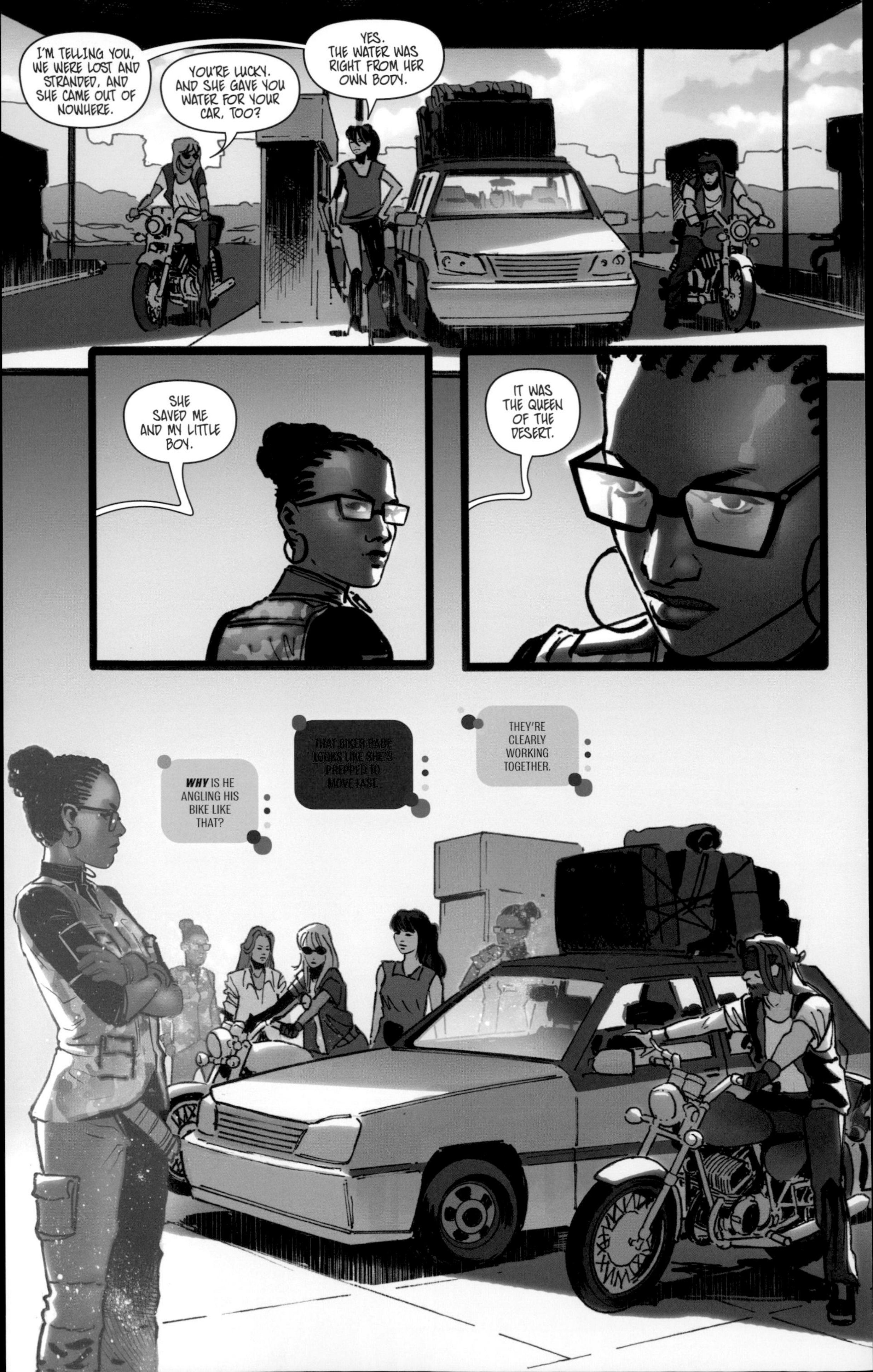
I'M TELLING YOU, WE WERE LOST AND STRANDED, AND SHE CAME OUT OF NOWHERE.
YOU'RE LUCKY. AND SHE GAVE YOU WATER FOR YOUR CAR, TOO?
YES. THE WATER WAS RIGHT FROM HER OWN BODY.
SHE SAVED ME AND MY LITTLE BOY.
IT WAS THE QUEEN OF THE DESERT.
WHY IS HE ANGLING HIS BIKE LIKE THAT?
THAT BIKER BABE LOOKS LIKE SHE'S PREPPED TO MOVE FAST.
THEY'RE CLEARLY WORKING TOGETHER.

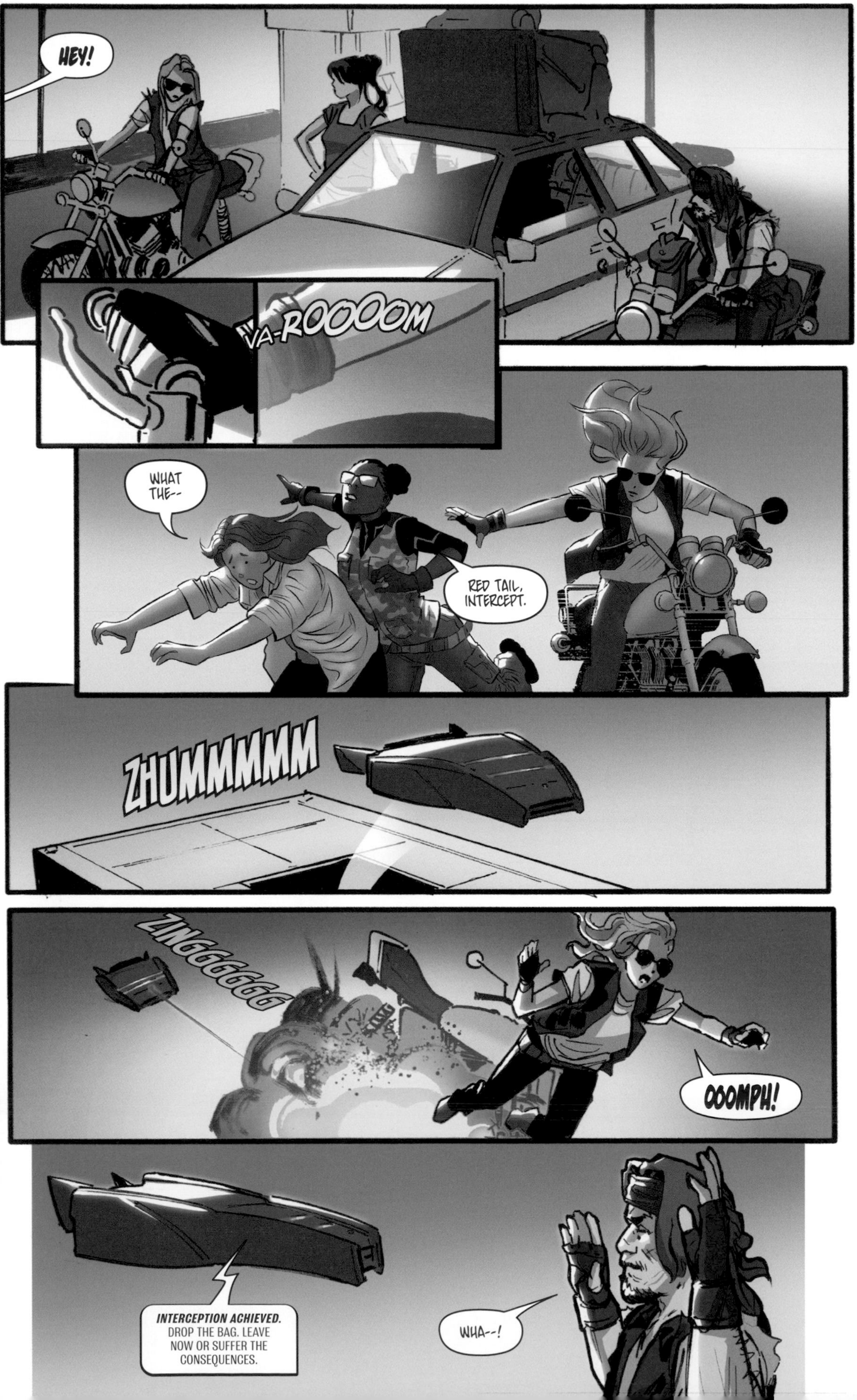
HEY!
VA-ROOOOOM
WHAT THE--
RED TAIL, INTERCEPT.
ZHUMMMMM
ZINGGGGGG
OOOMPH!
INTERCEPTION ACHIEVED. DROP THE BAG. LEAVE NOW OR SUFFER THE CONSEQUENCES.
WHA--!

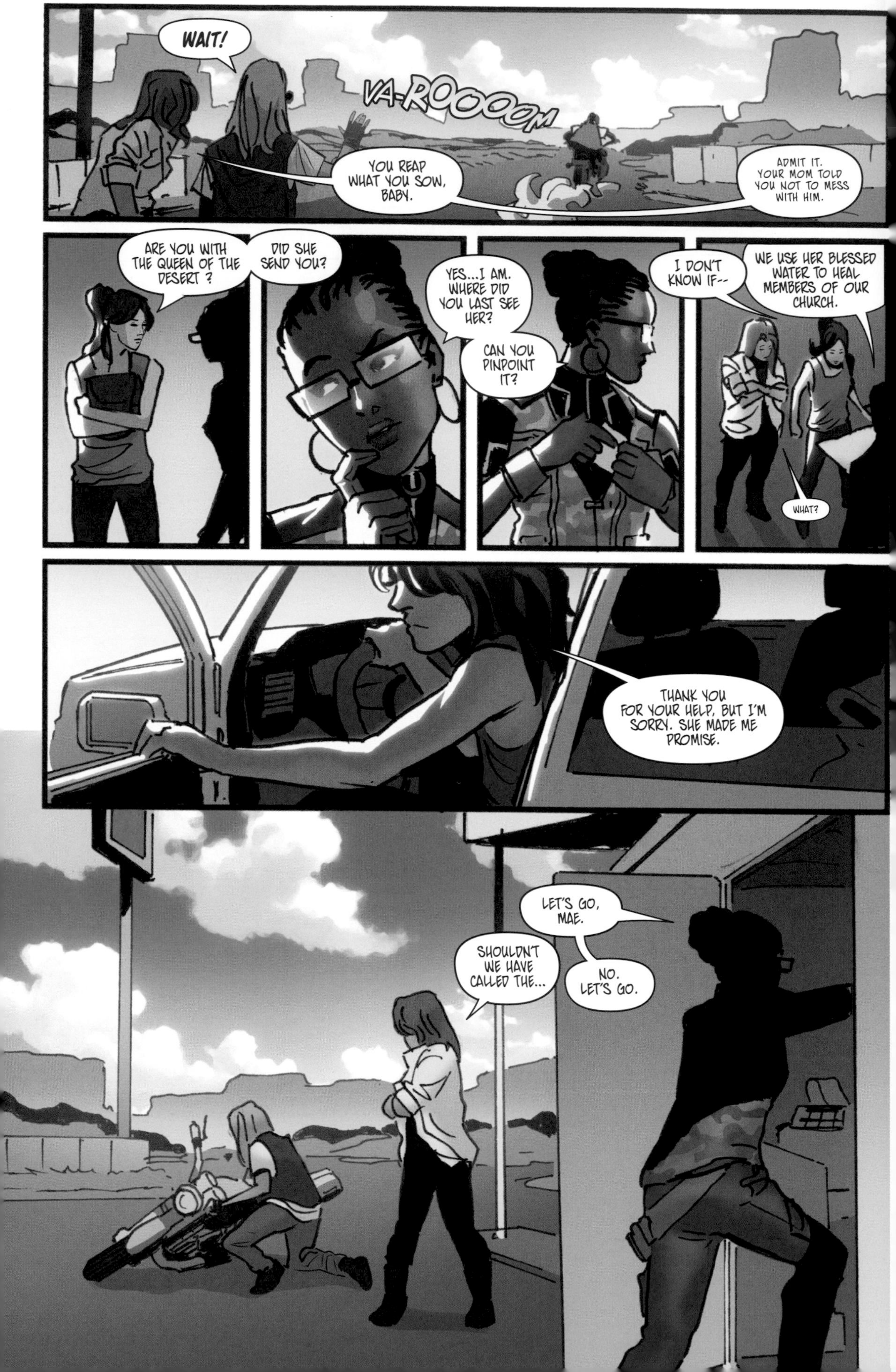
WAIT!
VA-ROOOOOM
YOU REAP WHAT YOU SOW, BABY.
ADMIT IT. YOUR MOM TOLD YOU NOT TO MESS WITH HIM.
ARE YOU WITH THE QUEEN OF THE DESERT ?
DID SHE SEND YOU?
YES...I AM. WHERE DID YOU LAST SEE HER?
CAN YOU PINPOINT IT?
I DON'T KNOW IF--
WE USE HER BLESSED WATER TO HEAL MEMBERS OF OUR CHURCH.
WHAT?
THANK YOU FOR YOUR HELP, BUT I'M SORRY. SHE MADE ME PROMISE.
LET'S GO, MAE.
SHOULDN'T WE HAVE CALLED THE...
NO. LET'S GO.

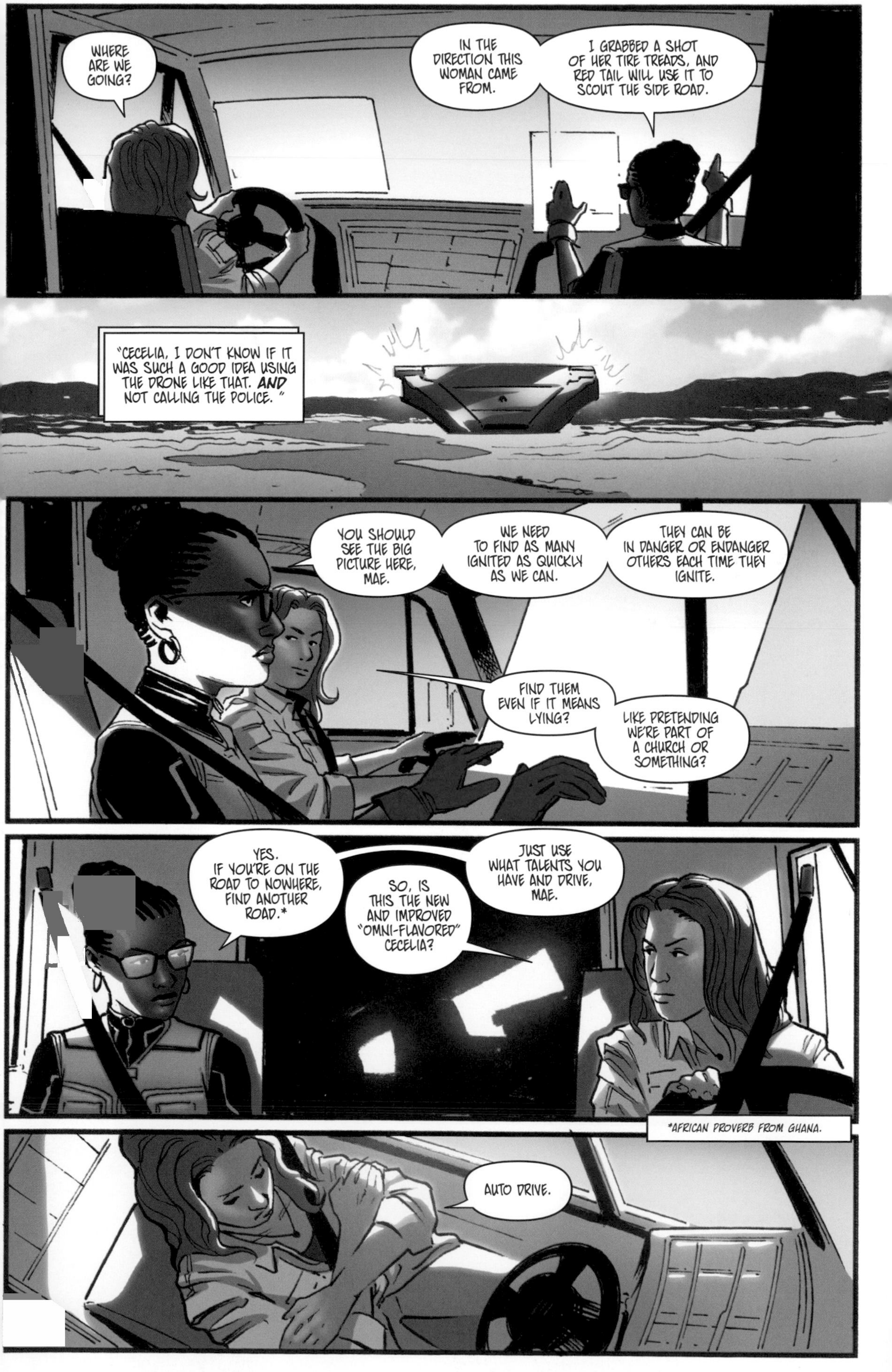
WHERE ARE WE GOING?
IN THE DIRECTION THIS WOMAN CAME FROM.
I GRABBED A SHOT OF HER TIRE TREADS, AND RED TAIL WILL USE IT TO SCOUT THE SIDE ROAD.
"CECELIA, I DON'T KNOW IF IT WAS SUCH A GOOD IDEA USING THE DRONE LIKE THAT. **AND** NOT CALLING THE POLICE."
YOU SHOULD SEE THE BIG PICTURE HERE, MAE.
WE NEED TO FIND AS MANY IGNITED AS QUICKLY AS WE CAN.
THEY CAN BE IN DANGER OR ENDANGER OTHERS EACH TIME THEY IGNITE.
FIND THEM EVEN IF IT MEANS LYING?
LIKE PRETENDING WE'RE PART OF A CHURCH OR SOMETHING?
YES. IF YOU'RE ON THE ROAD TO NOWHERE, FIND ANOTHER ROAD.*
JUST USE WHAT TALENTS YOU HAVE AND DRIVE, MAE.
SO, IS THIS THE NEW AND IMPROVED "OMNI-FLAVORED" CECELIA?
*AFRICAN PROVERB FROM GHANA.
AUTO DRIVE.

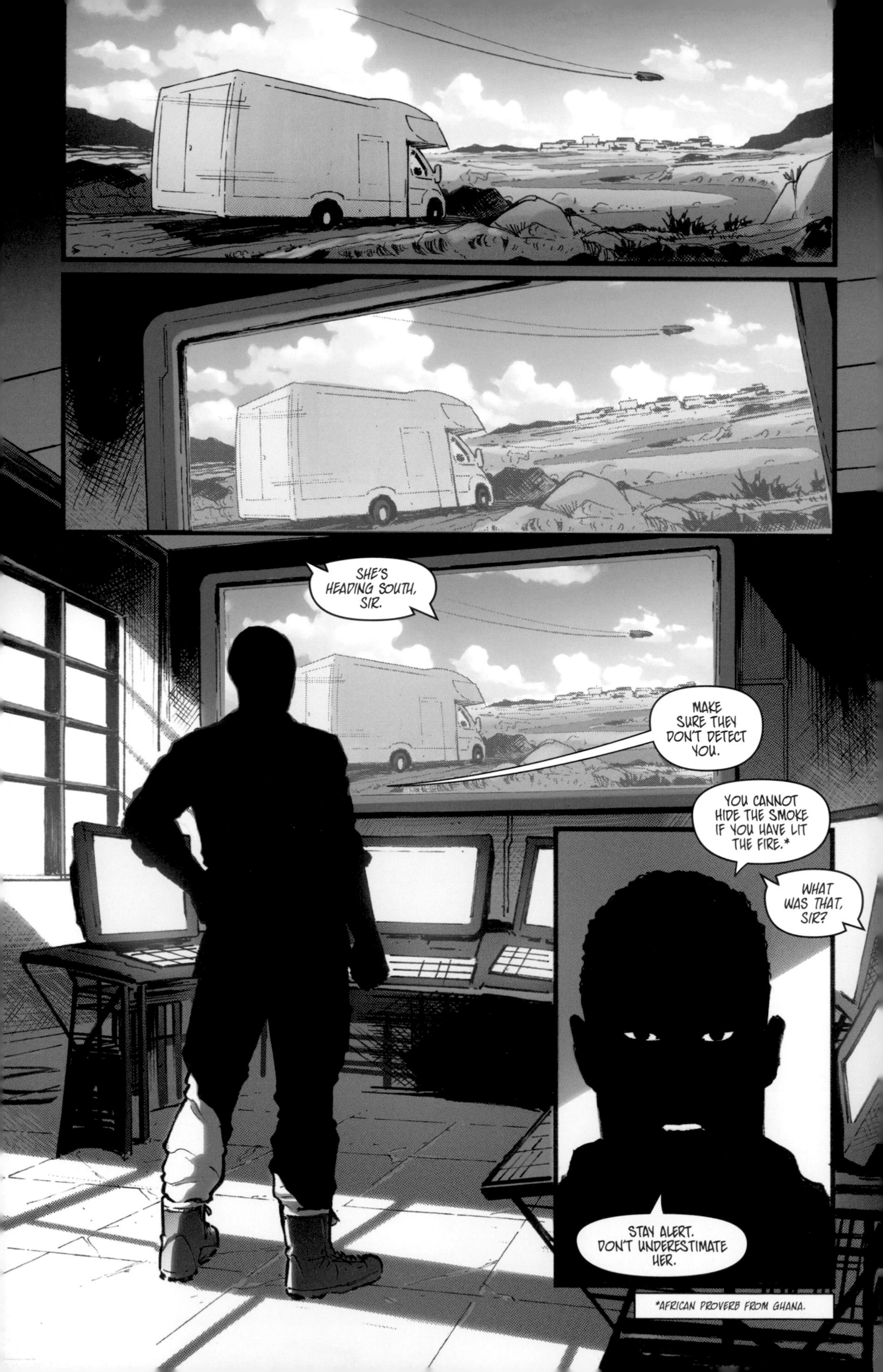
SHE'S HEADING SOUTH, SIR.
MAKE SURE THEY DON'T DETECT YOU.
YOU CANNOT HIDE THE SMOKE IF YOU HAVE LIT THE FIRE.*
WHAT WAS THAT, SIR?
STAY ALERT. DON'T UNDERESTIMATE HER.
*AFRICAN PROVERB FROM GHANA.

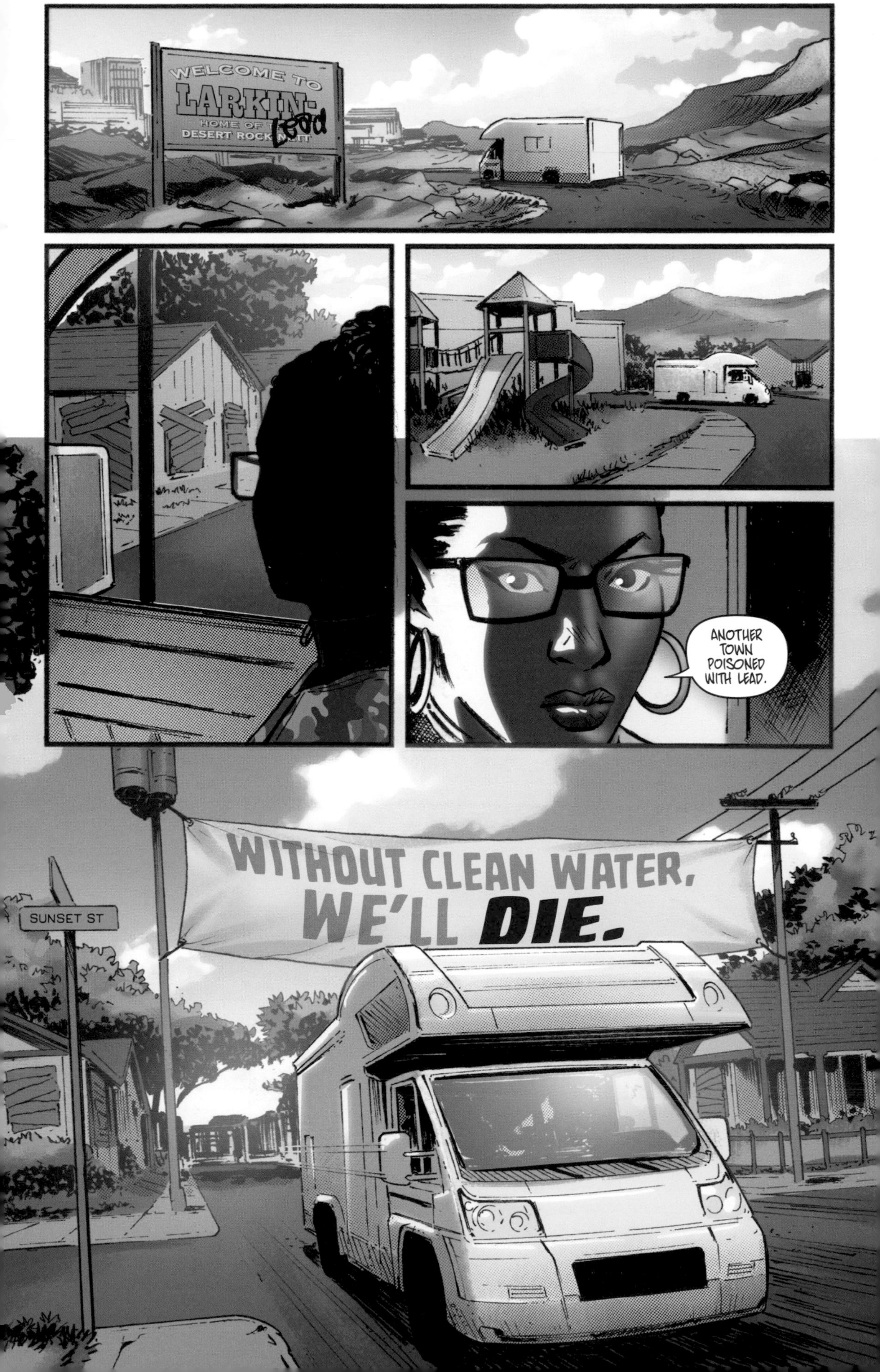
WELCOME TO
LARKIN-
Lead
ANOTHER TOWN POISONED WITH LEAD.
WITHOUT CLEAN WATER, WE'LL DIE.
SUNSET ST

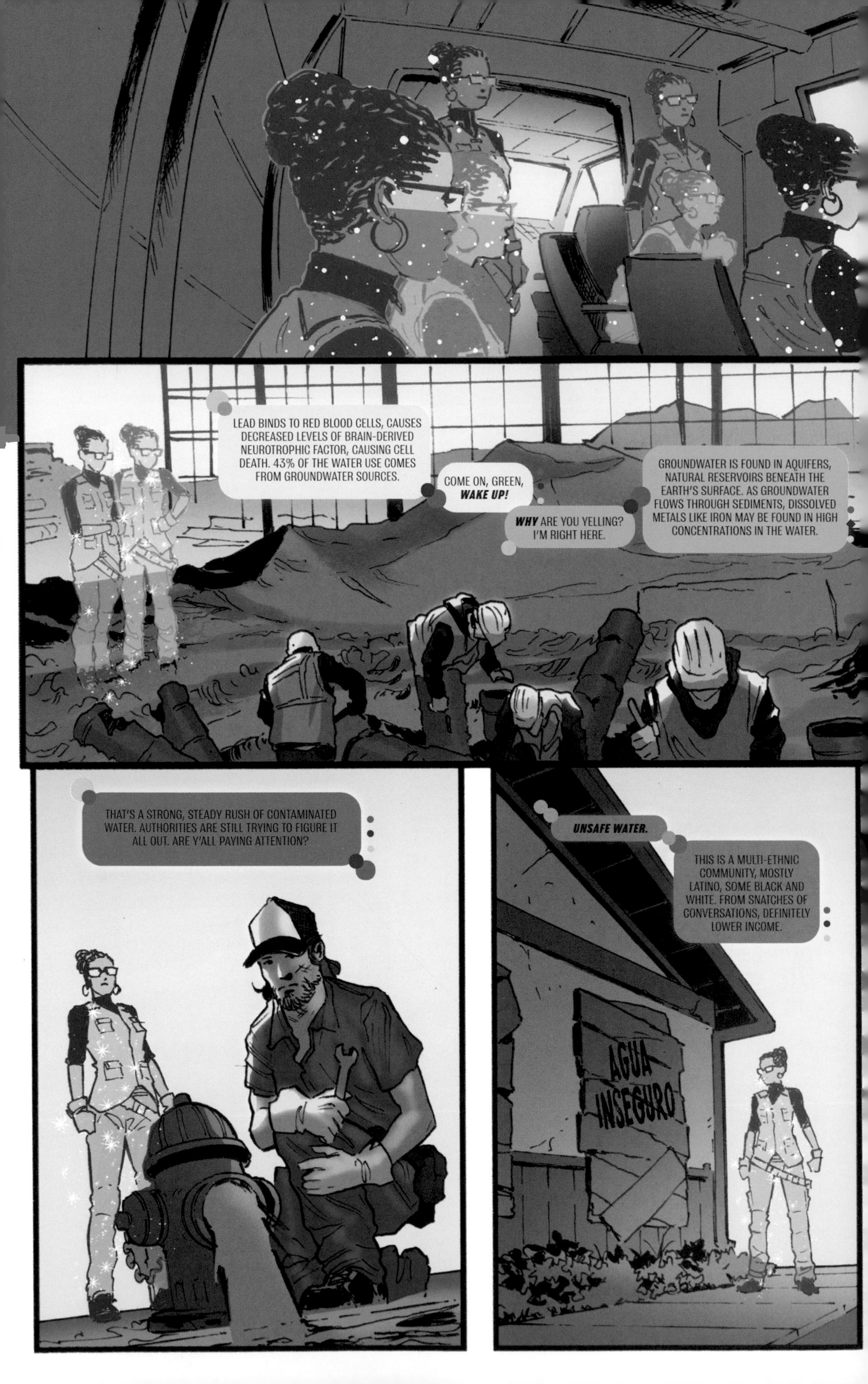
LEAD BINDS TO RED BLOOD CELLS, CAUSES DECREASED LEVELS OF BRAIN-DERIVED NEUROTROPHIC FACTOR, CAUSING CELL DEATH. 43% OF THE WATER USE COMES FROM GROUNDWATER SOURCES.
COME ON, GREEN, WAKE UP!
WHY ARE YOU YELLING? I'M RIGHT HERE.
GROUNDWATER IS FOUND IN AQUIFERS, NATURAL RESERVOIRS BENEATH THE EARTH'S SURFACE. AS GROUNDWATER FLOWS THROUGH SEDIMENTS, DISSOLVED METALS LIKE IRON MAY BE FOUND IN HIGH CONCENTRATIONS IN THE WATER.
THAT'S A STRONG, STEADY RUSH OF CONTAMINATED WATER. AUTHORITIES ARE STILL TRYING TO FIGURE IT ALL OUT. ARE Y'ALL PAYING ATTENTION?
UNSAFE WATER.
THIS IS A MULTI-ETHNIC COMMUNITY, MOSTLY LATINO, SOME BLACK AND WHITE. FROM SNATCHES OF CONVERSATIONS, DEFINITELY LOWER INCOME.
AGUA INSEGURO

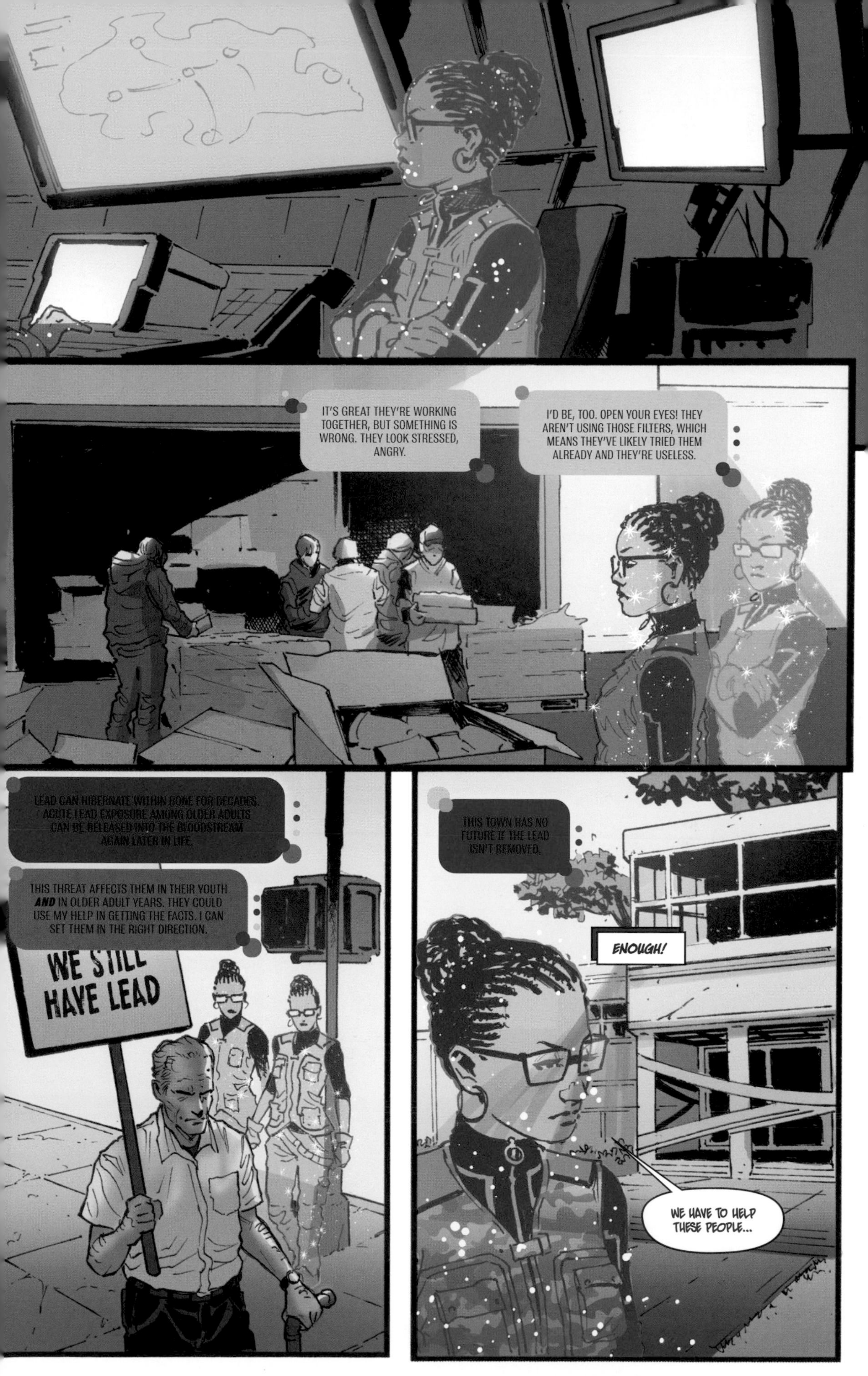
IT'S GREAT THEY'RE WORKING TOGETHER, BUT SOMETHING IS WRONG. THEY LOOK STRESSED, ANGRY.
I'D BE, TOO. OPEN YOUR EYES! THEY AREN'T USING THOSE FILTERS, WHICH MEANS THEY'VE LIKELY TRIED THEM ALREADY AND THEY'RE USELESS.
LEAD CAN HIBERNATE WITHIN BONE FOR DECADES. ACUTE LEAD EXPOSURE AMONG OLDER ADULTS CAN BE RELEASED INTO THE BLOODSTREAM AGAIN LATER IN LIFE.
THIS THREAT AFFECTS THEM IN THEIR YOUTH **AND** IN OLDER ADULT YEARS. THEY COULD USE MY HELP IN GETTING THE FACTS. I CAN SET THEM IN THE RIGHT DIRECTION.
WE STILL HAVE LEAD
THIS TOWN HAS NO FUTURE IF THE LEAD ISN'T REMOVED.
ENOUGH!
WE HAVE TO HELP THESE PEOPLE...

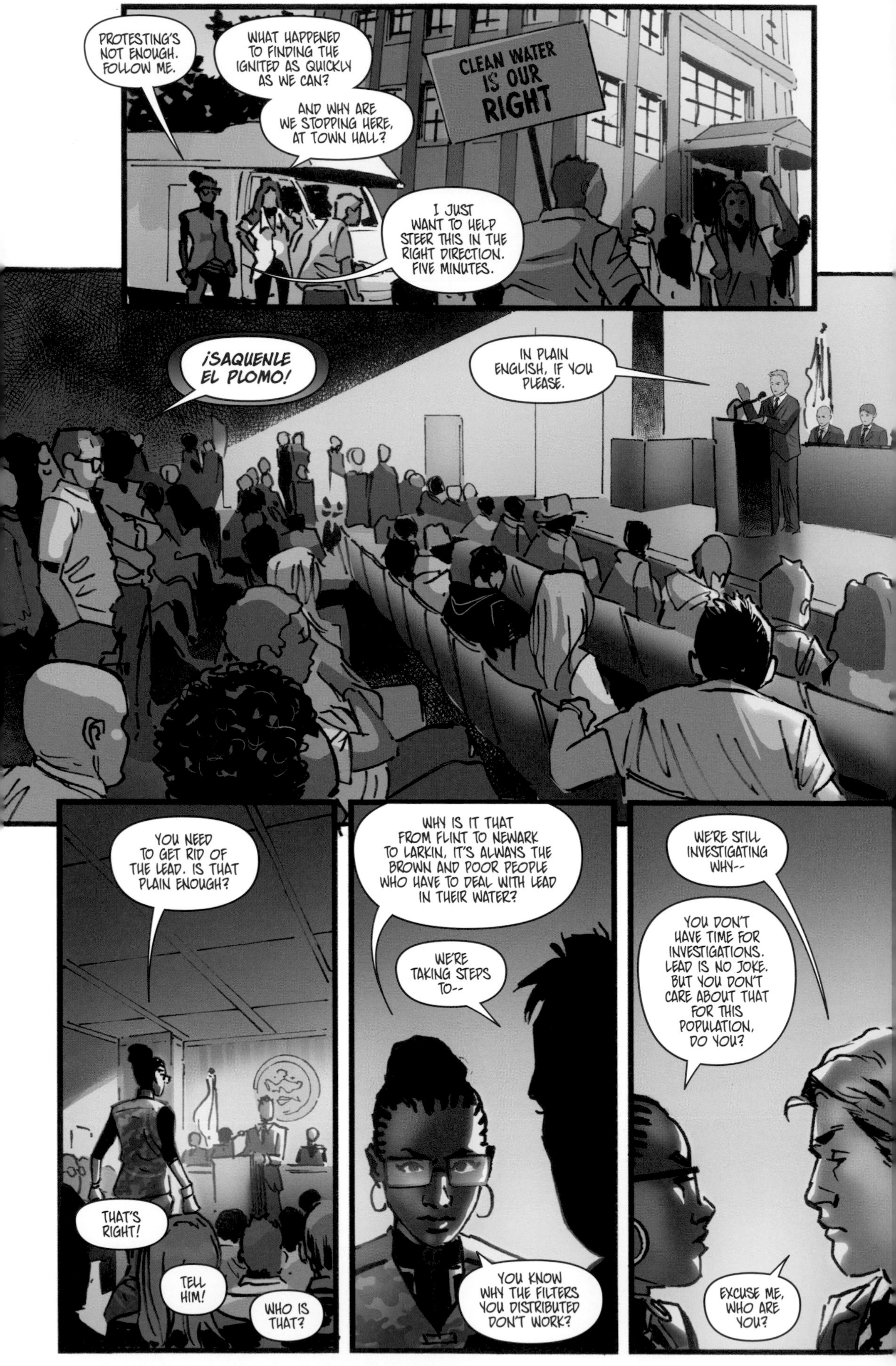
PROTESTING'S NOT ENOUGH. FOLLOW ME.
WHAT HAPPENED TO FINDING THE IGNITED AS QUICKLY AS WE CAN?
AND WHY ARE WE STOPPING HERE, AT TOWN HALL?
CLEAN WATER IS OUR RIGHT
I JUST WANT TO HELP STEER THIS IN THE RIGHT DIRECTION. FIVE MINUTES.
¡SAQUENLE EL PLOMO!
IN PLAIN ENGLISH, IF YOU PLEASE.
YOU NEED TO GET RID OF THE LEAD. IS THAT PLAIN ENOUGH?
THAT'S RIGHT!
TELL HIM!
WHO IS THAT?
WHY IS IT THAT FROM FLINT TO NEWARK TO LARKIN, IT'S ALWAYS THE BROWN AND POOR PEOPLE WHO HAVE TO DEAL WITH LEAD IN THEIR WATER?
WE'RE TAKING STEPS TO--
YOU KNOW WHY THE FILTERS YOU DISTRIBUTED DON'T WORK?
WE'RE STILL INVESTIGATING WHY--
YOU DON'T HAVE TIME FOR INVESTIGATIONS. LEAD IS NO JOKE. BUT YOU DON'T CARE ABOUT THAT FOR THIS POPULATION, DO YOU?
EXCUSE ME, WHO ARE YOU?

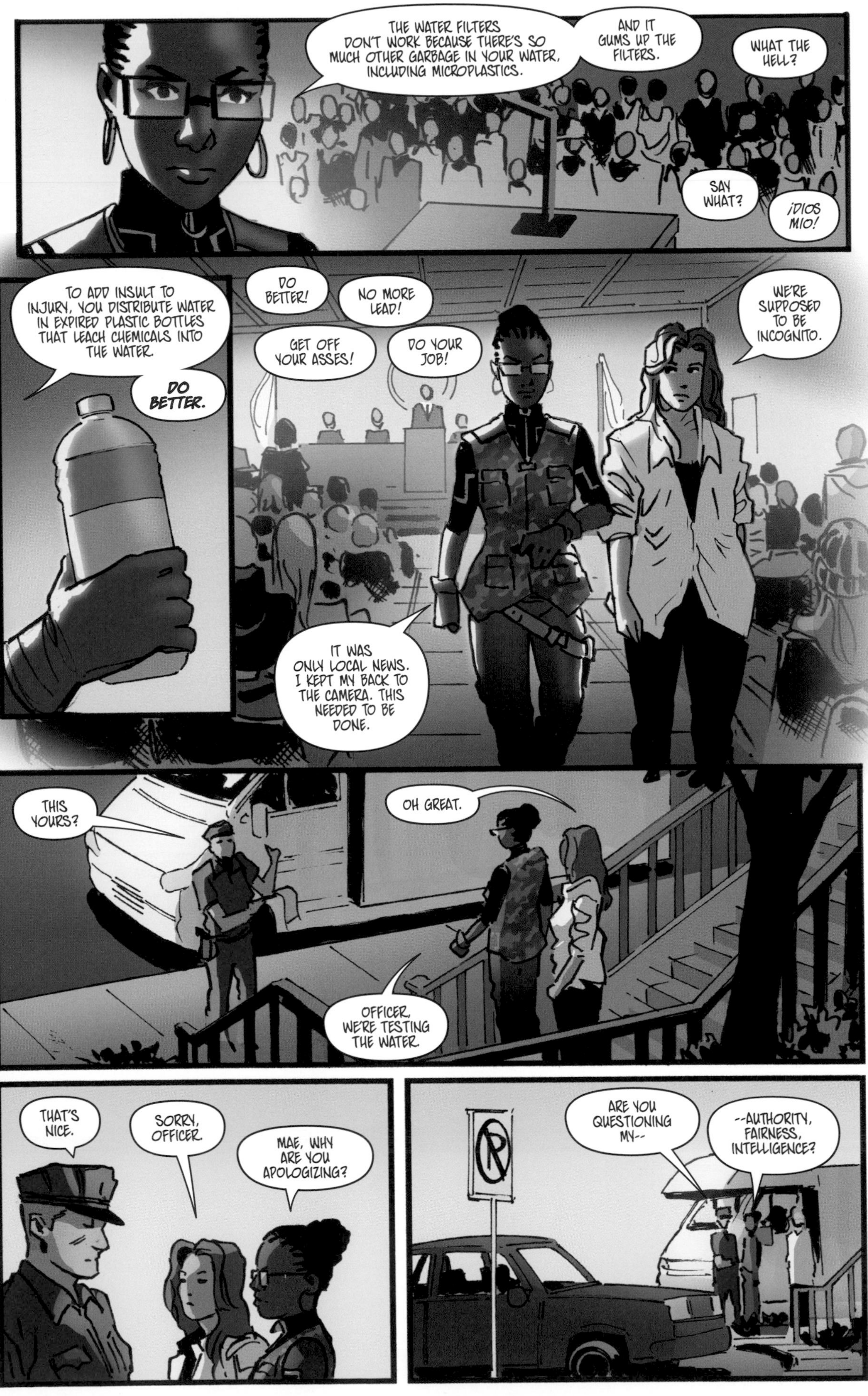
THE WATER FILTERS DON'T WORK BECAUSE THERE'S SO MUCH OTHER GARBAGE IN YOUR WATER, INCLUDING MICROPLASTICS.
AND IT GUMS UP THE FILTERS.
WHAT THE HELL?
SAY WHAT?
¡DIOS MIO!
TO ADD INSULT TO INJURY, YOU DISTRIBUTE WATER IN EXPIRED PLASTIC BOTTLES THAT LEACH CHEMICALS INTO THE WATER.
DO BETTER.
DO BETTER!
NO MORE LEAD!
GET OFF YOUR ASSES!
DO YOUR JOB!
WE'RE SUPPOSED TO BE INCOGNITO.
IT WAS ONLY LOCAL NEWS. I KEPT MY BACK TO THE CAMERA. THIS NEEDED TO BE DONE.
THIS YOURS?
OH GREAT.
OFFICER, WE'RE TESTING THE WATER.
THAT'S NICE.
SORRY, OFFICER.
MAE, WHY ARE YOU APOLOGIZING?
ARE YOU QUESTIONING MY--
--AUTHORITY, FAIRNESS, INTELLIGENCE?

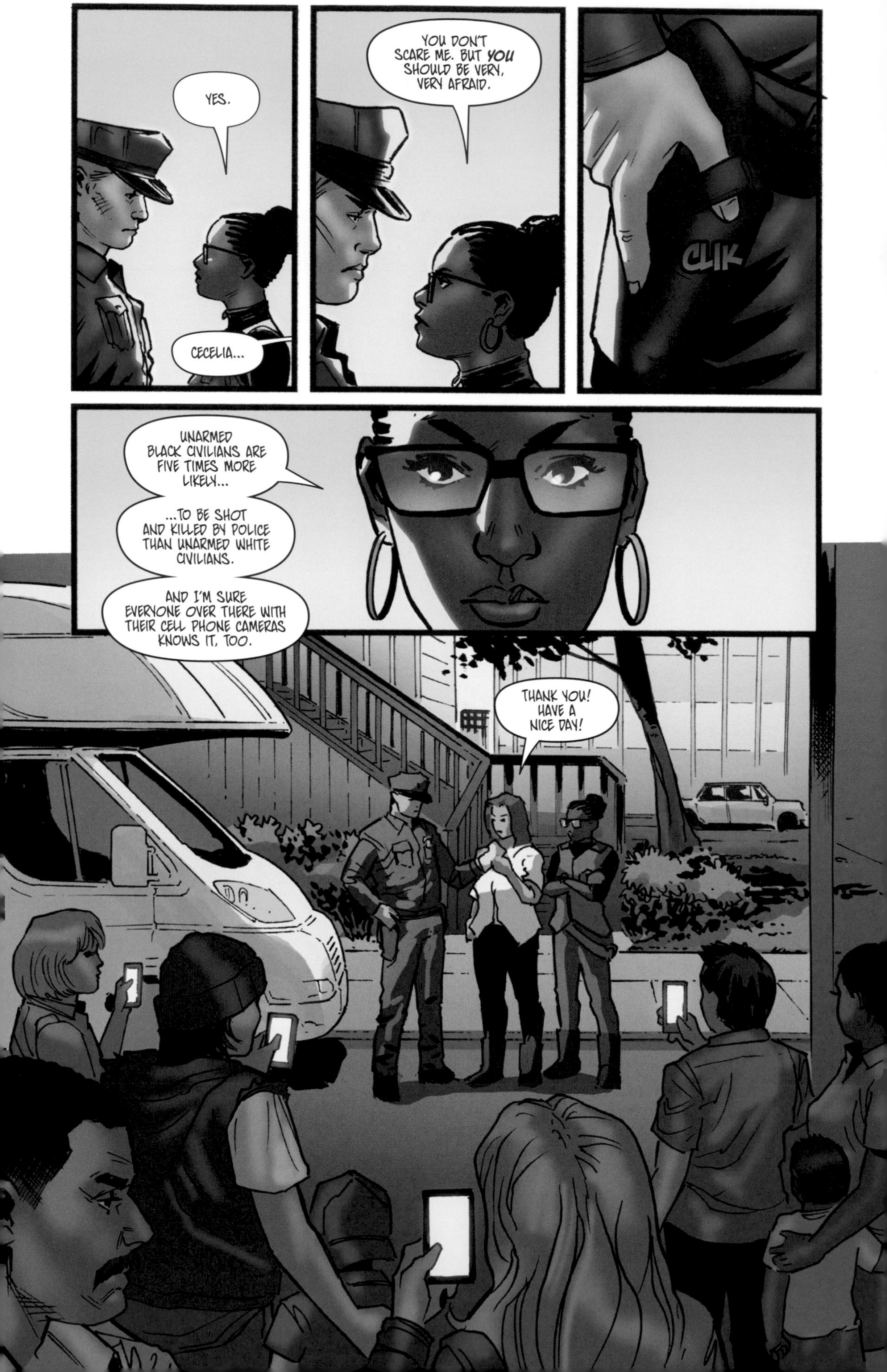
YES.
CECELIA...
YOU DON'T SCARE ME. BUT YOU SHOULD BE VERY, VERY AFRAID.
CLIK
UNARMED BLACK CIVILIANS ARE FIVE TIMES MORE LIKELY...
...TO BE SHOT AND KILLED BY POLICE THAN UNARMED WHITE CIVILIANS.
AND I'M SURE EVERYONE OVER THERE WITH THEIR CELL PHONE CAMERAS KNOWS IT, TOO.
THANK YOU! HAVE A NICE DAY!

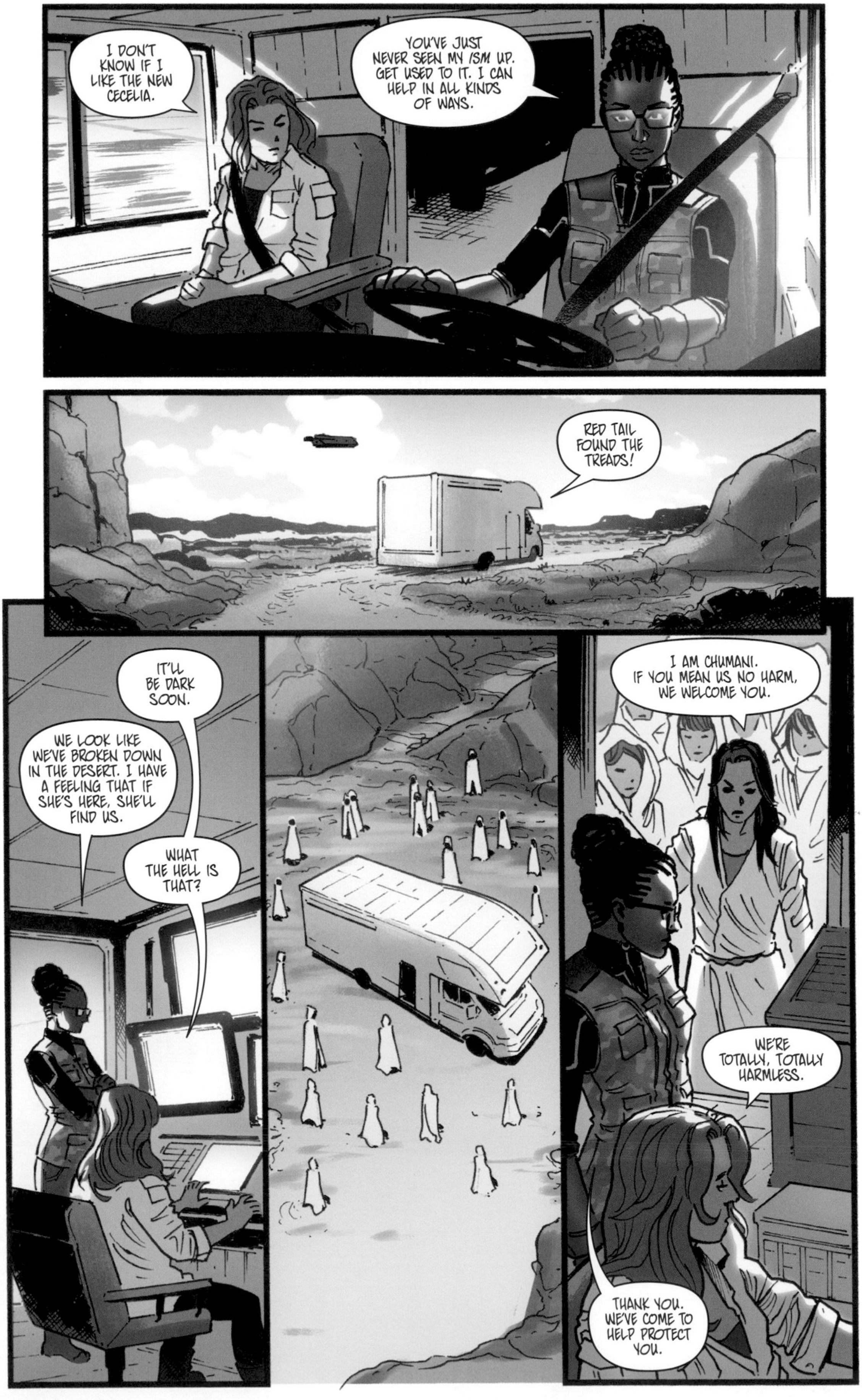
I DON'T KNOW IF I LIKE THE NEW CECELIA.
YOU'VE JUST NEVER SEEN MY ISM UP. GET USED TO IT. I CAN HELP IN ALL KINDS OF WAYS.
RED TAIL FOUND THE TREADS!
IT'LL BE DARK SOON.
WE LOOK LIKE WE'VE BROKEN DOWN IN THE DESERT. I HAVE A FEELING THAT IF SHE'S HERE, SHE'LL FIND US.
WHAT THE HELL IS THAT?
I AM CHUMANI. IF YOU MEAN US NO HARM, WE WELCOME YOU.
WE'RE TOTALLY, TOTALLY HARMLESS.
THANK YOU. WE'VE COME TO HELP PROTECT YOU.

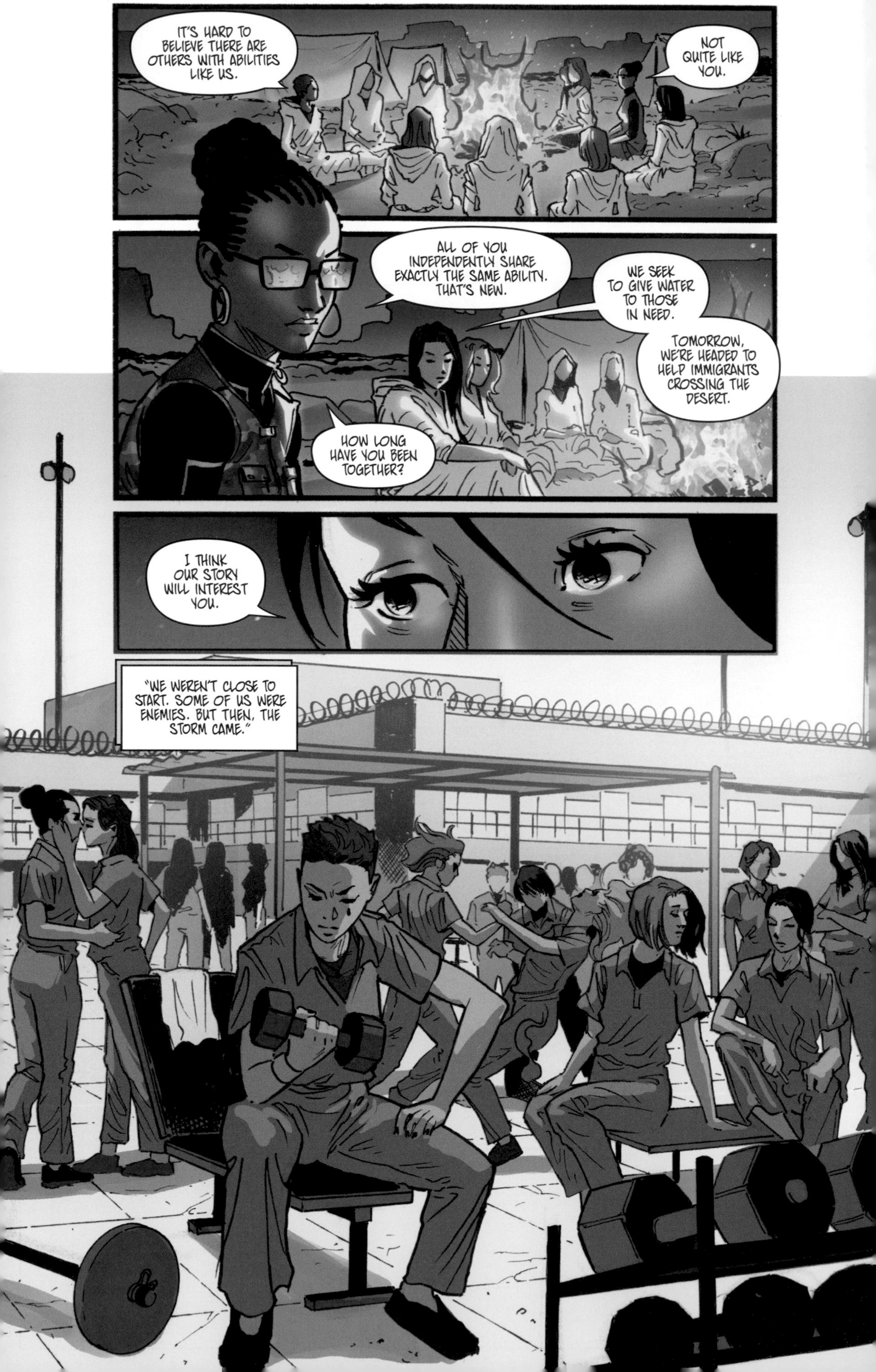
IT'S HARD TO BELIEVE THERE ARE OTHERS WITH ABILITIES LIKE US.
NOT QUITE LIKE YOU.
ALL OF YOU INDEPENDENTLY SHARE EXACTLY THE SAME ABILITY. THAT'S NEW.
WE SEEK TO GIVE WATER TO THOSE IN NEED.
TOMORROW, WE'RE HEADED TO HELP IMMIGRANTS CROSSING THE DESERT.
HOW LONG HAVE YOU BEEN TOGETHER?
I THINK OUR STORY WILL INTEREST YOU.
"WE WEREN'T CLOSE TO START. SOME OF US WERE ENEMIES. BUT THEN, THE STORM CAME."

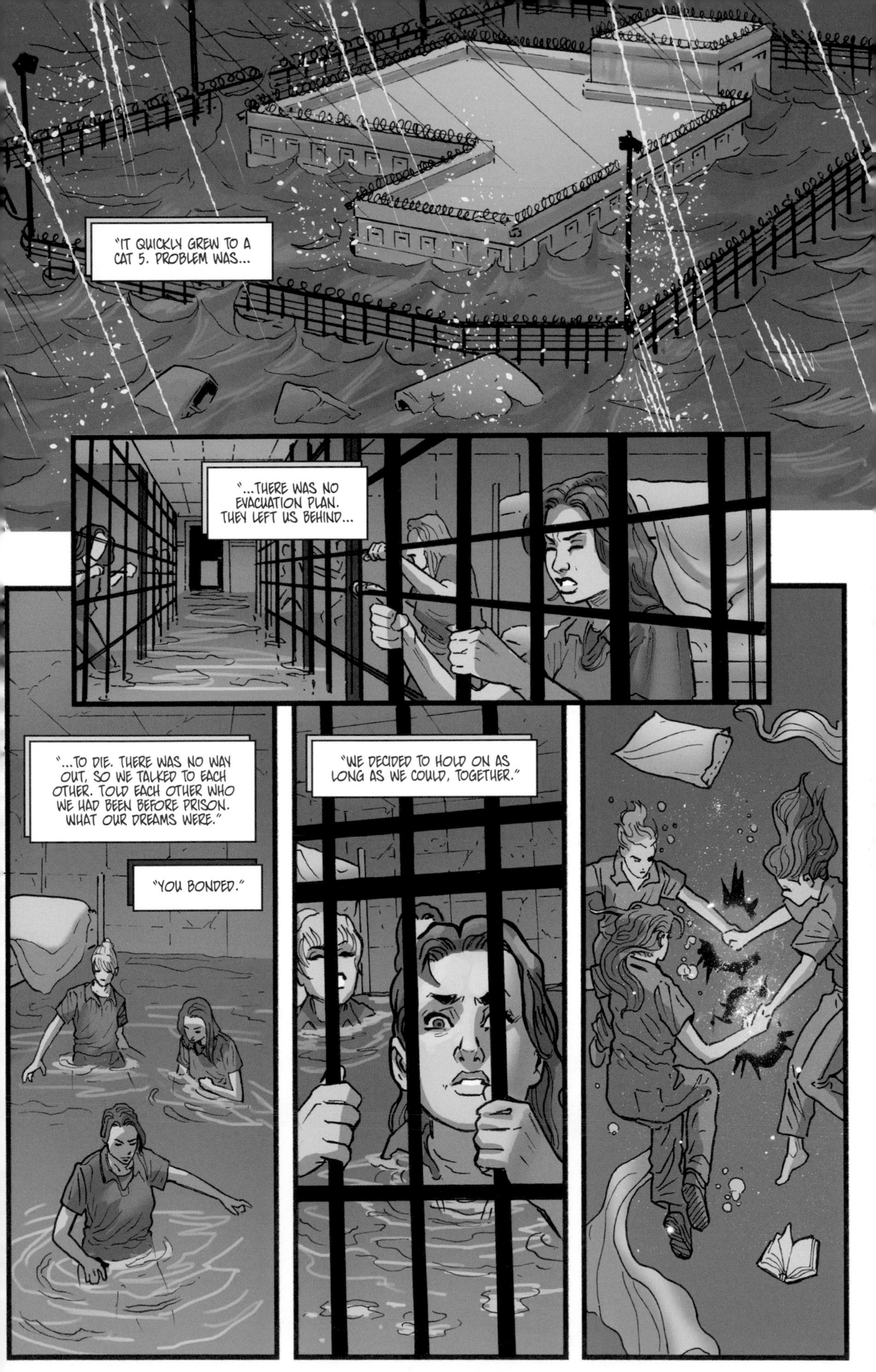
"IT QUICKLY GREW TO A CAT 5. PROBLEM WAS...
"...THERE WAS NO EVACUATION PLAN. THEY LEFT US BEHIND...
"...TO DIE. THERE WAS NO WAY OUT, SO WE TALKED TO EACH OTHER. TOLD EACH OTHER WHO WE HAD BEEN BEFORE PRISON. WHAT OUR DREAMS WERE."
"YOU BONDED."
"WE DECIDED TO HOLD ON AS LONG AS WE COULD, TOGETHER."

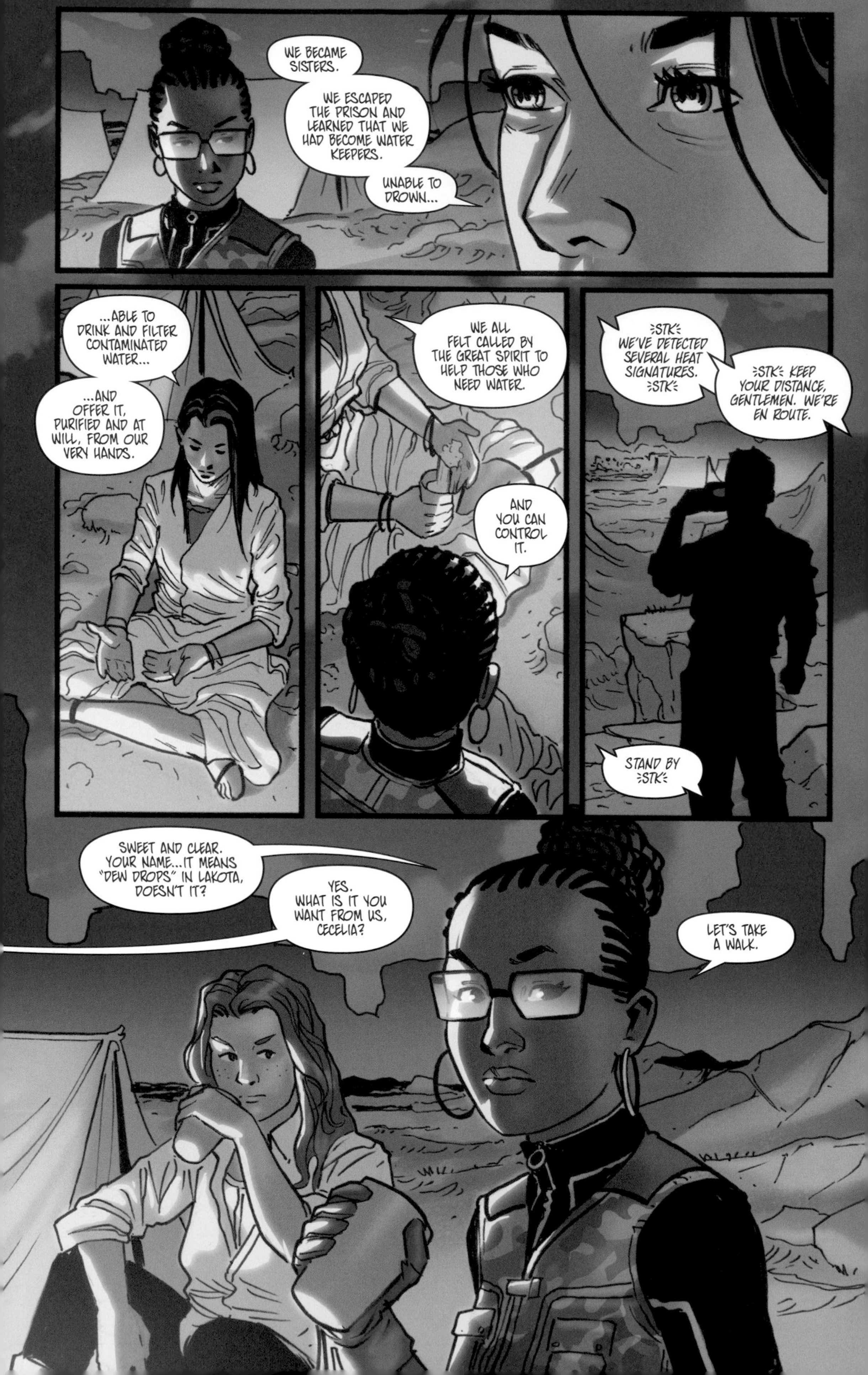
WE BECAME SISTERS.
WE ESCAPED THE PRISON AND LEARNED THAT WE HAD BECOME WATER KEEPERS.
UNABLE TO DROWN...
...ABLE TO DRINK AND FILTER CONTAMINATED WATER...
...AND OFFER IT, PURIFIED AND AT WILL, FROM OUR VERY HANDS.
WE ALL FELT CALLED BY THE GREAT SPIRIT TO HELP THOSE WHO NEED WATER.
AND YOU CAN CONTROL IT.
STK WE'VE DETECTED SEVERAL HEAT SIGNATURES. STK
STK KEEP YOUR DISTANCE, GENTLEMEN. WE'RE EN ROUTE.
STAND BY STK
SWEET AND CLEAR. YOUR NAME...IT MEANS "DEW DROPS" IN LAKOTA, DOESN'T IT?
YES. WHAT IS IT YOU WANT FROM US, CECELIA?
LET'S TAKE A WALK.

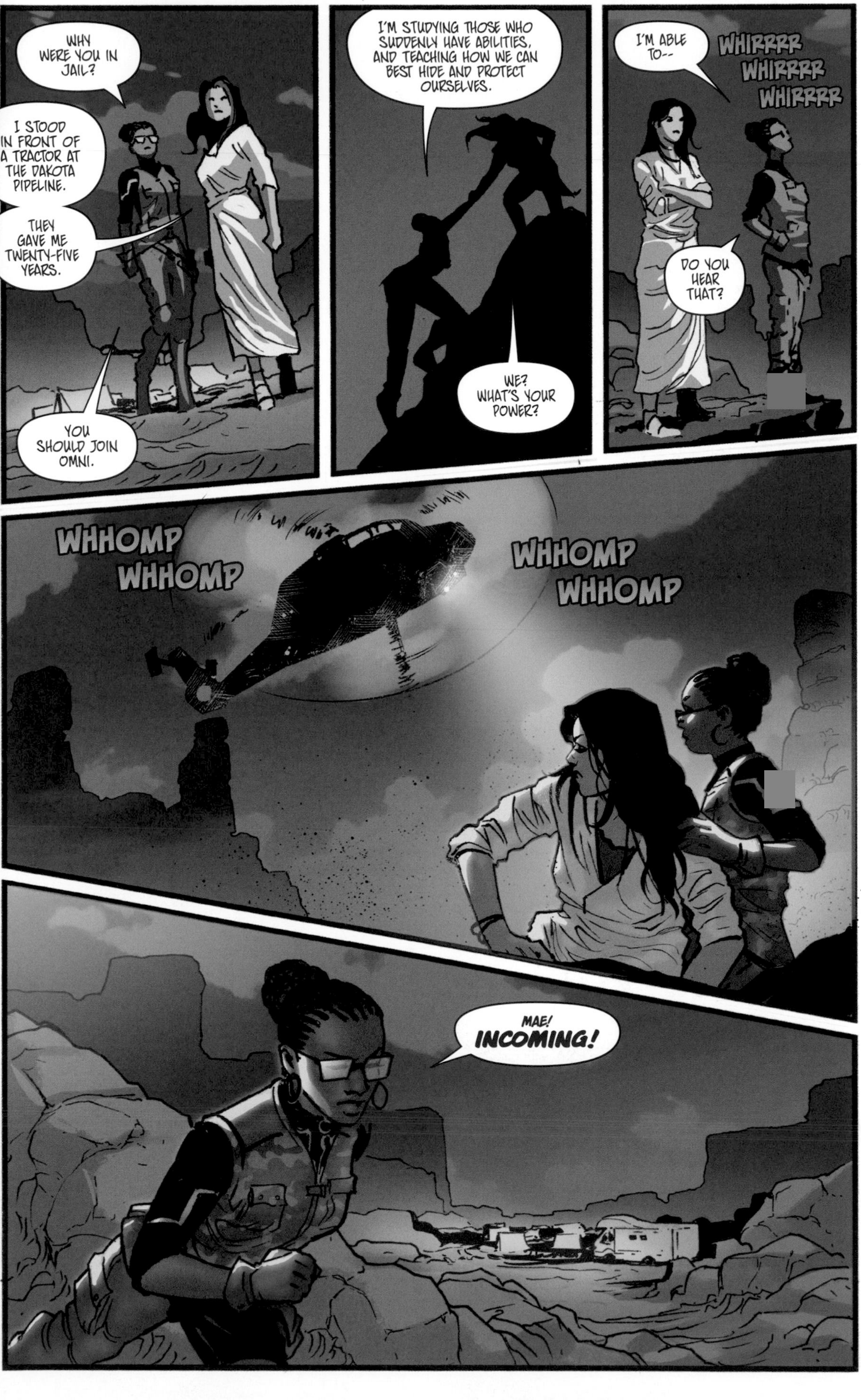
WHY WERE YOU IN JAIL?
I STOOD IN FRONT OF A TRACTOR AT THE DAKOTA PIPELINE.
THEY GAVE ME TWENTY-FIVE YEARS.
YOU SHOULD JOIN OMNI.
I'M STUDYING THOSE WHO SUDDENLY HAVE ABILITIES, AND TEACHING HOW WE CAN BEST HIDE AND PROTECT OURSELVES.
WE? WHAT'S YOUR POWER?
I'M ABLE TO--
WHIRRRR WHIRRRR WHIRRRR
DO YOU HEAR THAT?
WHHOMP WHHOMP
WHHOMP WHHOMP
MAE! INCOMING!

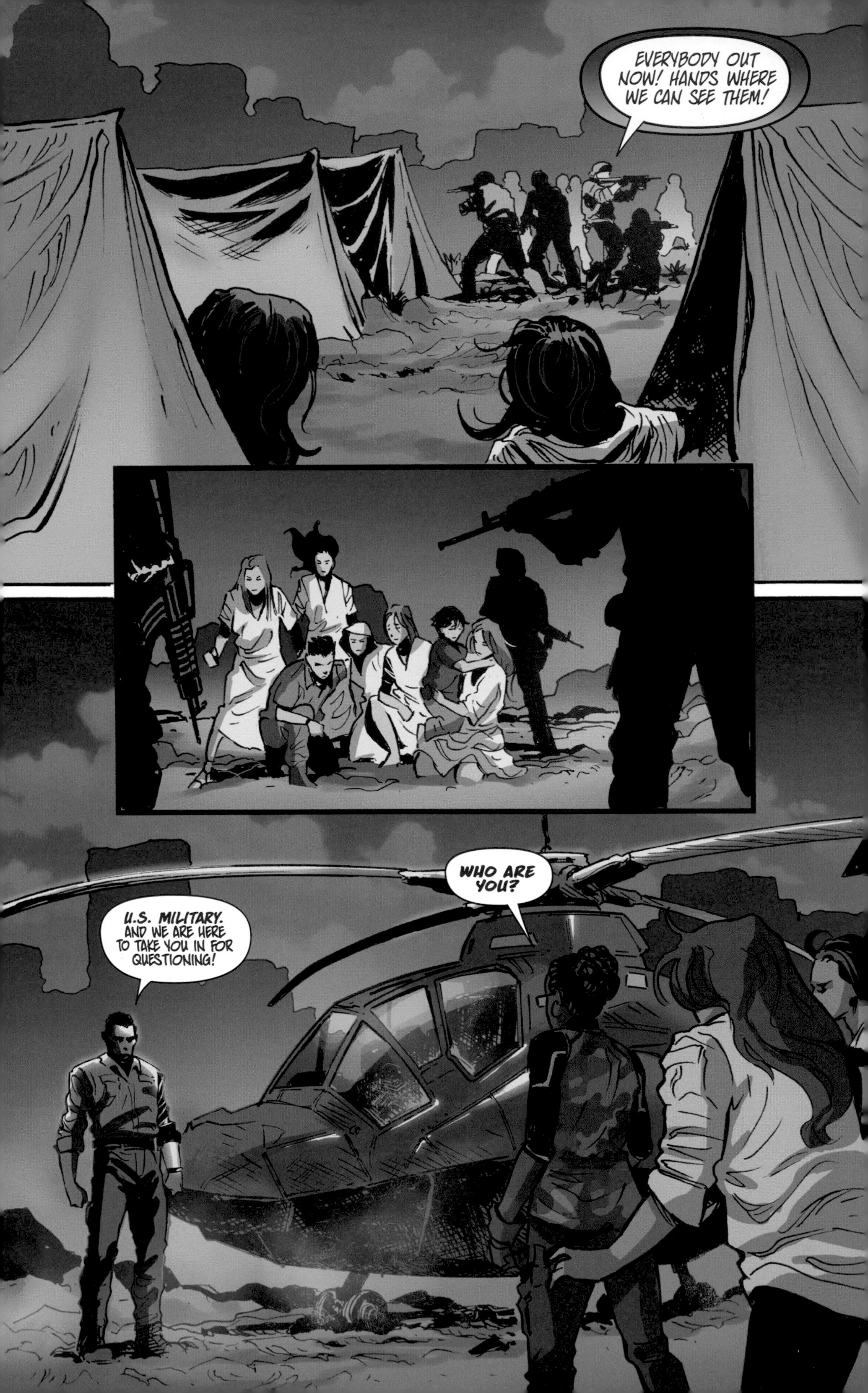
EVERYBODY OUT NOW! HANDS WHERE WE CAN SEE THEM!
WHO ARE YOU?
U.S. MILITARY. AND WE ARE HERE TO TAKE YOU IN FOR QUESTIONING!

ARIZONA DESERT

THIS IS THE U.S. MILITARY, AND WE ARE HERE TO TAKE YOU IN FOR QUESTIONING.

QUESTIONING FOR WHAT?

CHUMANI, WAIT...

LET ME HANDLE THIS.

No Records Found.

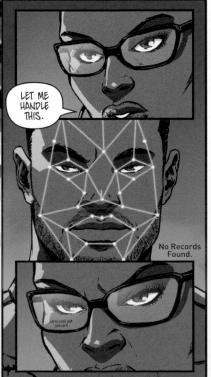

SO HERE'S WHAT'S GOING TO HAPPEN, LADIES...

YOU WILL ALL LINE UP SO WE CAN GET YOU READY TO--

I DON'T THINK SO.

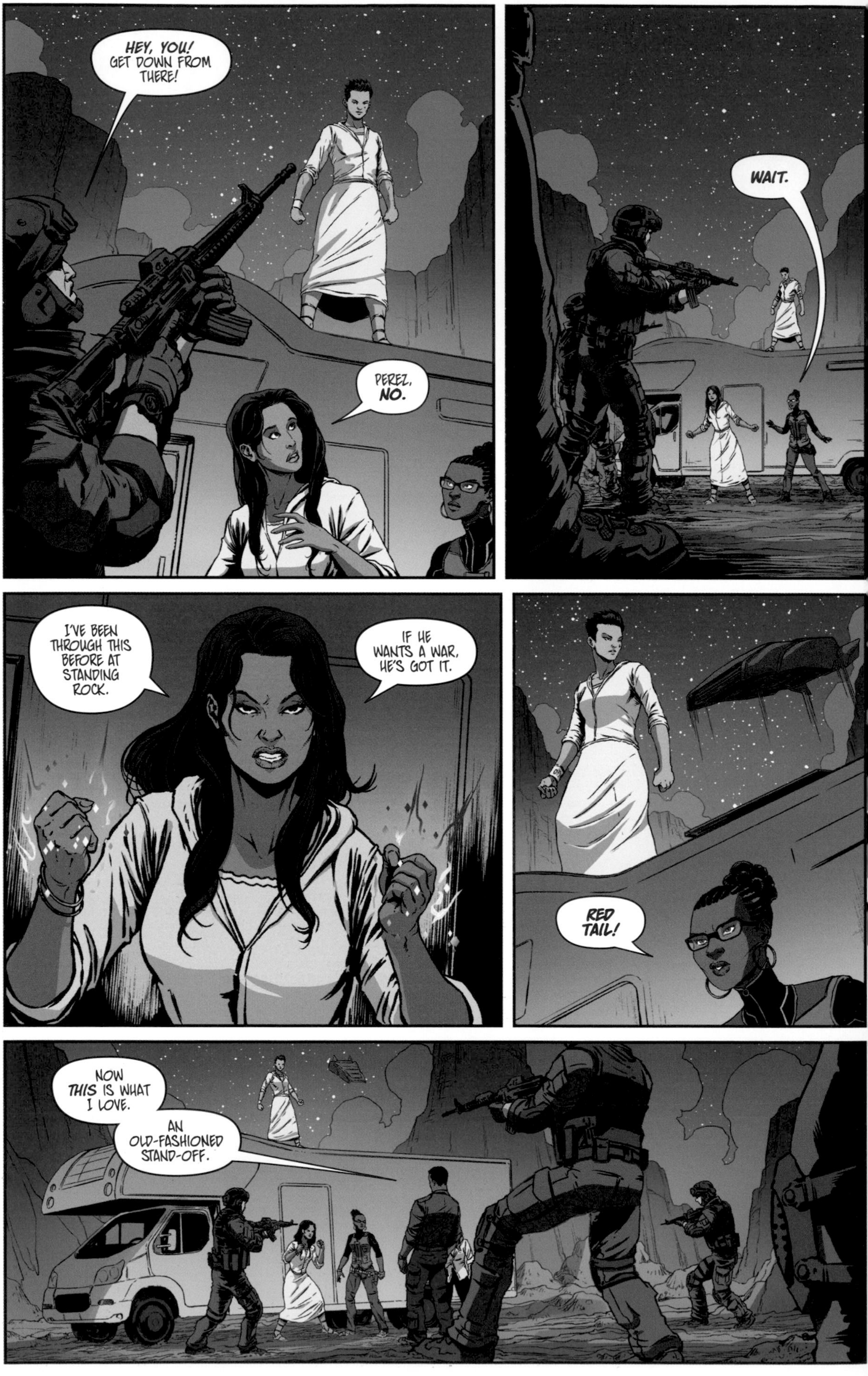
HEY, YOU! GET DOWN FROM THERE!
PEREZ, NO.
WAIT.
I'VE BEEN THROUGH THIS BEFORE AT STANDING ROCK.
IF HE WANTS A WAR, HE'S GOT IT.
RED TAIL!
NOW THIS IS WHAT I LOVE.
AN OLD-FASHIONED STAND-OFF.

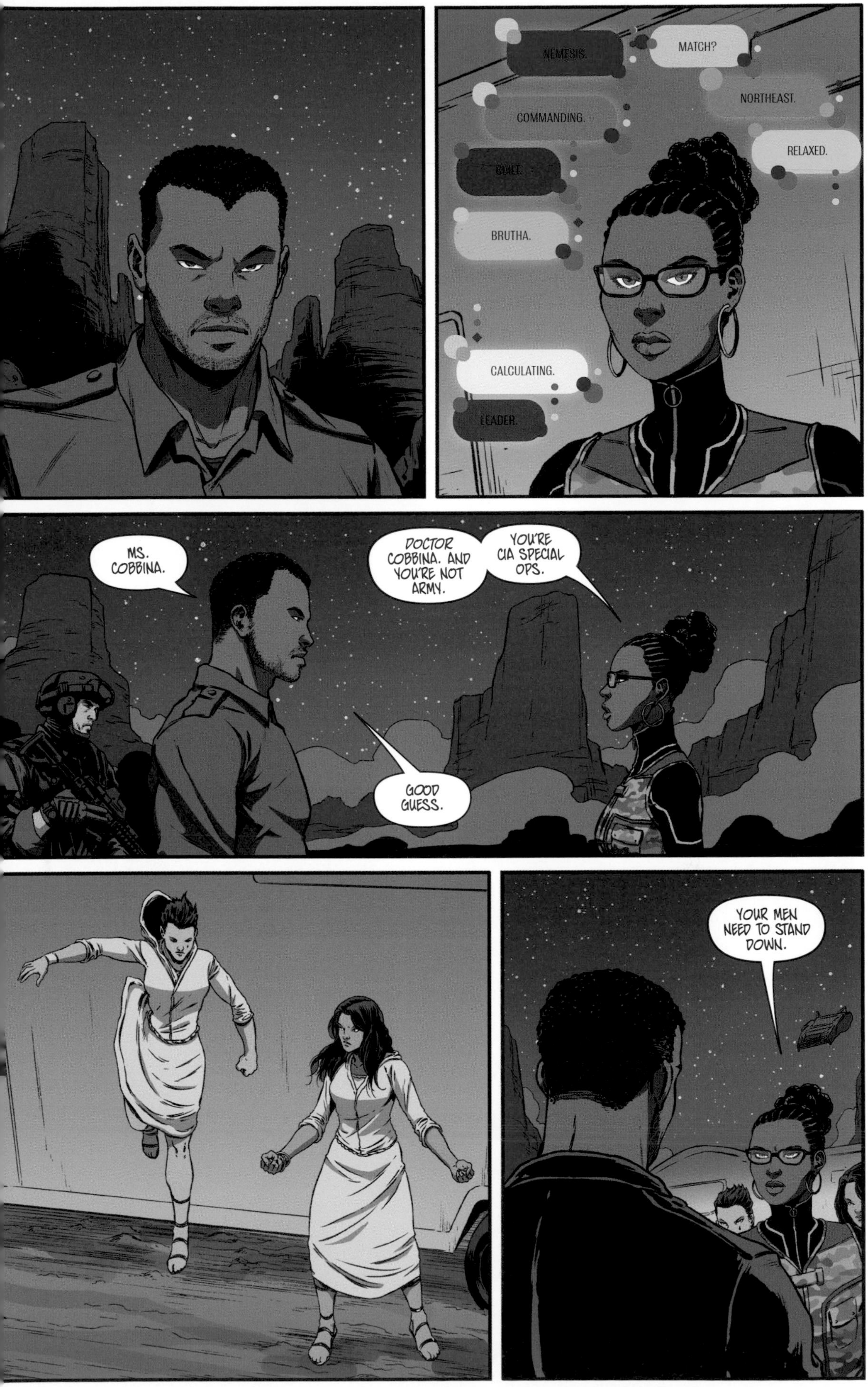
NEMESIS.
MATCH?
COMMANDING.
NORTHEAST.
GUILT.
RELAXED.
BRUTHA.
CALCULATING.
LEADER.
MS. COBBINA.
DOCTOR COBBINA. AND YOU'RE NOT ARMY.
YOU'RE CIA SPECIAL OPS.
GOOD GUESS.
YOUR MEN NEED TO STAND DOWN.

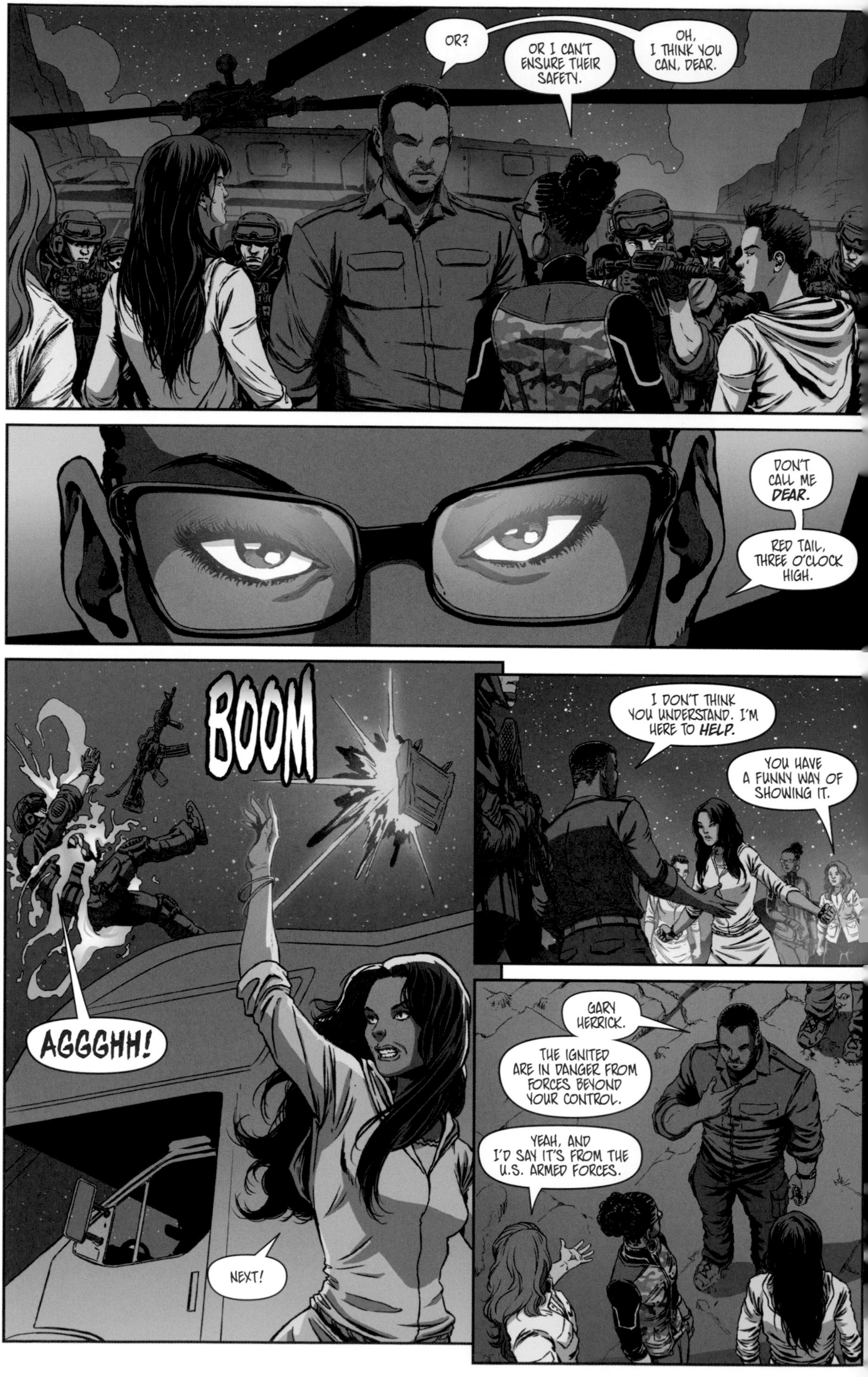
OR?
OR I CAN'T ENSURE THEIR SAFETY.
OH, I THINK YOU CAN, DEAR.
DON'T CALL ME **DEAR.**
RED TAIL, THREE O'CLOCK HIGH.
BOOM
AGGGHH!
NEXT!
I DON'T THINK YOU UNDERSTAND. I'M HERE TO **HELP.**
YOU HAVE A FUNNY WAY OF SHOWING IT.
GARY HERRICK.
THE IGNITED ARE IN DANGER FROM FORCES BEYOND YOUR CONTROL.
YEAH, AND I'D SAY IT'S FROM THE U.S. ARMED FORCES.

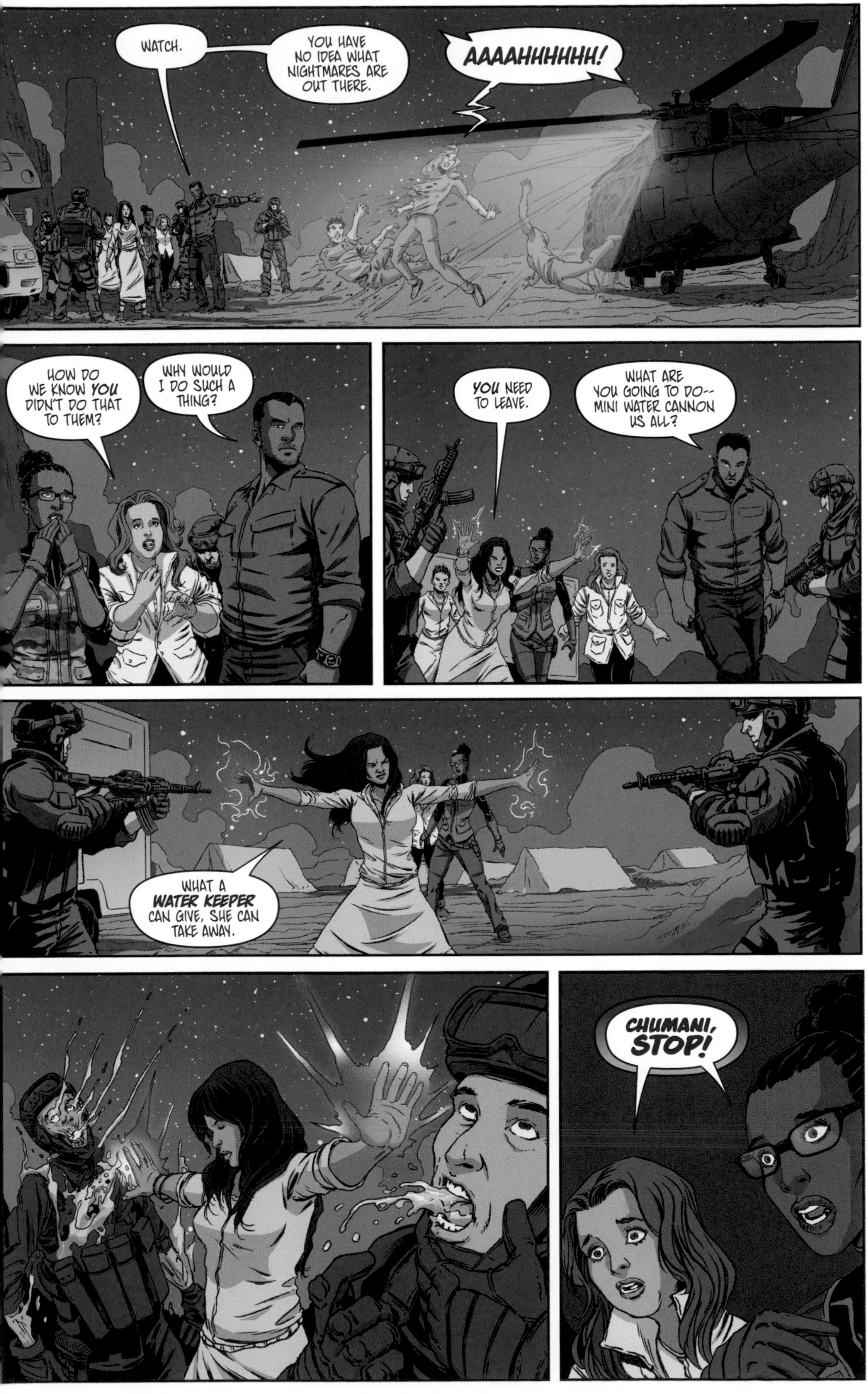
WATCH.
YOU HAVE NO IDEA WHAT NIGHTMARES ARE OUT THERE.
AAAAHHHHHH!
HOW DO WE KNOW YOU DIDN'T DO THAT TO THEM?
WHY WOULD I DO SUCH A THING?
YOU NEED TO LEAVE.
WHAT ARE YOU GOING TO DO-- MINI WATER CANNON US ALL?
WHAT A WATER KEEPER CAN GIVE, SHE CAN TAKE AWAY.
CHUMANI, STOP!

CHUMANI, YOUR ABILITIES NEED TO BE CHANNELED TO *HELP* OTHERS, NOT *HARM* THEM.

AND THAT'S EXACTLY WHY WE'RE HERE, CECELIA.

WE WANT TO HELP YOU STUDY WHAT'S HAPPENING TO THESE WOMEN...

...AND ALL THE OTHERS YOU'VE BEEN TRACKING.

WHY SHOULD I TRUST YOU?

BECAUSE WE HAVE *MORE* IN *COMMON* THAN YOU REALIZE.

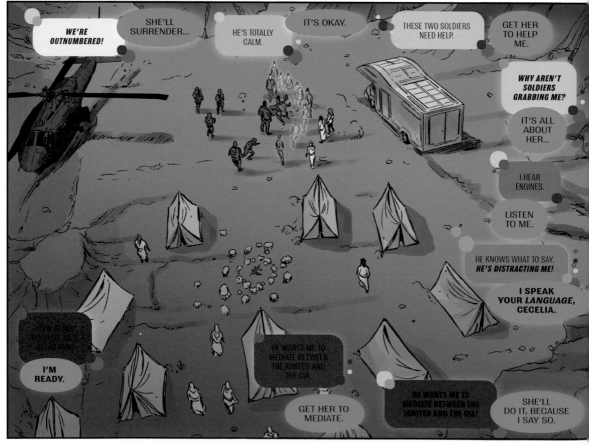

WE'RE OUTNUMBERED!

SHE'LL SURRENDER...

HE'S TOTALLY CALM.

IT'S OKAY.

THESE TWO SOLDIERS NEED HELP.

GET HER TO HELP ME.

WHY AREN'T SOLDIERS GRABBING ME?

IT'S ALL ABOUT HER...

I HEAR ENGINES.

LISTEN TO ME.

HE KNOWS WHAT TO SAY. *HE'S DISTRACTING ME!*

I SPEAK YOUR *LANGUAGE*, CECELIA.

LOOK AT HER. POSITIVE HE'S SET IT DOWN.

I'M READY.

HE WANTS ME TO MEDIATE BETWEEN THE IGNITED AND THE CIA.

HE WANTS ME TO MEDIATE BETWEEN THE IGNITED AND THE CIA!

GET HER TO MEDIATE.

SHE'LL DO IT, BECAUSE I SAY SO.

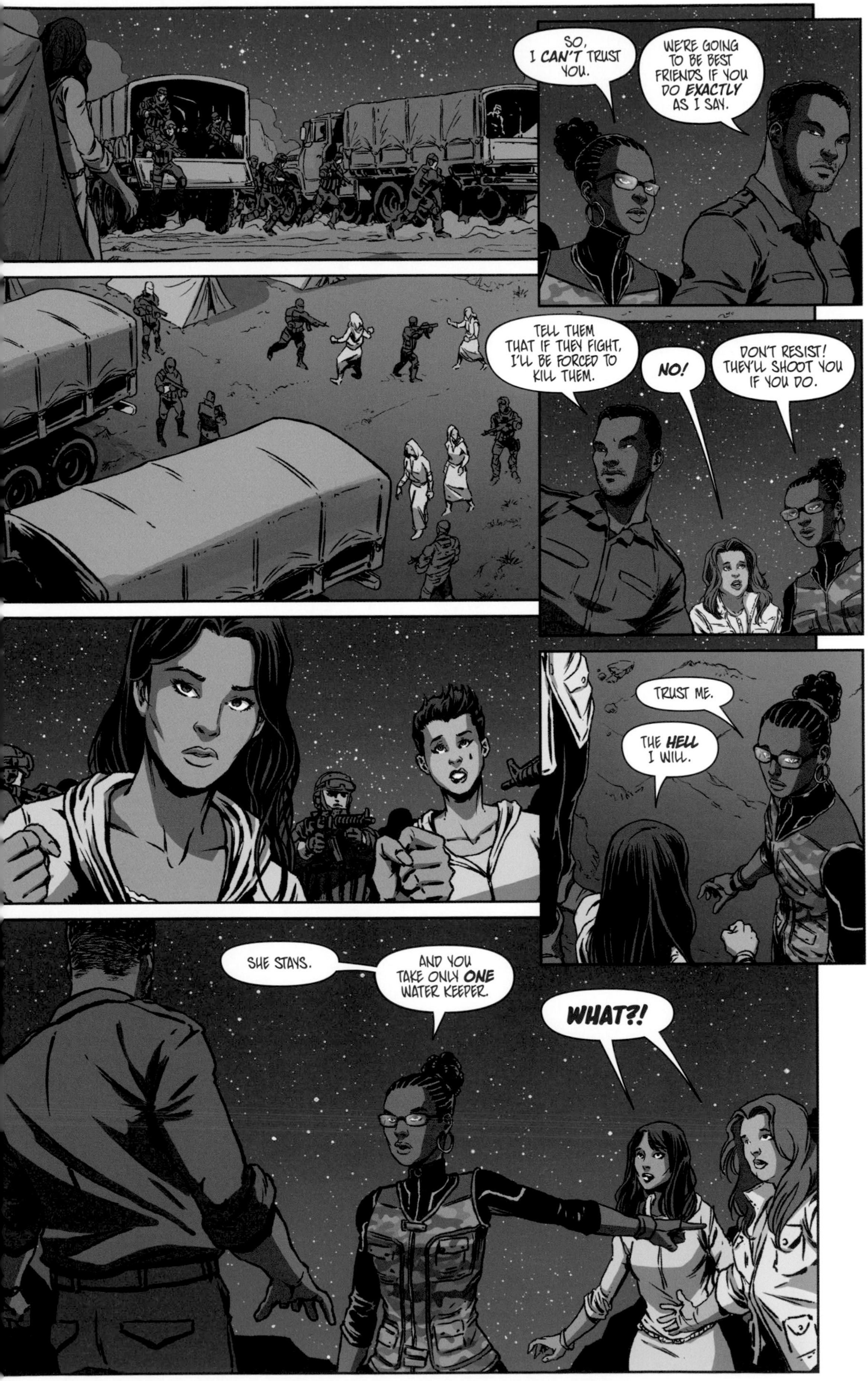
SO, I **CAN'T** TRUST YOU.
WE'RE GOING TO BE BEST FRIENDS IF YOU DO **EXACTLY** AS I SAY.
TELL THEM THAT IF THEY FIGHT, I'LL BE FORCED TO KILL THEM.
NO!
DON'T RESIST! THEY'LL SHOOT YOU IF YOU DO.
TRUST ME.
THE **HELL** I WILL.
SHE STAYS.
AND YOU TAKE ONLY **ONE** WATER KEEPER.
WHAT?!

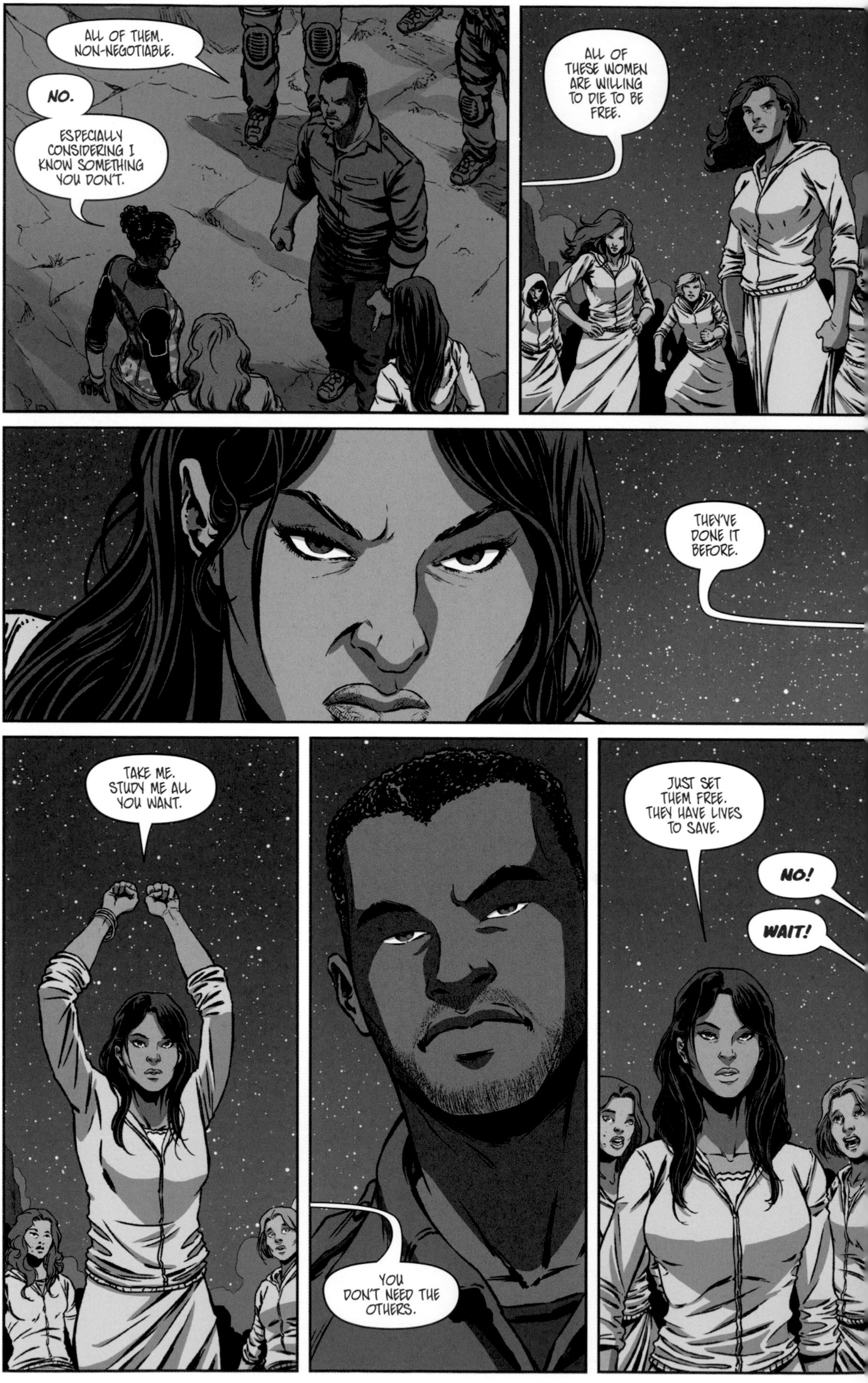
ALL OF THEM. NON-NEGOTIABLE.
NO.
ESPECIALLY CONSIDERING I KNOW SOMETHING YOU DON'T.
ALL OF THESE WOMEN ARE WILLING TO DIE TO BE FREE.
THEY'VE DONE IT BEFORE.
TAKE ME. STUDY ME ALL YOU WANT.
YOU DON'T NEED THE OTHERS.
JUST SET THEM FREE. THEY HAVE LIVES TO SAVE.
NO!
WAIT!

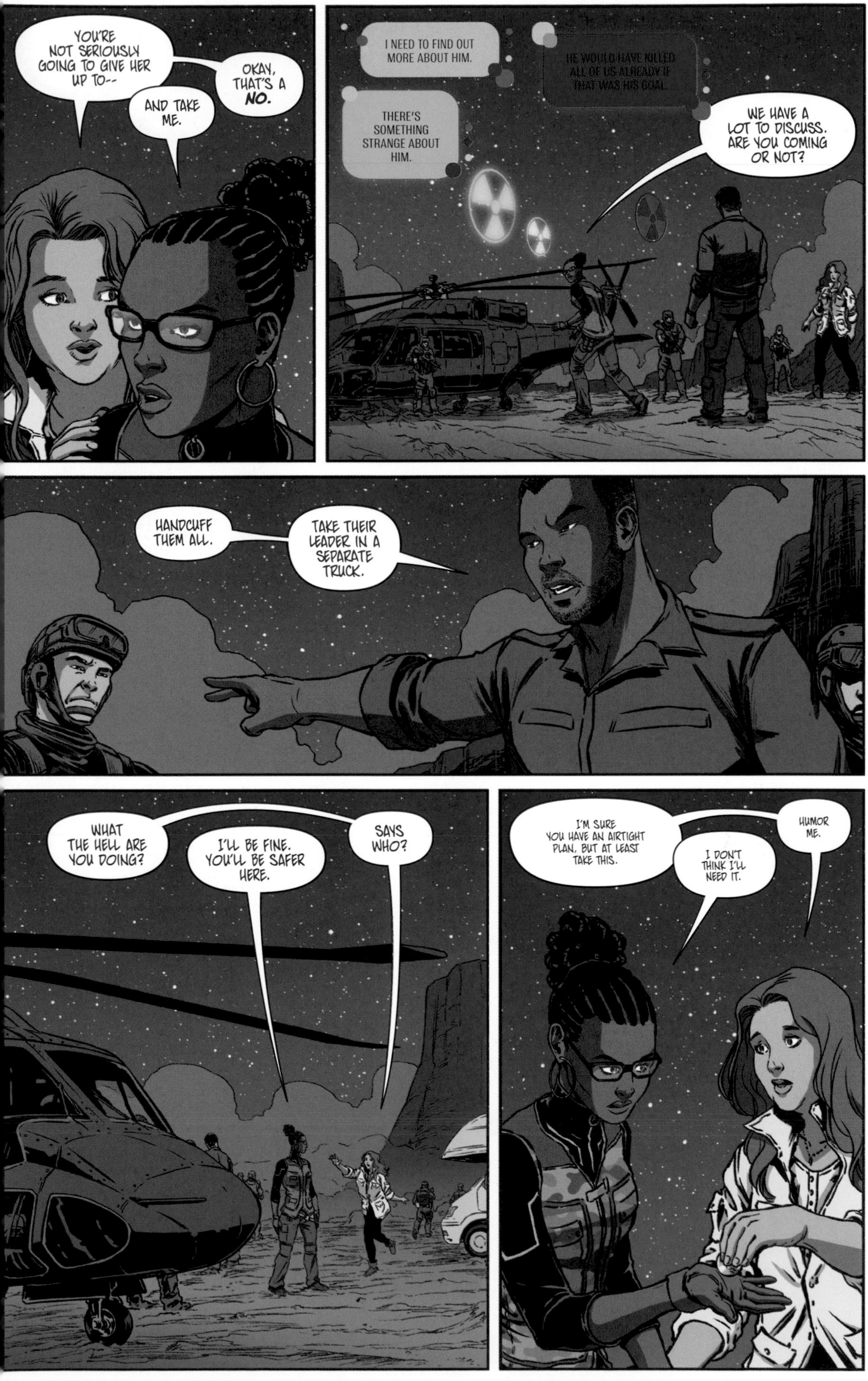

YOU'RE NOT SERIOUSLY GOING TO GIVE HER UP TO--
AND TAKE ME.
OKAY, THAT'S A NO.
I NEED TO FIND OUT MORE ABOUT HIM.
THERE'S SOMETHING STRANGE ABOUT HIM.
HE WOULD HAVE KILLED ALL OF US ALREADY IF THAT WAS HIS GOAL.
WE HAVE A LOT TO DISCUSS. ARE YOU COMING OR NOT?
HANDCUFF THEM ALL.
TAKE THEIR LEADER IN A SEPARATE TRUCK.
WHAT THE HELL ARE YOU DOING?
I'LL BE FINE. YOU'LL BE SAFER HERE.
SAYS WHO?
I'M SURE YOU HAVE AN AIRTIGHT PLAN, BUT AT LEAST TAKE THIS.
I DON'T THINK I'LL NEED IT.
HUMOR ME.

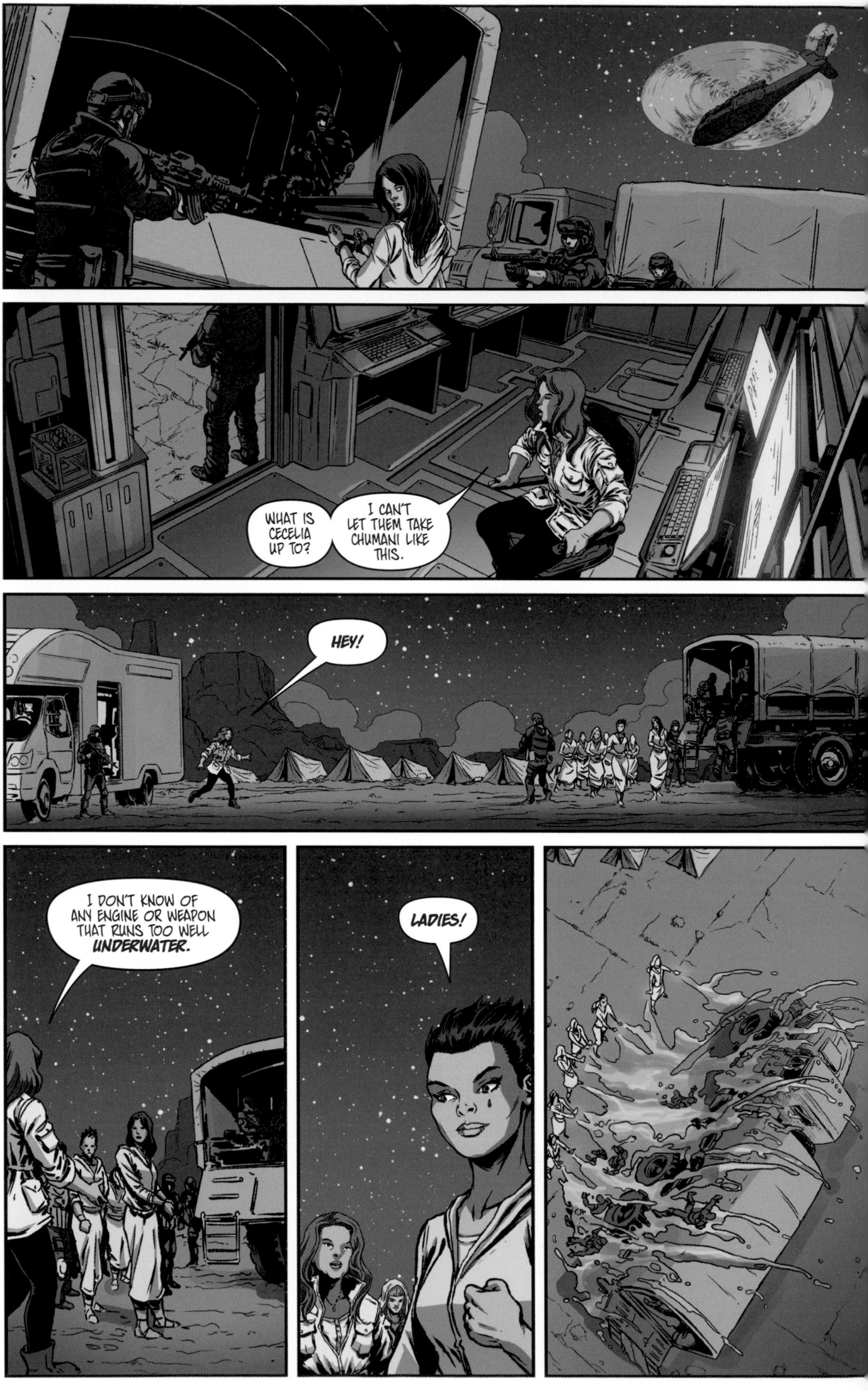
WHAT IS CECELIA UP TO?
I CAN'T LET THEM TAKE CHUMANI LIKE THIS.
HEY!
I DON'T KNOW OF ANY ENGINE OR WEAPON THAT RUNS TOO WELL UNDERWATER.
LADIES!

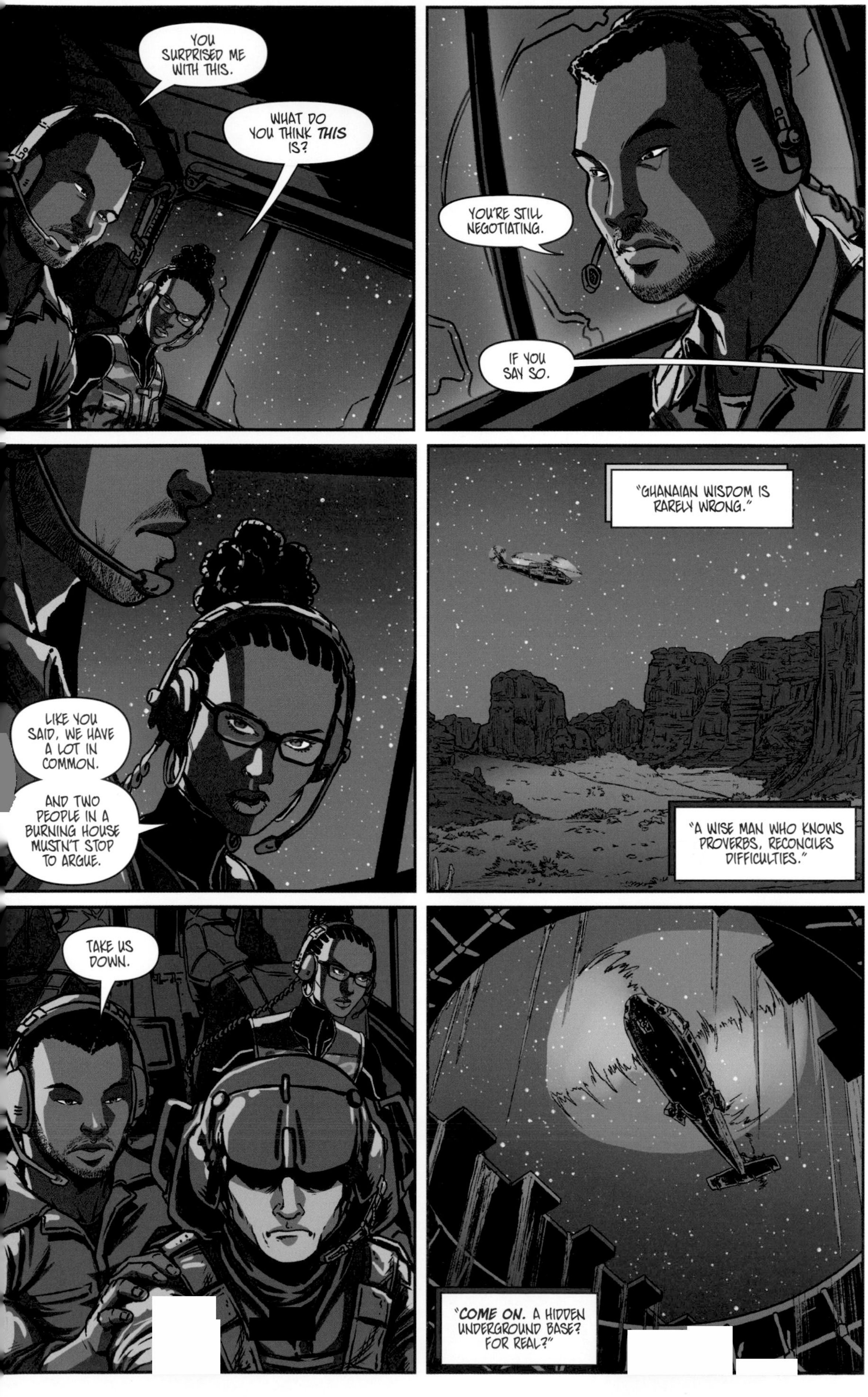
YOU SURPRISED ME WITH THIS.
WHAT DO YOU THINK ***THIS*** IS?
YOU'RE STILL NEGOTIATING.
IF YOU SAY SO.
LIKE YOU SAID, WE HAVE A LOT IN COMMON.
AND TWO PEOPLE IN A BURNING HOUSE MUSTN'T STOP TO ARGUE.
"GHANAIAN WISDOM IS RARELY WRONG."
"A WISE MAN WHO KNOWS PROVERBS, RECONCILES DIFFICULTIES."
TAKE US DOWN.
"***COME ON.*** A HIDDEN UNDERGROUND BASE? FOR REAL?"

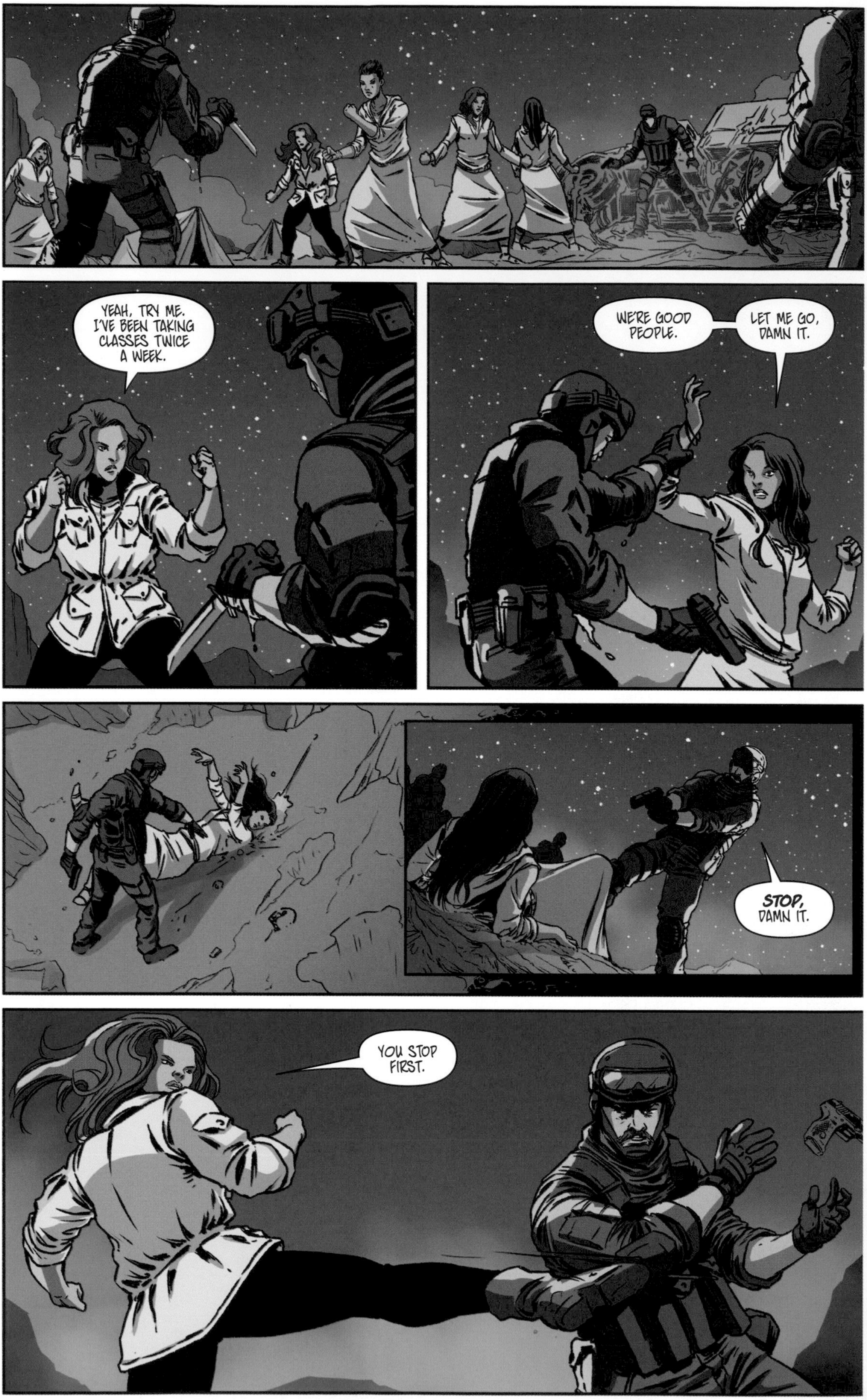
YEAH, TRY ME. I'VE BEEN TAKING CLASSES TWICE A WEEK.
WE'RE GOOD PEOPLE.
LET ME GO, DAMN IT.
STOP, DAMN IT.
YOU STOP FIRST.

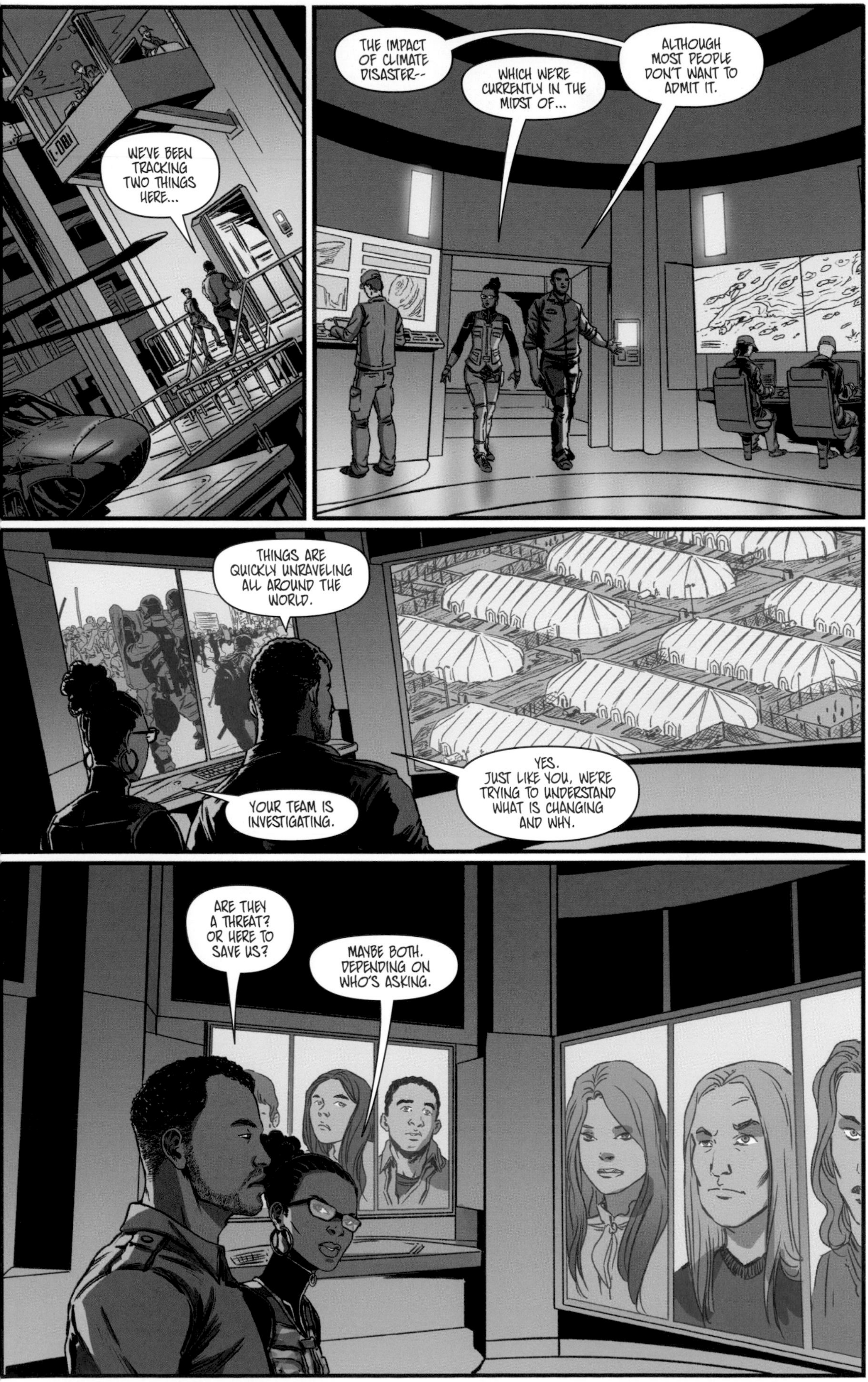
WE'VE BEEN TRACKING TWO THINGS HERE...
THE IMPACT OF CLIMATE DISASTER--
WHICH WE'RE CURRENTLY IN THE MIDST OF...
ALTHOUGH MOST PEOPLE DON'T WANT TO ADMIT IT.
THINGS ARE QUICKLY UNRAVELING ALL AROUND THE WORLD.
YOUR TEAM IS INVESTIGATING.
YES. JUST LIKE YOU, WE'RE TRYING TO UNDERSTAND WHAT IS CHANGING AND WHY.
ARE THEY A THREAT? OR HERE TO SAVE US?
MAYBE BOTH. DEPENDING ON WHO'S ASKING.

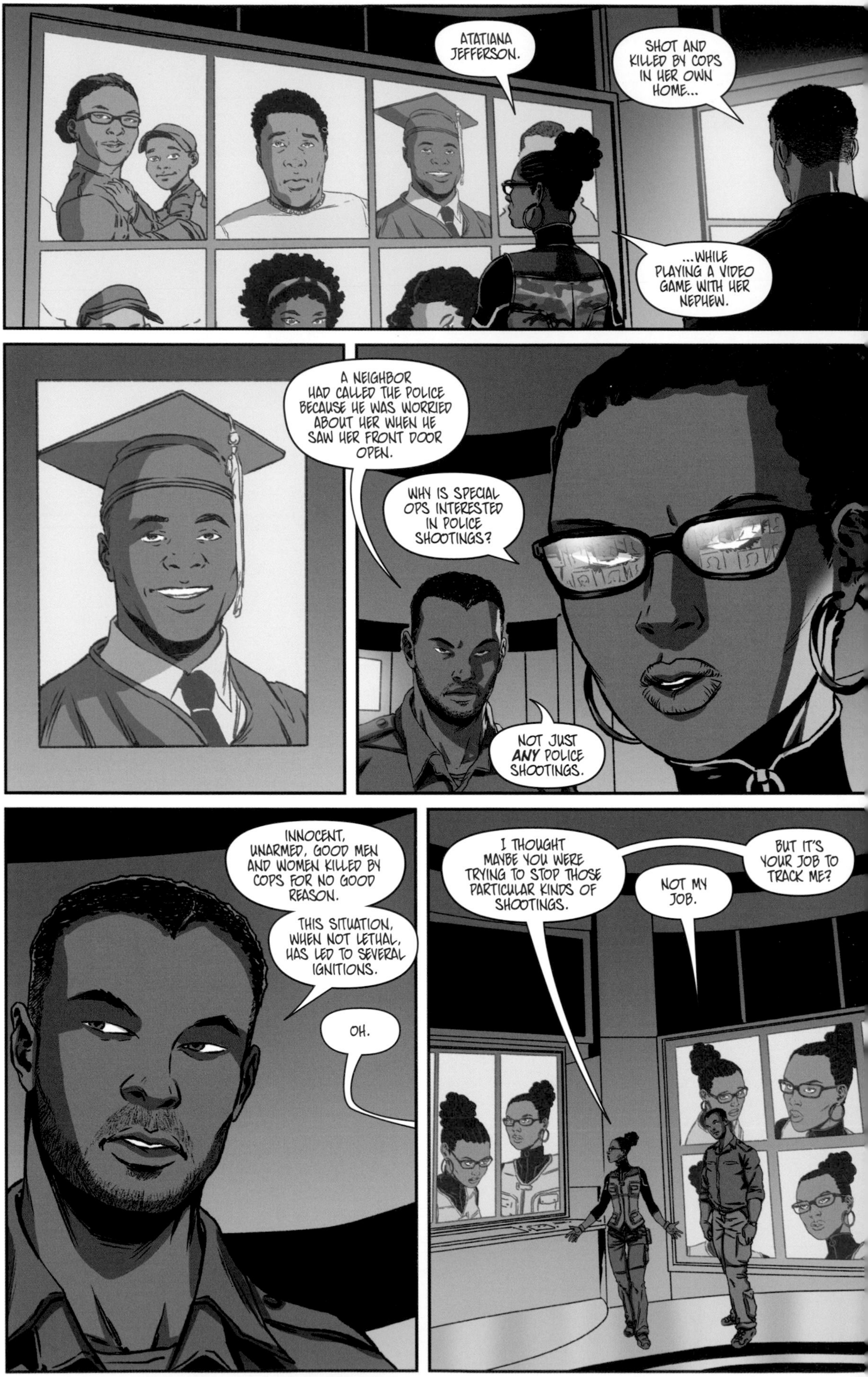
ATATIANA JEFFERSON.
SHOT AND KILLED BY COPS IN HER OWN HOME...
...WHILE PLAYING A VIDEO GAME WITH HER NEPHEW.
A NEIGHBOR HAD CALLED THE POLICE BECAUSE HE WAS WORRIED ABOUT HER WHEN HE SAW HER FRONT DOOR OPEN.
WHY IS SPECIAL OPS INTERESTED IN POLICE SHOOTINGS?
NOT JUST **ANY** POLICE SHOOTINGS.
INNOCENT, UNARMED, GOOD MEN AND WOMEN KILLED BY COPS FOR NO GOOD REASON.
THIS SITUATION, WHEN NOT LETHAL, HAS LED TO SEVERAL IGNITIONS.
OH.
I THOUGHT MAYBE YOU WERE TRYING TO STOP THOSE PARTICULAR KINDS OF SHOOTINGS.
NOT MY JOB.
BUT IT'S YOUR JOB TO TRACK ME?

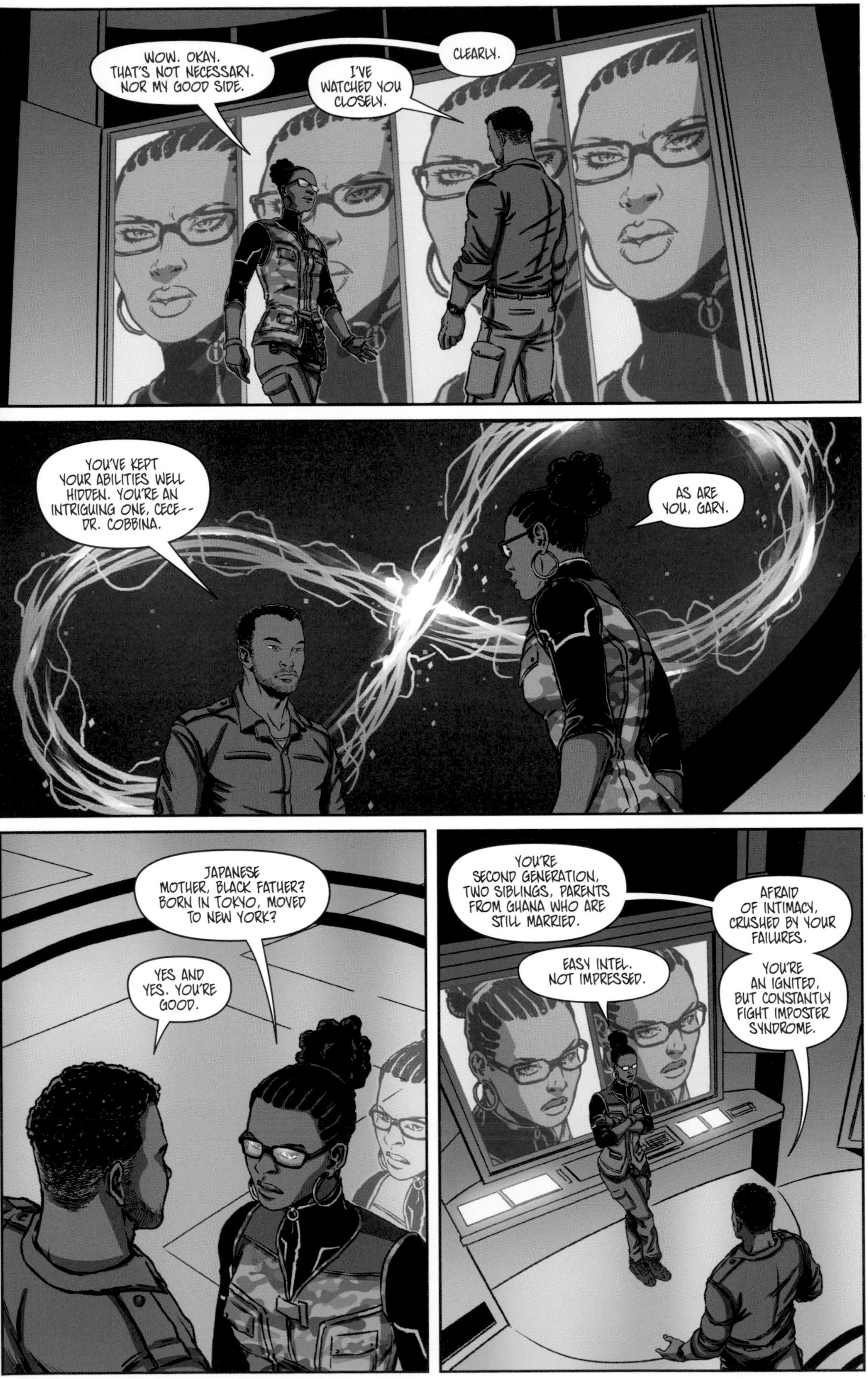
WOW. OKAY. THAT'S NOT NECESSARY. NOR MY GOOD SIDE.
CLEARLY.
I'VE WATCHED YOU CLOSELY.
YOU'VE KEPT YOUR ABILITIES WELL HIDDEN. YOU'RE AN INTRIGUING ONE, CECE-- DR. COBBINA.
AS ARE YOU, GARY.
JAPANESE MOTHER, BLACK FATHER? BORN IN TOKYO, MOVED TO NEW YORK?
YES AND YES. YOU'RE GOOD.
YOU'RE SECOND GENERATION, TWO SIBLINGS, PARENTS FROM GHANA WHO ARE STILL MARRIED.
EASY INTEL. NOT IMPRESSED.
AFRAID OF INTIMACY, CRUSHED BY YOUR FAILURES.
YOU'RE AN IGNITED, BUT CONSTANTLY FIGHT IMPOSTER SYNDROME.

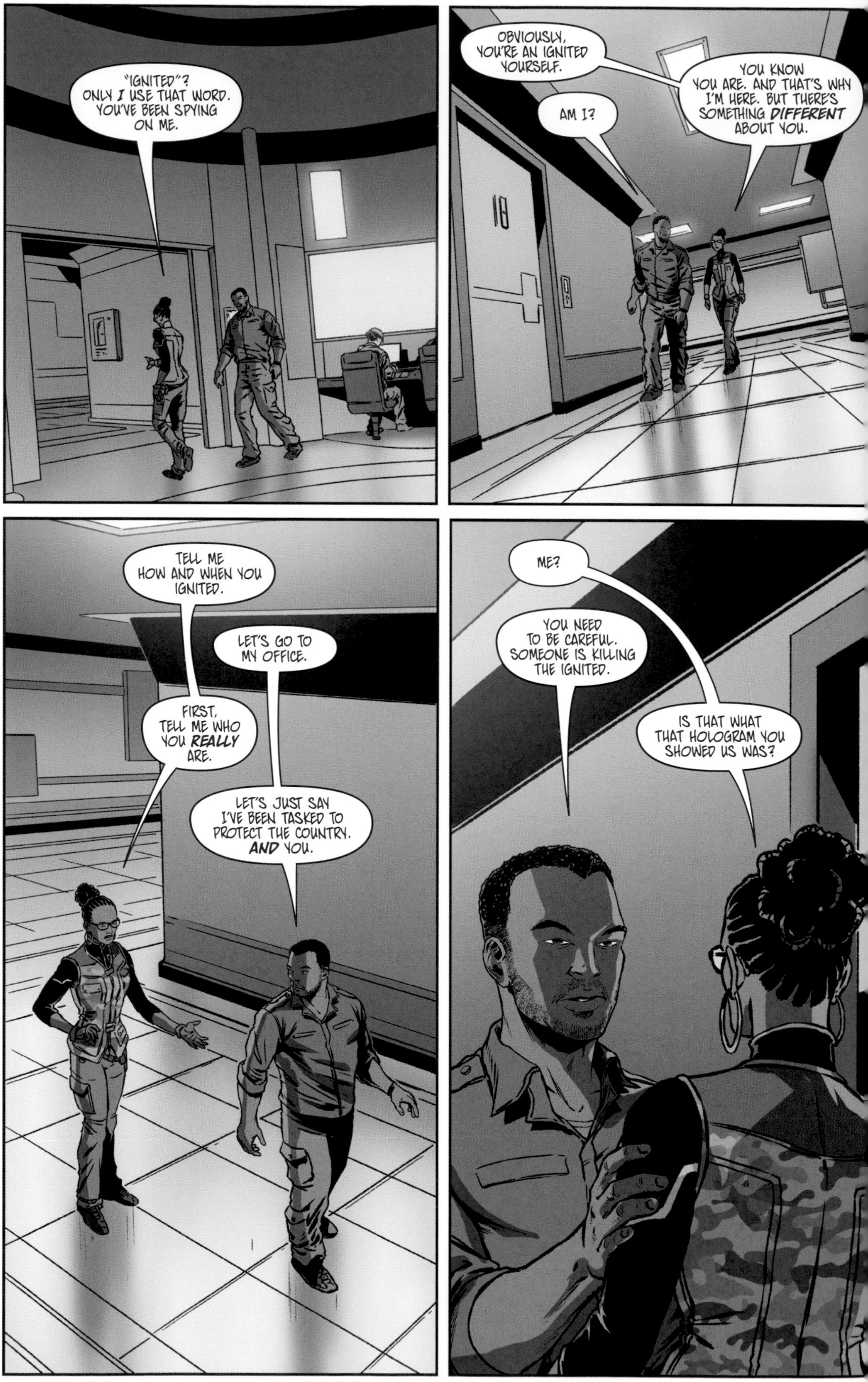
"IGNITED"? ONLY *I* USE THAT WORD. YOU'VE BEEN SPYING ON ME.
OBVIOUSLY, YOU'RE AN IGNITED YOURSELF.
AM I?
YOU KNOW YOU ARE. AND THAT'S WHY I'M HERE. BUT THERE'S SOMETHING **DIFFERENT** ABOUT YOU.
TELL ME HOW AND WHEN YOU IGNITED.
LET'S GO TO MY OFFICE.
FIRST, TELL ME WHO YOU **REALLY** ARE.
LET'S JUST SAY I'VE BEEN TASKED TO PROTECT THE COUNTRY. **AND** YOU.
ME?
YOU NEED TO BE CAREFUL. SOMEONE IS KILLING THE IGNITED.
IS THAT WHAT THAT HOLOGRAM YOU SHOWED US WAS?

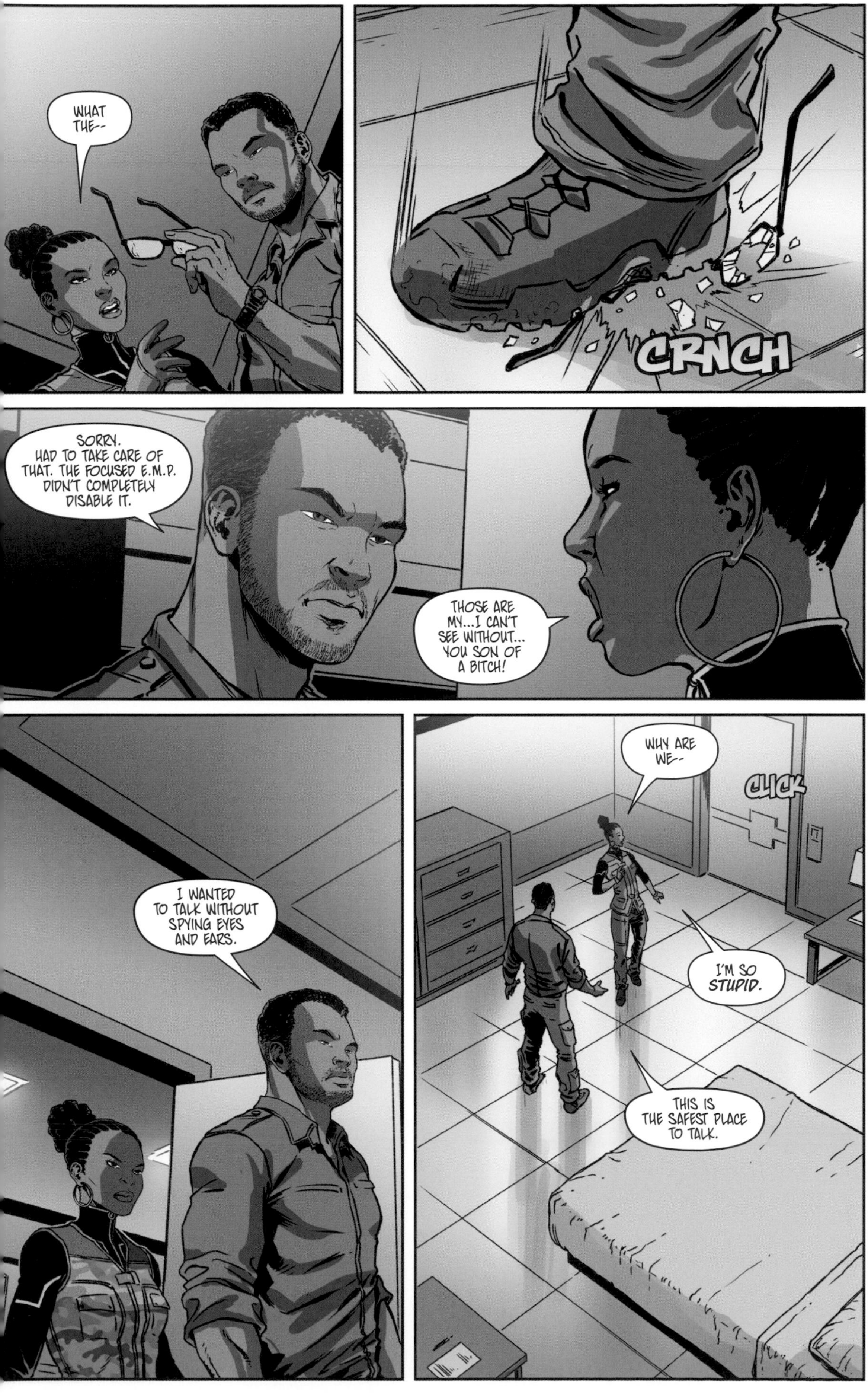
WHAT THE--
CRNCH
SORRY. HAD TO TAKE CARE OF THAT. THE FOCUSED E.M.P. DIDN'T COMPLETELY DISABLE IT.
THOSE ARE MY...I CAN'T SEE WITHOUT... YOU SON OF A BITCH!
I WANTED TO TALK WITHOUT SPYING EYES AND EARS.
WHY ARE WE--
CLICK
I'M SO STUPID.
THIS IS THE SAFEST PLACE TO TALK.

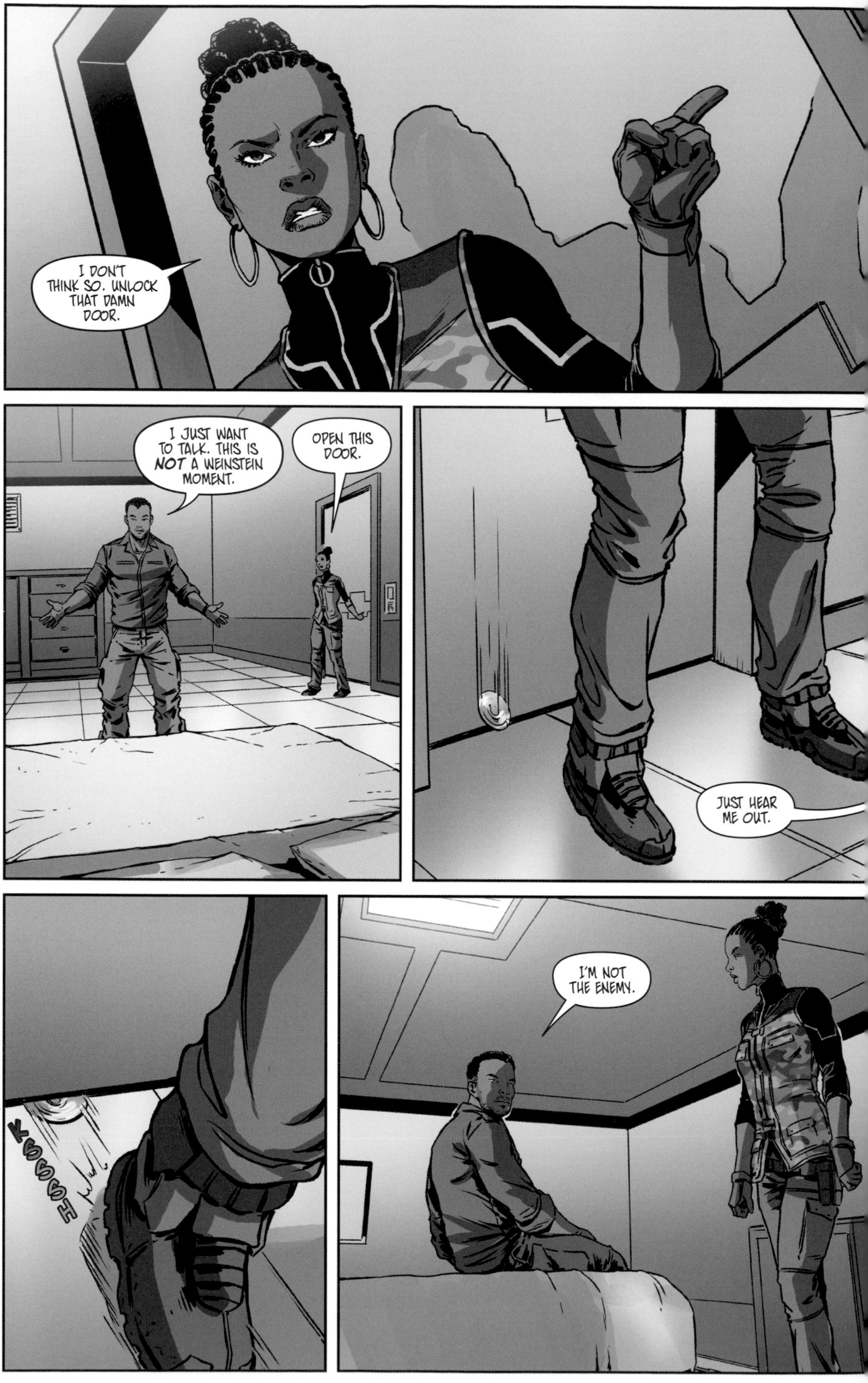
I DON'T THINK SO. UNLOCK THAT DAMN DOOR.
I JUST WANT TO TALK. THIS IS **NOT** A WEINSTEIN MOMENT.
OPEN THIS DOOR.
JUST HEAR ME OUT.
KSSSH
I'M NOT THE ENEMY.

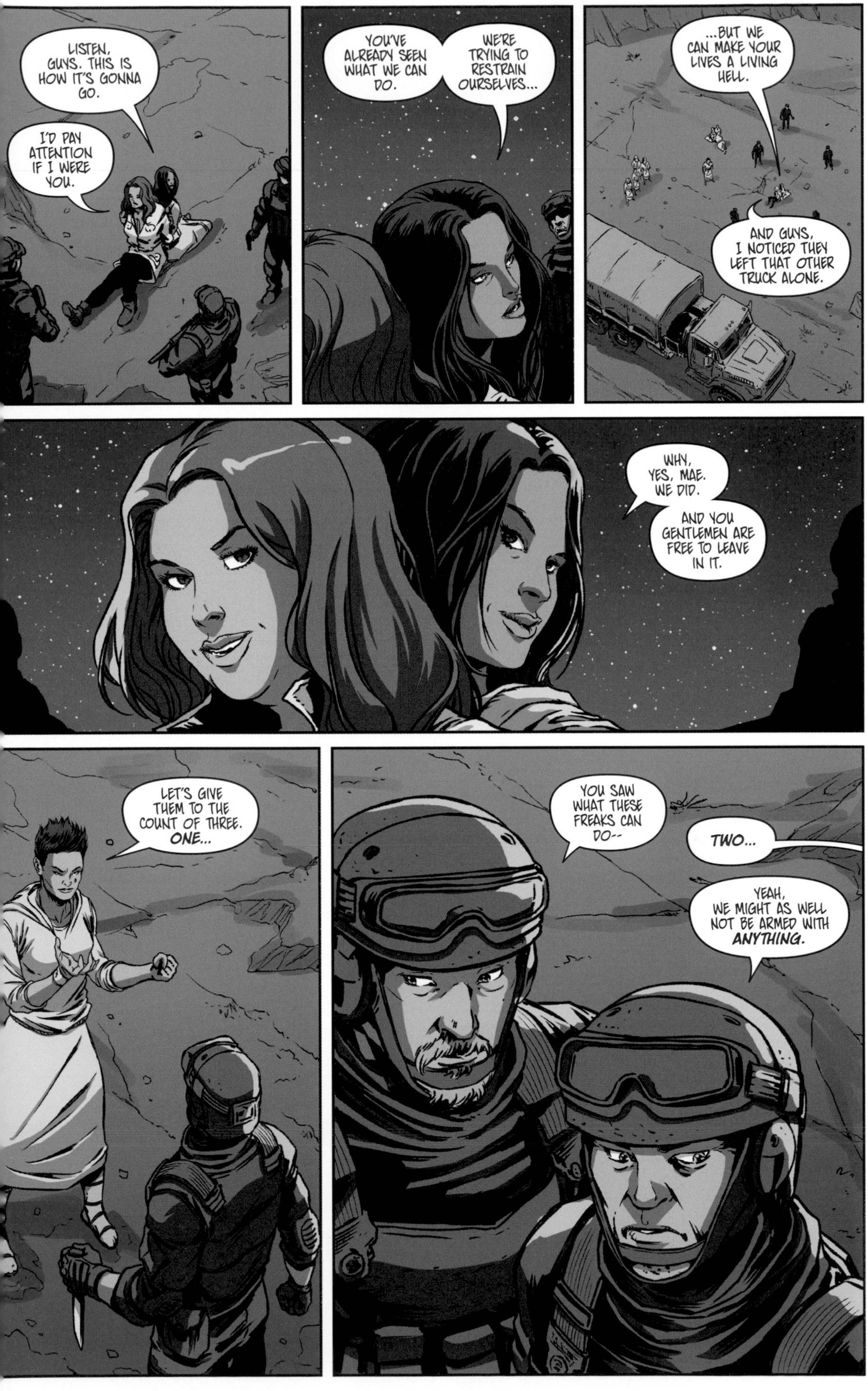
LISTEN, GUYS. THIS IS HOW IT'S GONNA GO.
I'D PAY ATTENTION IF I WERE YOU.
YOU'VE ALREADY SEEN WHAT WE CAN DO.
WE'RE TRYING TO RESTRAIN OURSELVES...
...BUT WE CAN MAKE YOUR LIVES A LIVING HELL.
AND GUYS, I NOTICED THEY LEFT THAT OTHER TRUCK ALONE.
WHY, YES, MAE. WE DID.
AND YOU GENTLEMEN ARE FREE TO LEAVE IN IT.
LET'S GIVE THEM TO THE COUNT OF THREE. **ONE...**
YOU SAW WHAT THESE FREAKS CAN DO--
TWO...
YEAH, WE MIGHT AS WELL NOT BE ARMED WITH **ANYTHING.**

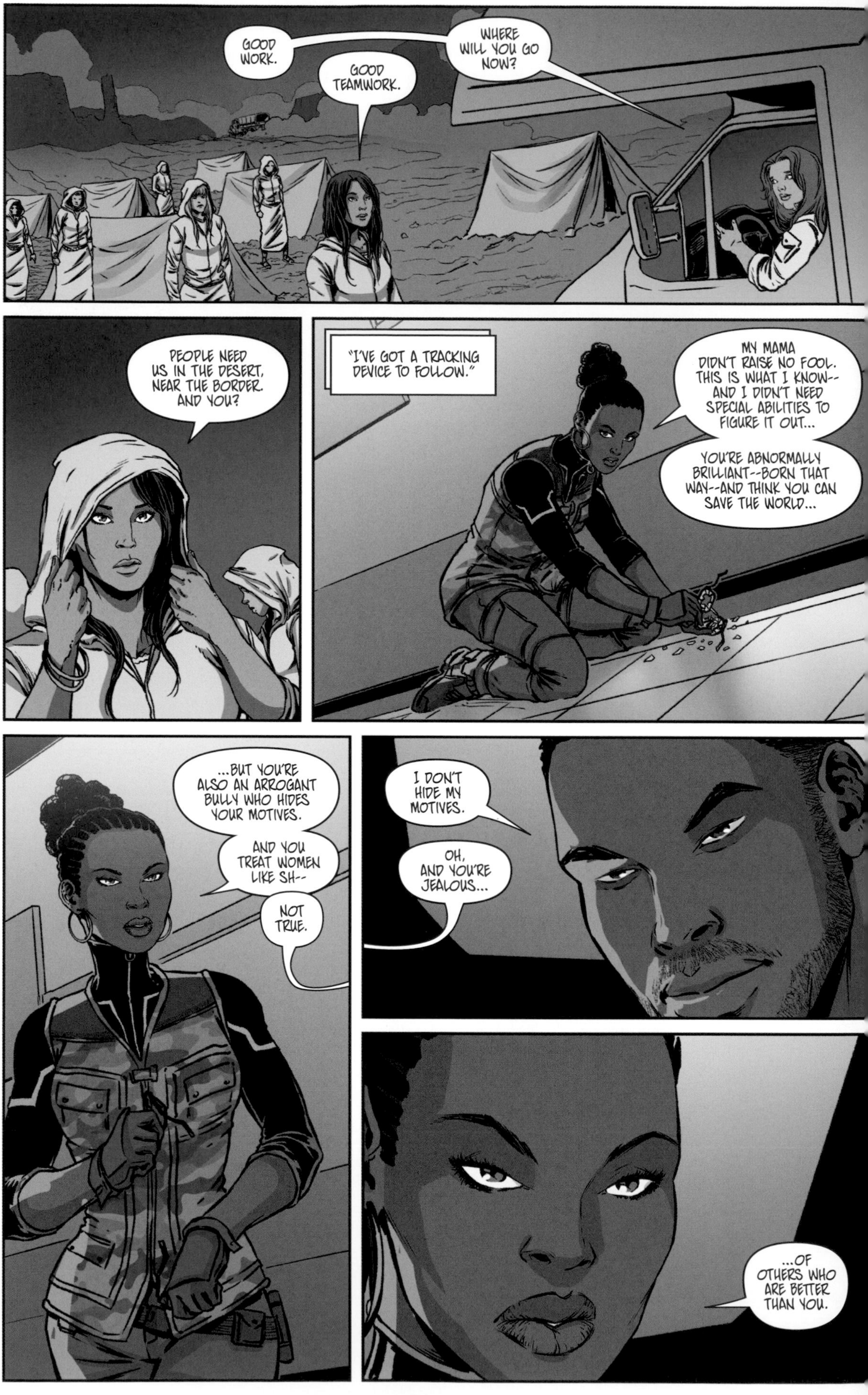
GOOD WORK.
GOOD TEAMWORK.
WHERE WILL YOU GO NOW?
PEOPLE NEED US IN THE DESERT, NEAR THE BORDER. AND YOU?
"I'VE GOT A TRACKING DEVICE TO FOLLOW."
MY MAMA DIDN'T RAISE NO FOOL. THIS IS WHAT I KNOW--AND I DIDN'T NEED SPECIAL ABILITIES TO FIGURE IT OUT...
YOU'RE ABNORMALLY BRILLIANT--BORN THAT WAY--AND THINK YOU CAN SAVE THE WORLD...
...BUT YOU'RE ALSO AN ARROGANT BULLY WHO HIDES YOUR MOTIVES.
AND YOU TREAT WOMEN LIKE SH--
NOT TRUE.
I DON'T HIDE MY MOTIVES.
OH, AND YOU'RE JEALOUS...
...OF OTHERS WHO ARE BETTER THAN YOU.

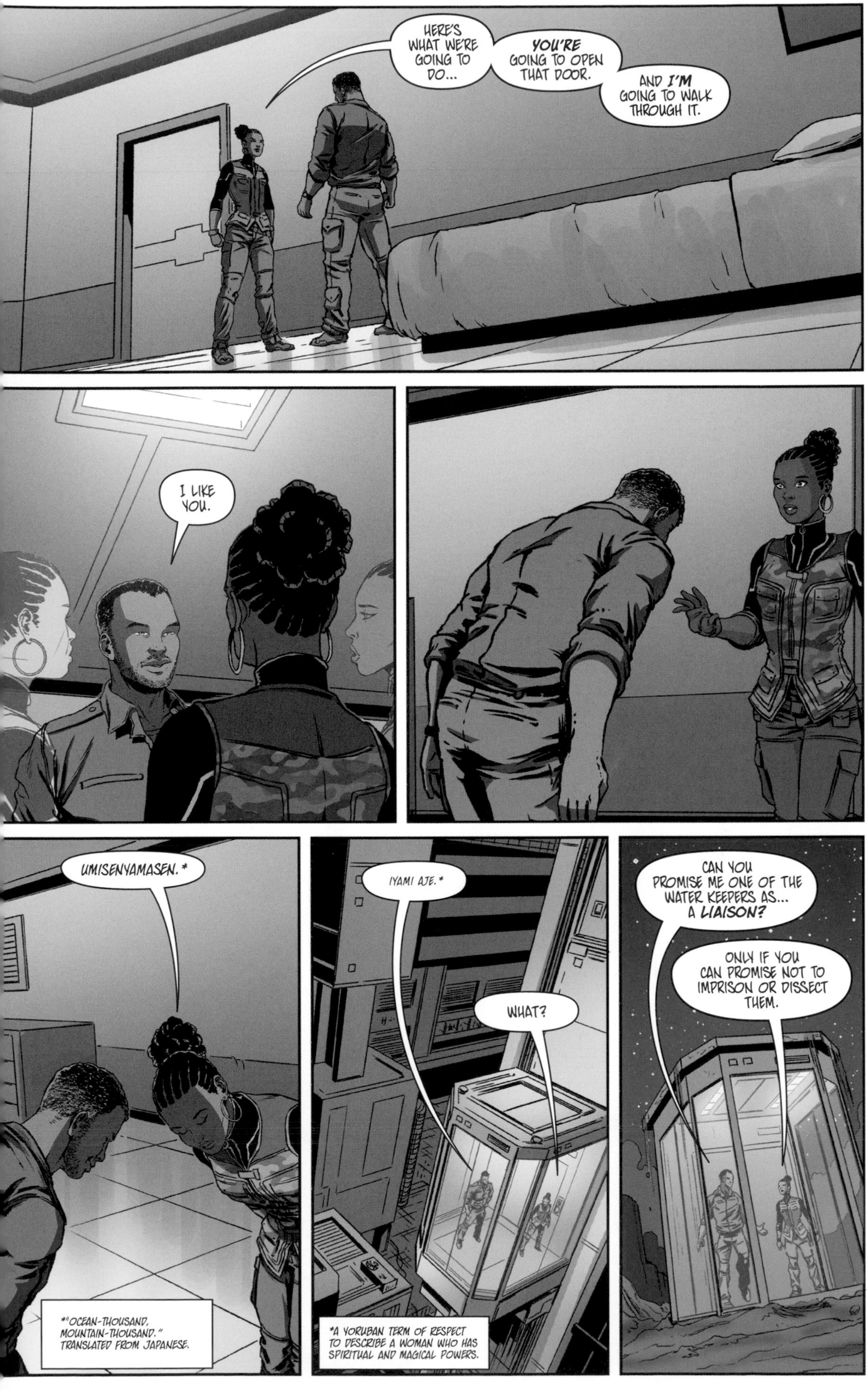
HERE'S WHAT WE'RE GOING TO DO...
YOU'RE GOING TO OPEN THAT DOOR.
AND I'M GOING TO WALK THROUGH IT.
I LIKE YOU.
UMISENYAMASEN.*
*"OCEAN-THOUSAND, MOUNTAIN-THOUSAND." TRANSLATED FROM JAPANESE.
IYAMI AJE.*
WHAT?
*A YORUBAN TERM OF RESPECT TO DESCRIBE A WOMAN WHO HAS SPIRITUAL AND MAGICAL POWERS.
CAN YOU PROMISE ME ONE OF THE WATER KEEPERS AS... A LIAISON?
ONLY IF YOU CAN PROMISE NOT TO IMPRISON OR DISSECT THEM.

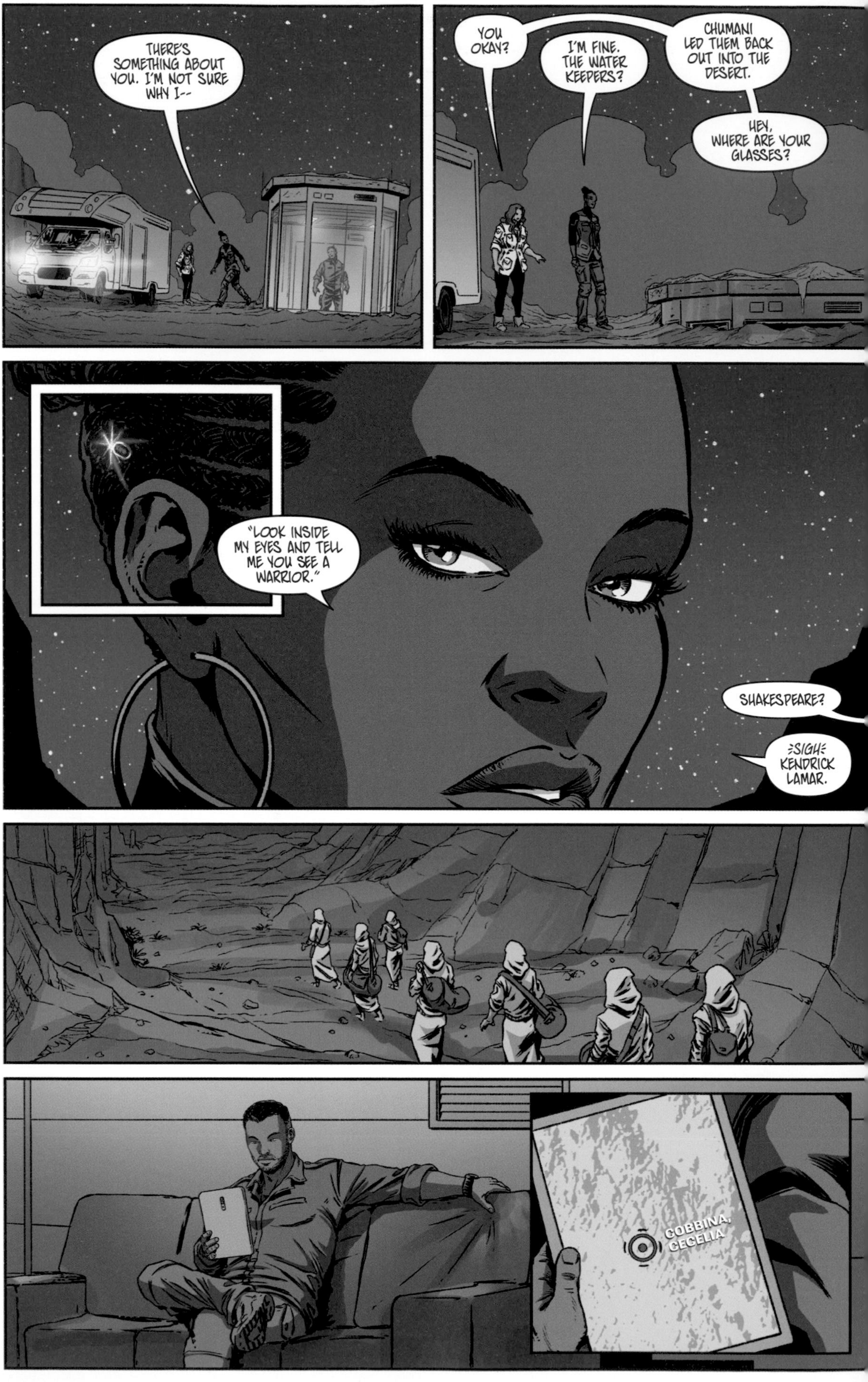
THERE'S SOMETHING ABOUT YOU. I'M NOT SURE WHY I--
YOU OKAY?
I'M FINE. THE WATER KEEPERS?
CHUMANI LED THEM BACK OUT INTO THE DESERT.
HEY, WHERE ARE YOUR GLASSES?
"LOOK INSIDE MY EYES AND TELL ME YOU SEE A WARRIOR."
SHAKESPEARE?
SIGH KENDRICK LAMAR.
GOBBINA, CECELIA

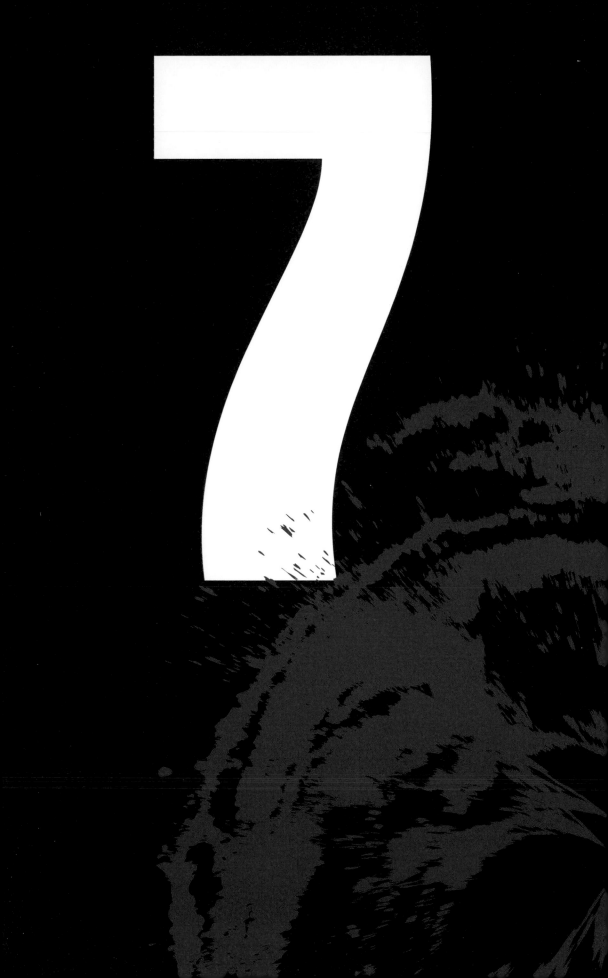

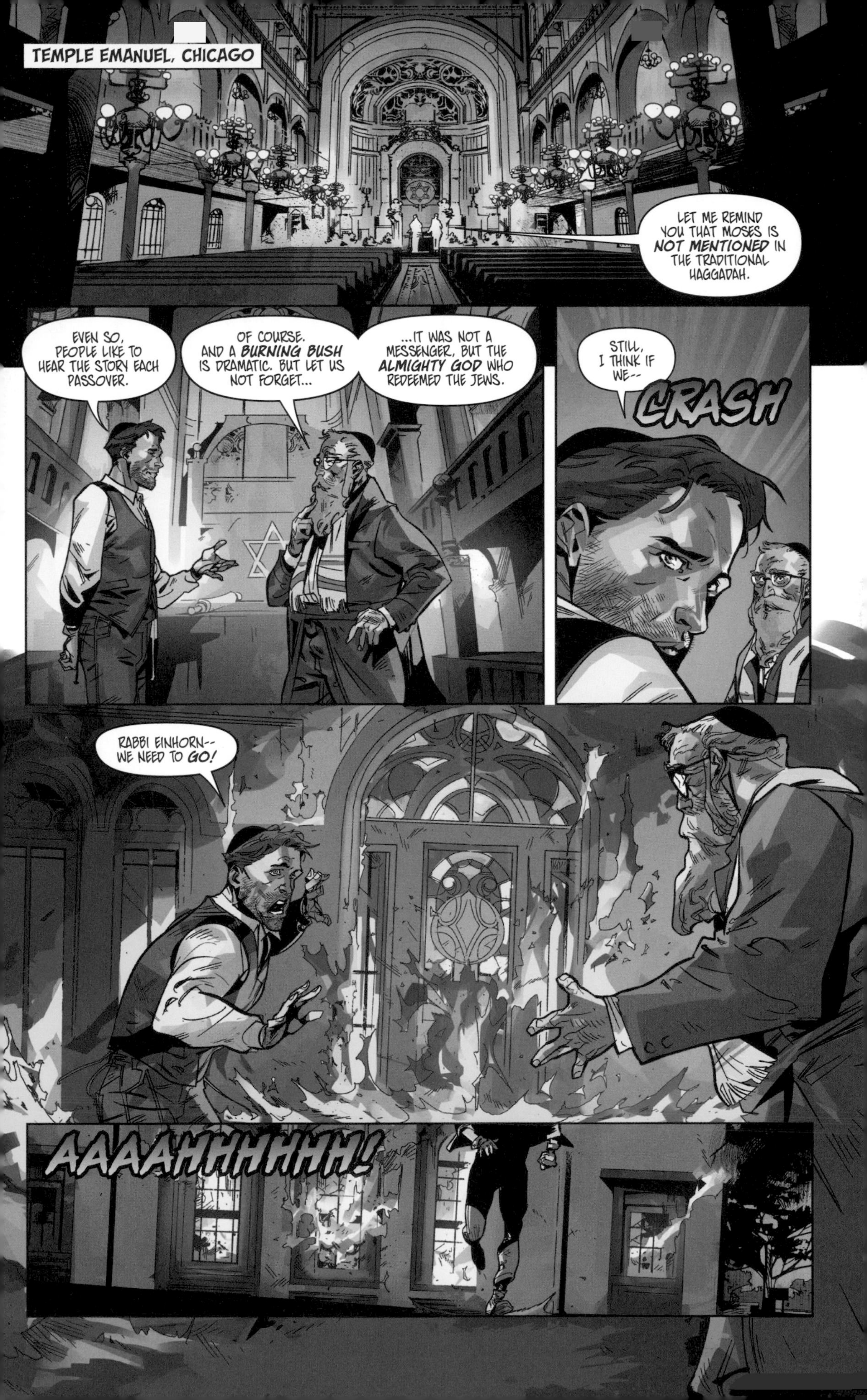
TEMPLE EMANUEL, CHICAGO
LET ME REMIND YOU THAT MOSES IS NOT MENTIONED IN THE TRADITIONAL HAGGADAH.
EVEN SO, PEOPLE LIKE TO HEAR THE STORY EACH PASSOVER.
OF COURSE. AND A BURNING BUSH IS DRAMATIC. BUT LET US NOT FORGET...
...IT WAS NOT A MESSENGER, BUT THE ALMIGHTY GOD WHO REDEEMED THE JEWS.
STILL, I THINK IF WE--
CRASH
RABBI EINHORN--WE NEED TO GO!
AAAAHHHHHHH!

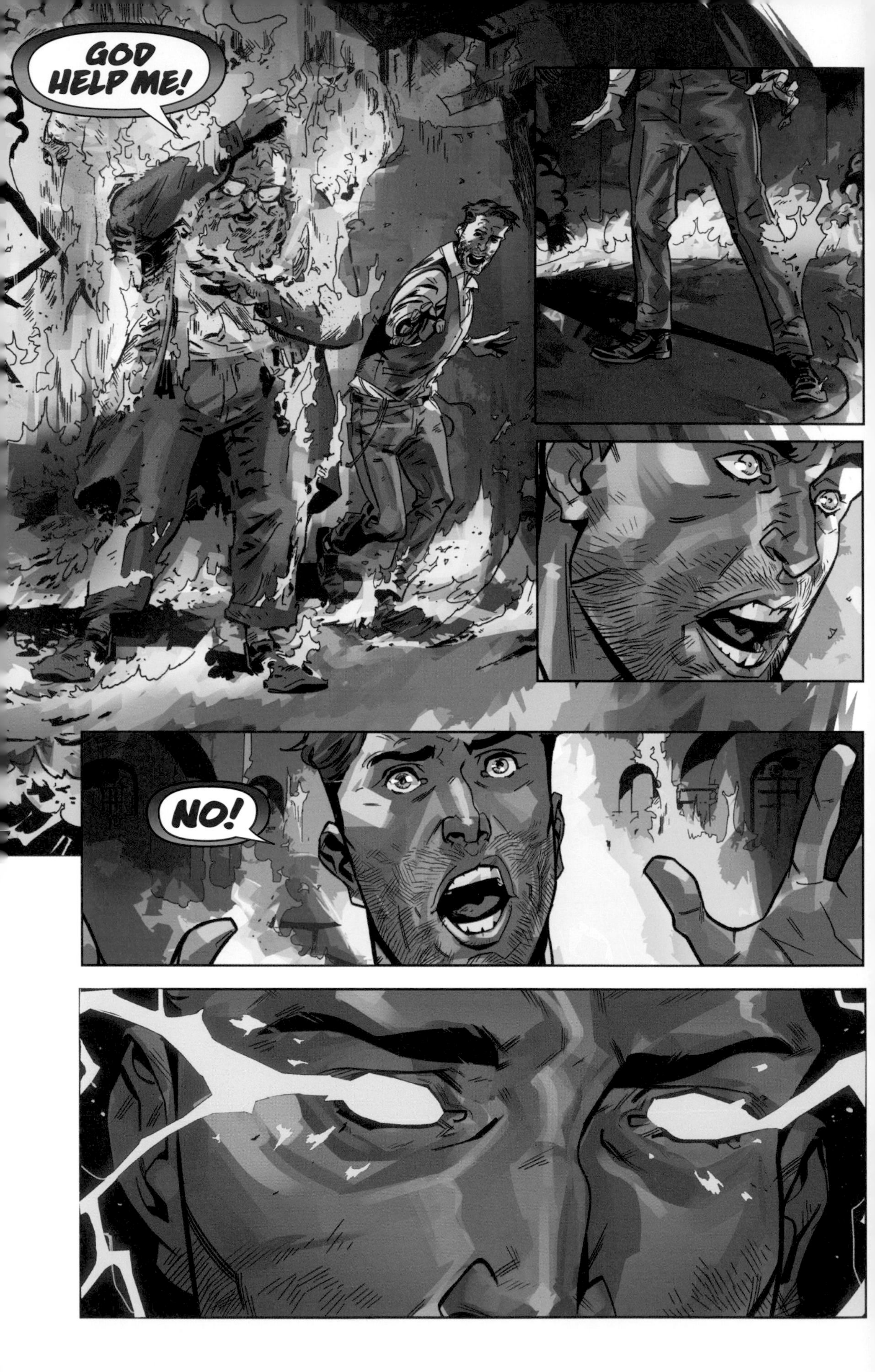
GOD HELP ME!
NO!

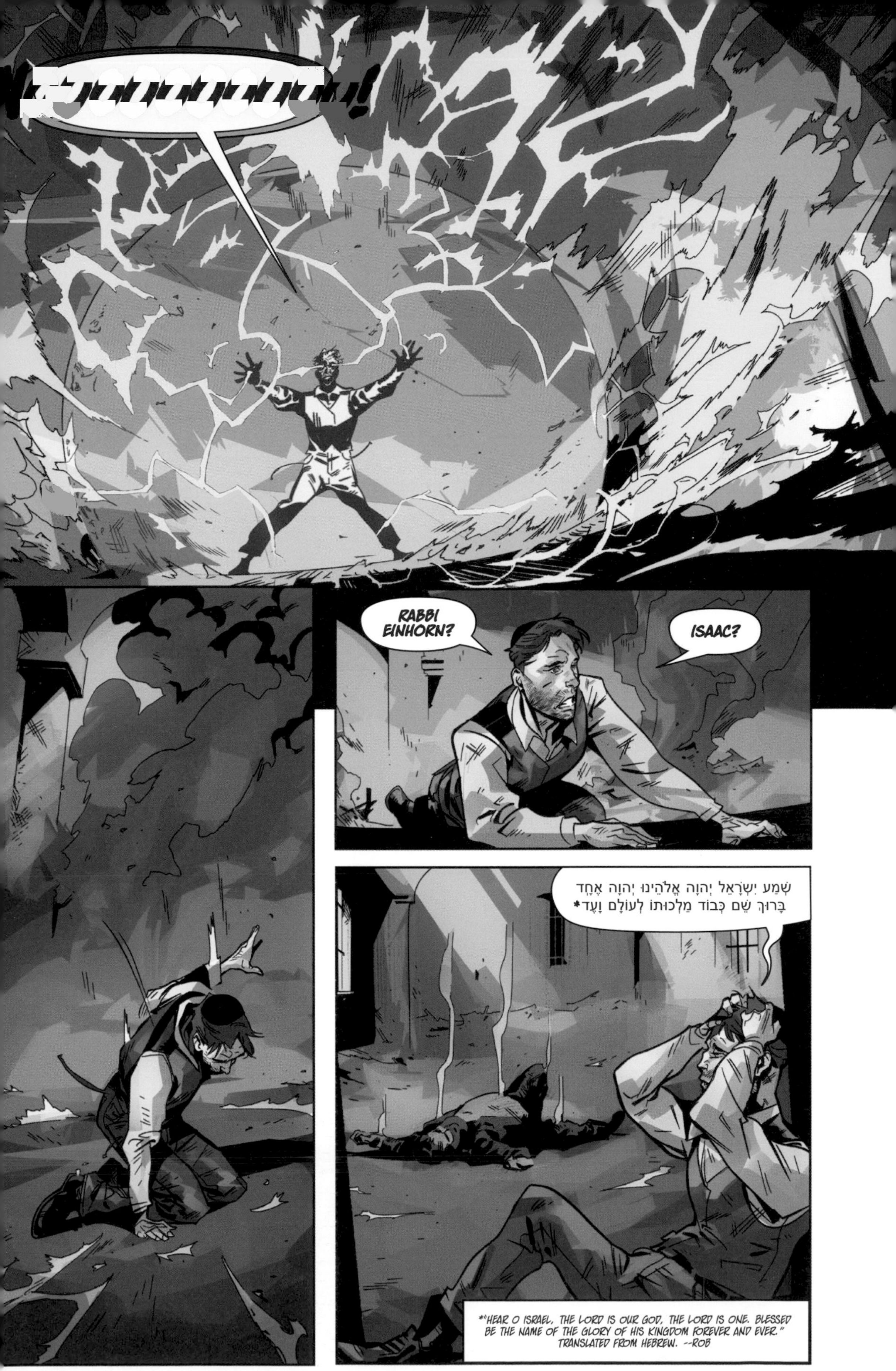

RABBI EINHORN?
ISAAC?
שְׁמַע יִשְׂרָאֵל יְהוָה אֱלֹהֵינוּ יְהוָה אֶחָד
בָּרוּךְ שֵׁם כְּבוֹד מַלְכוּתוֹ לְעוֹלָם וָעֶד*
*"HEAR O ISRAEL, THE LORD IS OUR GOD, THE LORD IS ONE. BLESSED BE THE NAME OF THE GLORY OF HIS KINGDOM FOREVER AND EVER." TRANSLATED FROM HEBREW. --ROB

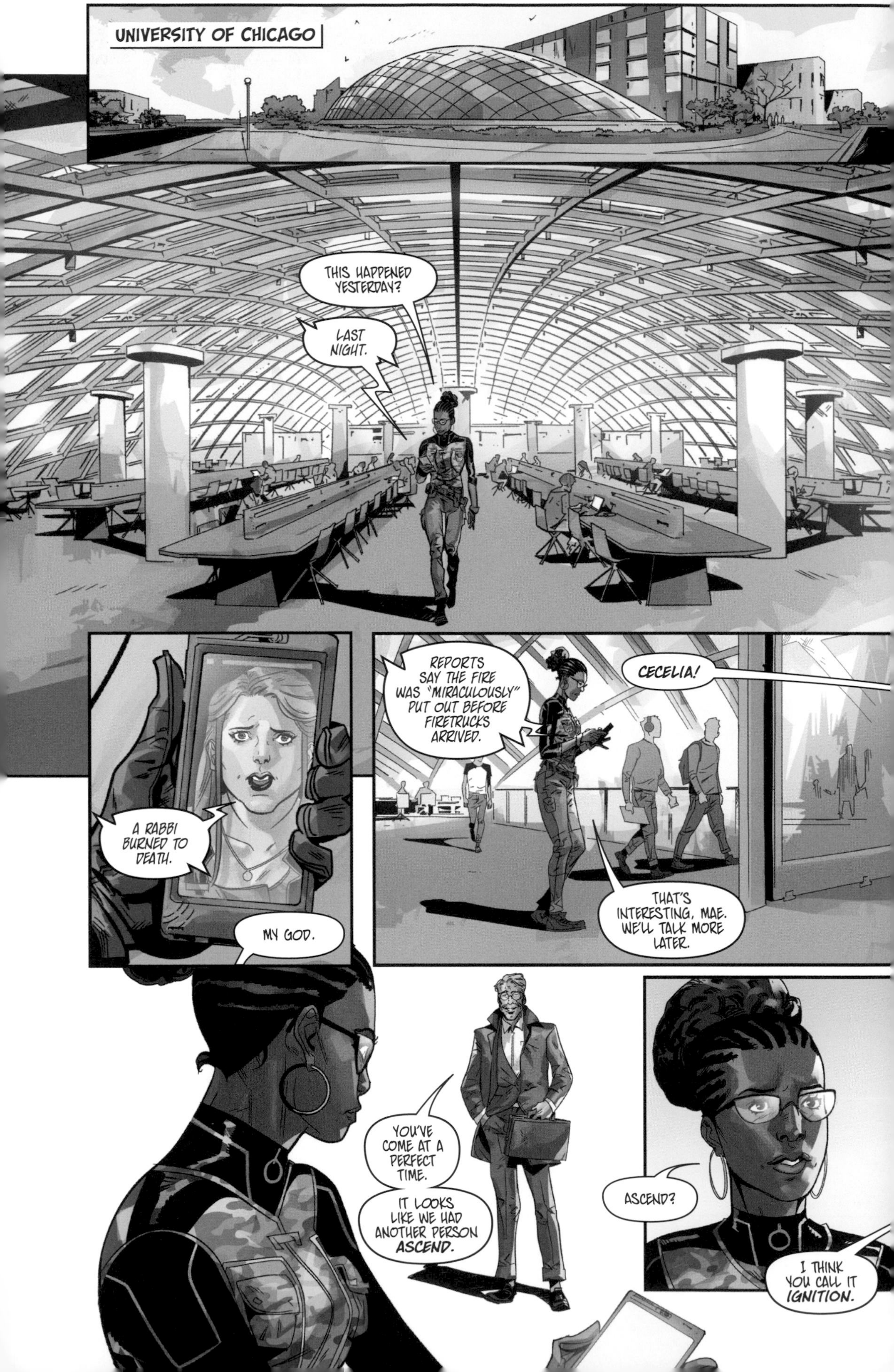
UNIVERSITY OF CHICAGO
THIS HAPPENED YESTERDAY?
LAST NIGHT.
A RABBI BURNED TO DEATH.
MY GOD.
REPORTS SAY THE FIRE WAS "MIRACULOUSLY" PUT OUT BEFORE FIRETRUCKS ARRIVED.
CECELIA!
THAT'S INTERESTING, MAE. WE'LL TALK MORE LATER.
YOU'VE COME AT A PERFECT TIME.
IT LOOKS LIKE WE HAD ANOTHER PERSON **ASCEND**.
ASCEND?
I THINK YOU CALL IT **IGNITION**.

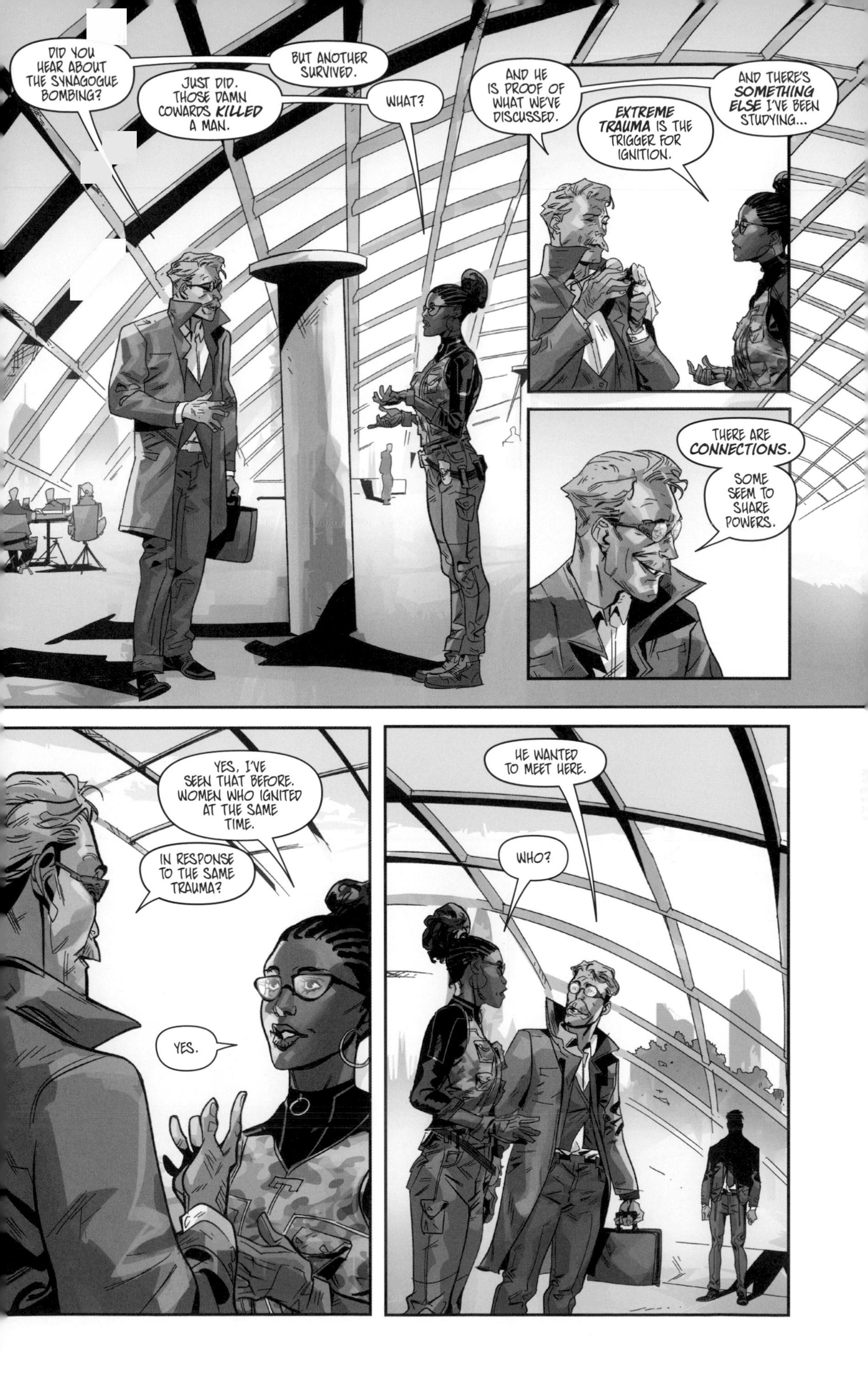
DID YOU HEAR ABOUT THE SYNAGOGUE BOMBING?
JUST DID. THOSE DAMN COWARDS KILLED A MAN.
BUT ANOTHER SURVIVED.
WHAT?
AND HE IS PROOF OF WHAT WE'VE DISCUSSED.
EXTREME TRAUMA IS THE TRIGGER FOR IGNITION.
AND THERE'S SOMETHING ELSE I'VE BEEN STUDYING...
THERE ARE CONNECTIONS.
SOME SEEM TO SHARE POWERS.
YES, I'VE SEEN THAT BEFORE. WOMEN WHO IGNITED AT THE SAME TIME.
IN RESPONSE TO THE SAME TRAUMA?
YES.
HE WANTED TO MEET HERE.
WHO?

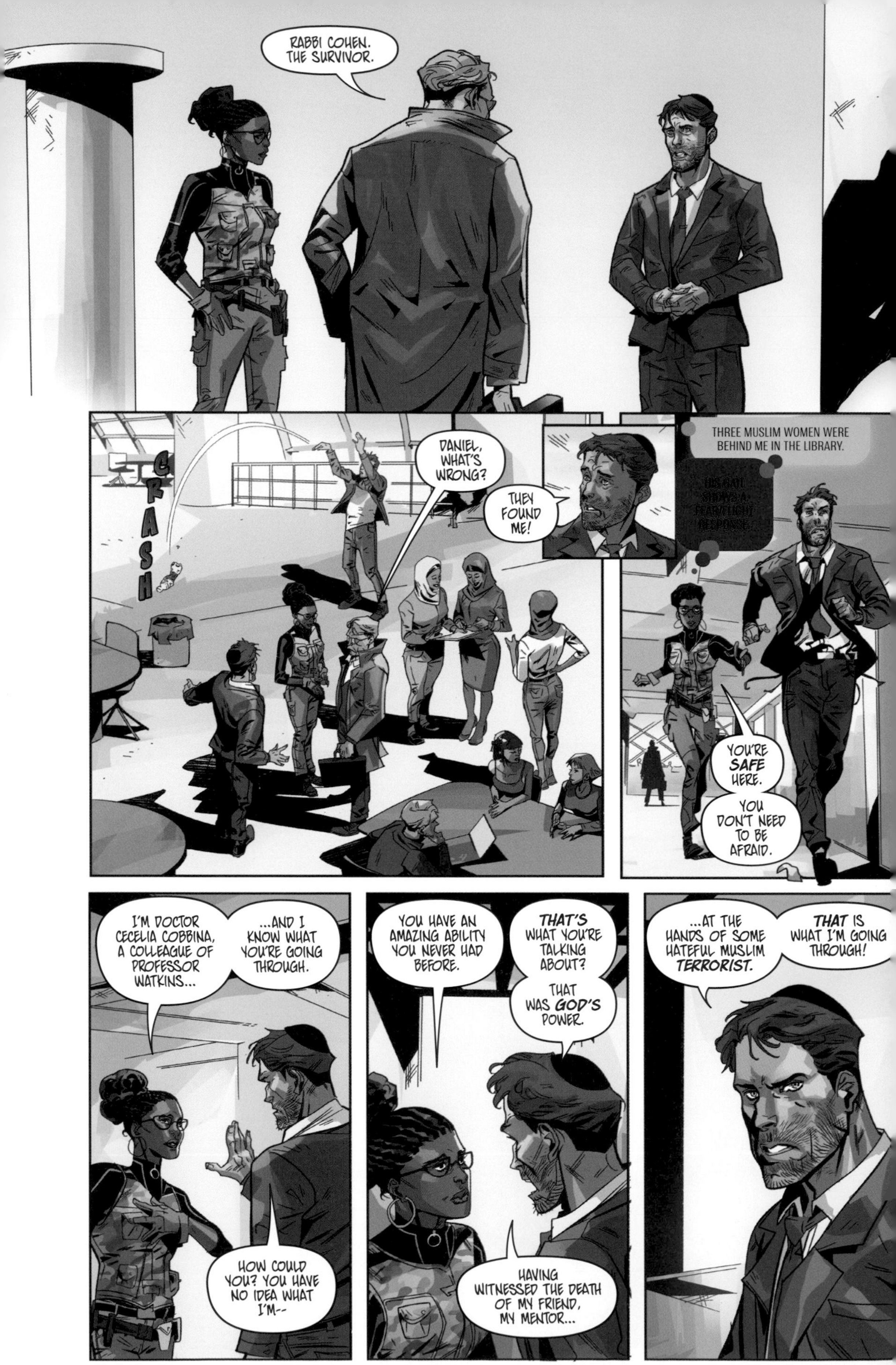

RABBI COHEN. THE SURVIVOR.
CRASH
DANIEL, WHAT'S WRONG?
THEY FOUND ME!
THREE MUSLIM WOMEN WERE BEHIND ME IN THE LIBRARY.
HIS GAIT SHOWS A FEAR/FLIGHT RESPONSE.
YOU'RE **SAFE** HERE.
YOU DON'T NEED TO BE AFRAID.
I'M DOCTOR CECELIA COBBINA, A COLLEAGUE OF PROFESSOR WATKINS...
...AND I KNOW WHAT YOU'RE GOING THROUGH.
HOW COULD YOU? YOU HAVE NO IDEA WHAT I'M--
YOU HAVE AN AMAZING ABILITY YOU NEVER HAD BEFORE.
THAT'S WHAT YOU'RE TALKING ABOUT?
THAT WAS **GOD'S** POWER.
HAVING WITNESSED THE DEATH OF MY FRIEND, MY MENTOR...
...AT THE HANDS OF SOME HATEFUL MUSLIM ***TERRORIST.***
THAT IS WHAT I'M GOING THROUGH!

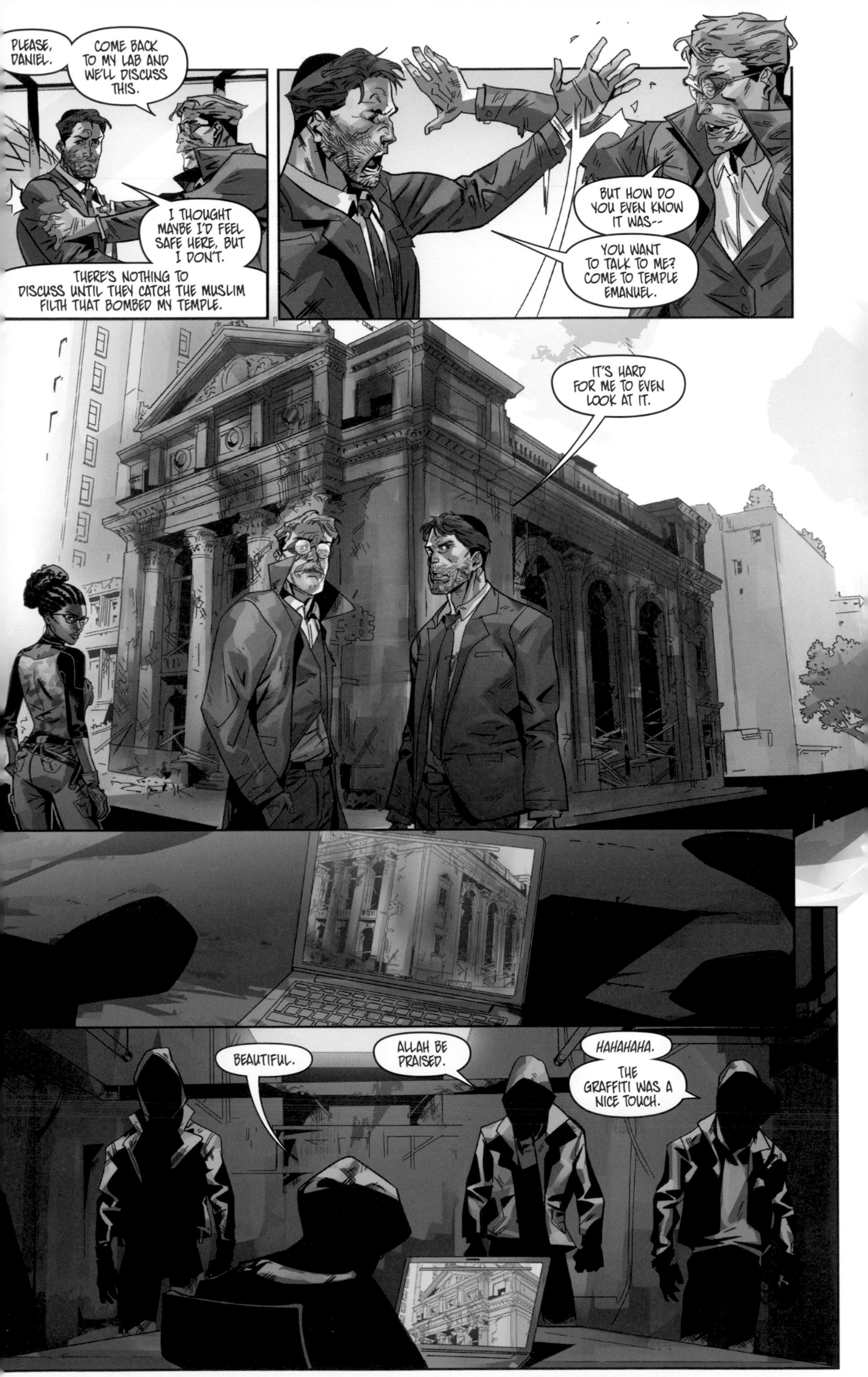
PLEASE, DANIEL.
COME BACK TO MY LAB AND WE'LL DISCUSS THIS.
I THOUGHT MAYBE I'D FEEL SAFE HERE, BUT I DON'T.
THERE'S NOTHING TO DISCUSS UNTIL THEY CATCH THE MUSLIM FILTH THAT BOMBED MY TEMPLE.
BUT HOW DO YOU EVEN KNOW IT WAS--
YOU WANT TO TALK TO ME? COME TO TEMPLE EMANUEL.
IT'S HARD FOR ME TO EVEN LOOK AT IT.
BEAUTIFUL.
ALLAH BE PRAISED.
HAHAHAHA.
THE GRAFFITI WAS A NICE TOUCH.

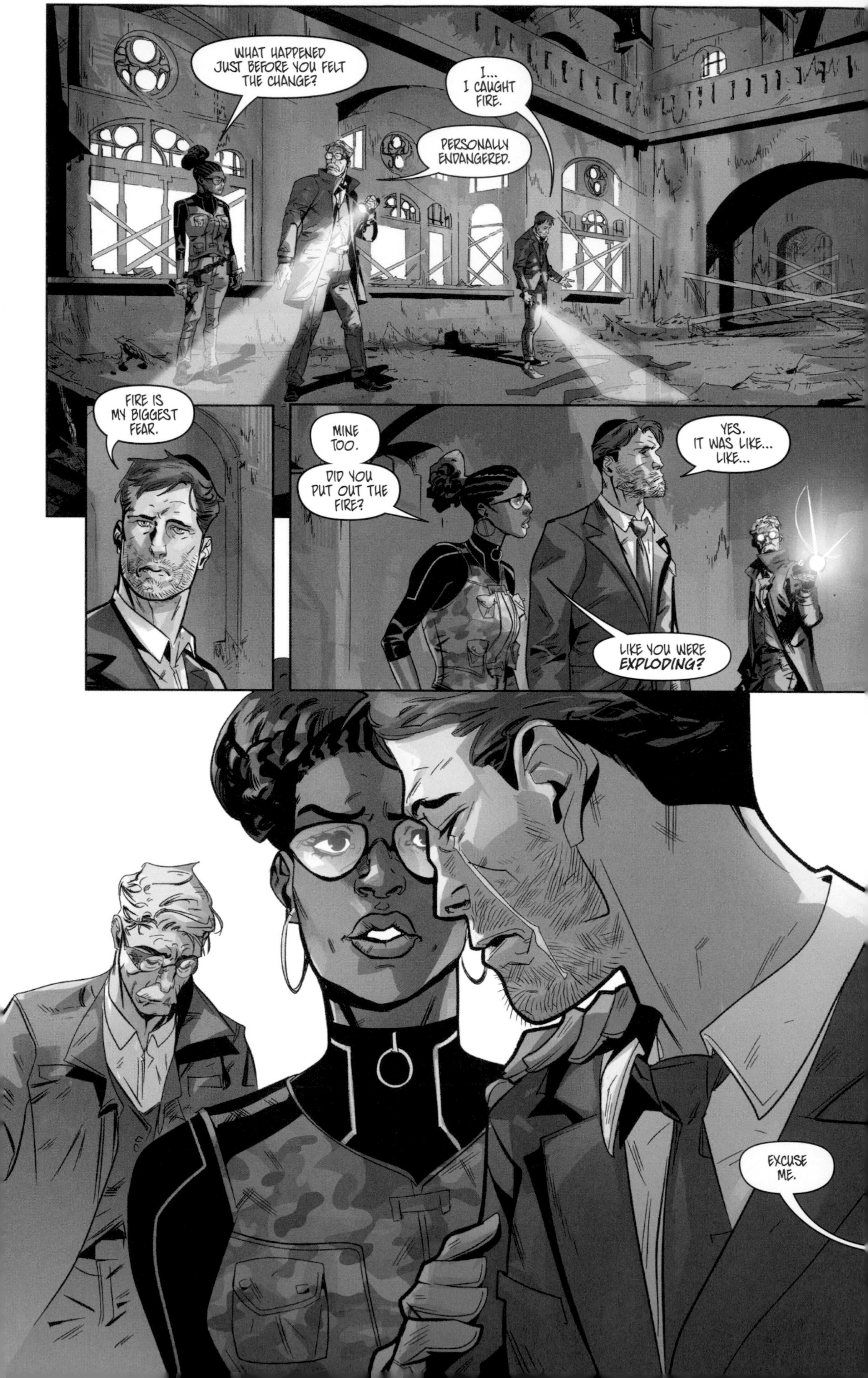
WHAT HAPPENED JUST BEFORE YOU FELT THE CHANGE?
I... I CAUGHT FIRE.
PERSONALLY ENDANGERED.
FIRE IS MY BIGGEST FEAR.
MINE TOO.
DID YOU PUT OUT THE FIRE?
YES. IT WAS LIKE... LIKE...
LIKE YOU WERE EXPLODING?
EXCUSE ME.

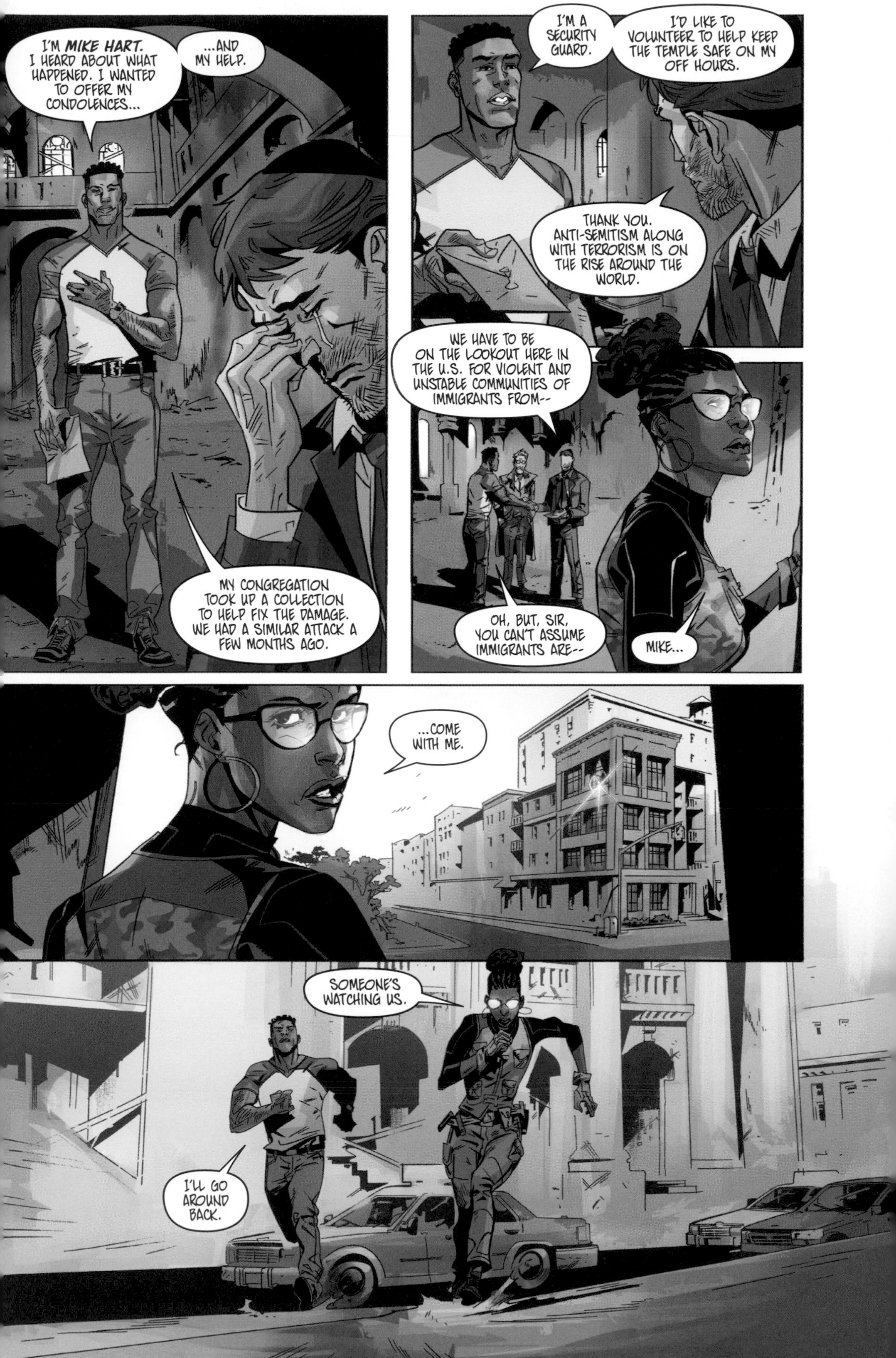
I'M MIKE HART. I HEARD ABOUT WHAT HAPPENED. I WANTED TO OFFER MY CONDOLENCES...
...AND MY HELP.
MY CONGREGATION TOOK UP A COLLECTION TO HELP FIX THE DAMAGE. WE HAD A SIMILAR ATTACK A FEW MONTHS AGO.
I'M A SECURITY GUARD.
I'D LIKE TO VOLUNTEER TO HELP KEEP THE TEMPLE SAFE ON MY OFF HOURS.
THANK YOU. ANTI-SEMITISM ALONG WITH TERRORISM IS ON THE RISE AROUND THE WORLD.
WE HAVE TO BE ON THE LOOKOUT HERE IN THE U.S. FOR VIOLENT AND UNSTABLE COMMUNITIES OF IMMIGRANTS FROM--
OH, BUT, SIR, YOU CAN'T ASSUME IMMIGRANTS ARE--
MIKE...
...COME WITH ME.
SOMEONE'S WATCHING US.
I'LL GO AROUND BACK.

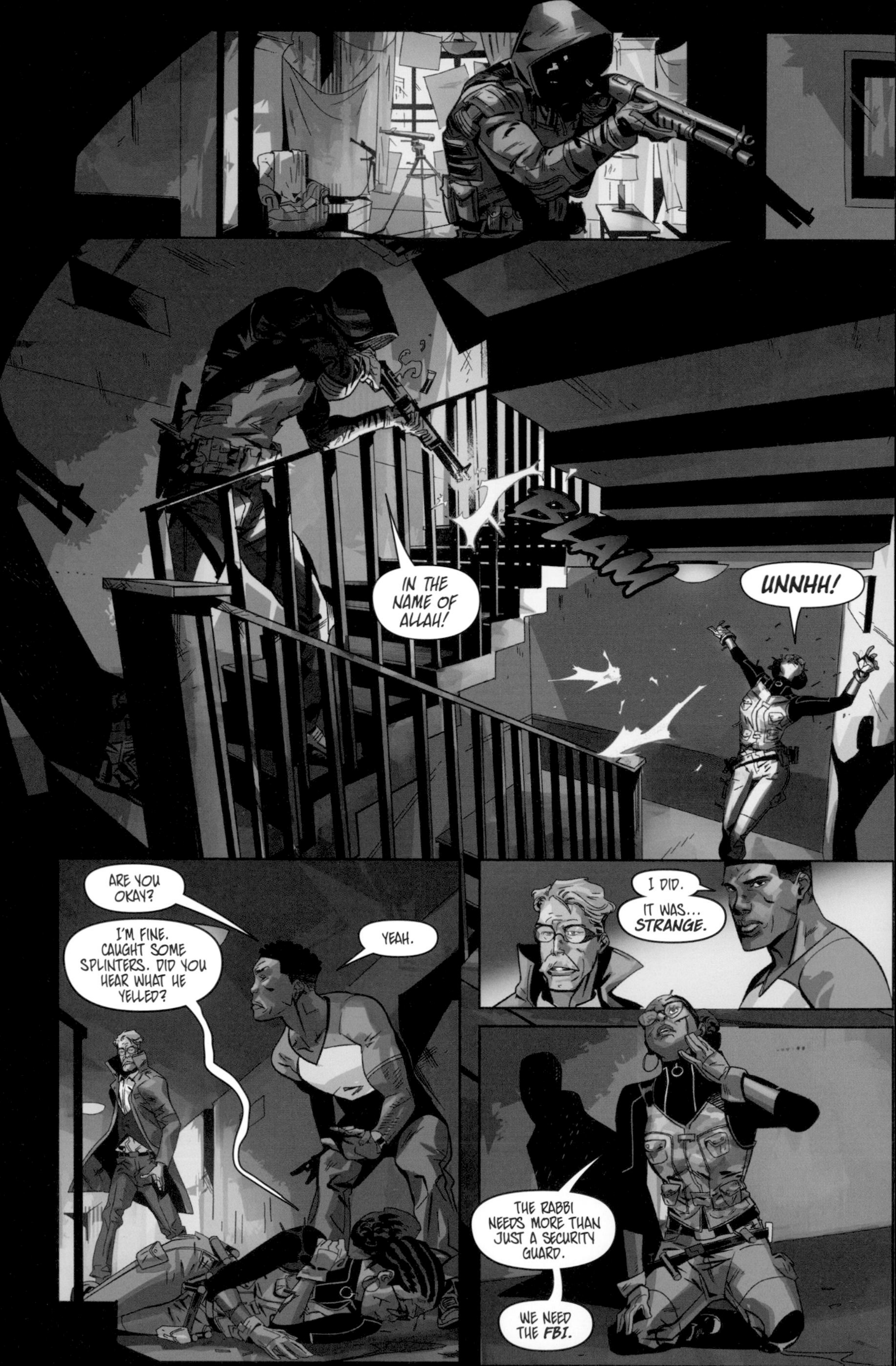
IN THE NAME OF ALLAH!
BLAM
UNNHH!
ARE YOU OKAY?
I'M FINE. CAUGHT SOME SPLINTERS. DID YOU HEAR WHAT HE YELLED?
YEAH.
I DID.
IT WAS... STRANGE.
THE RABBI NEEDS MORE THAN JUST A SECURITY GUARD.
WE NEED THE FBI.

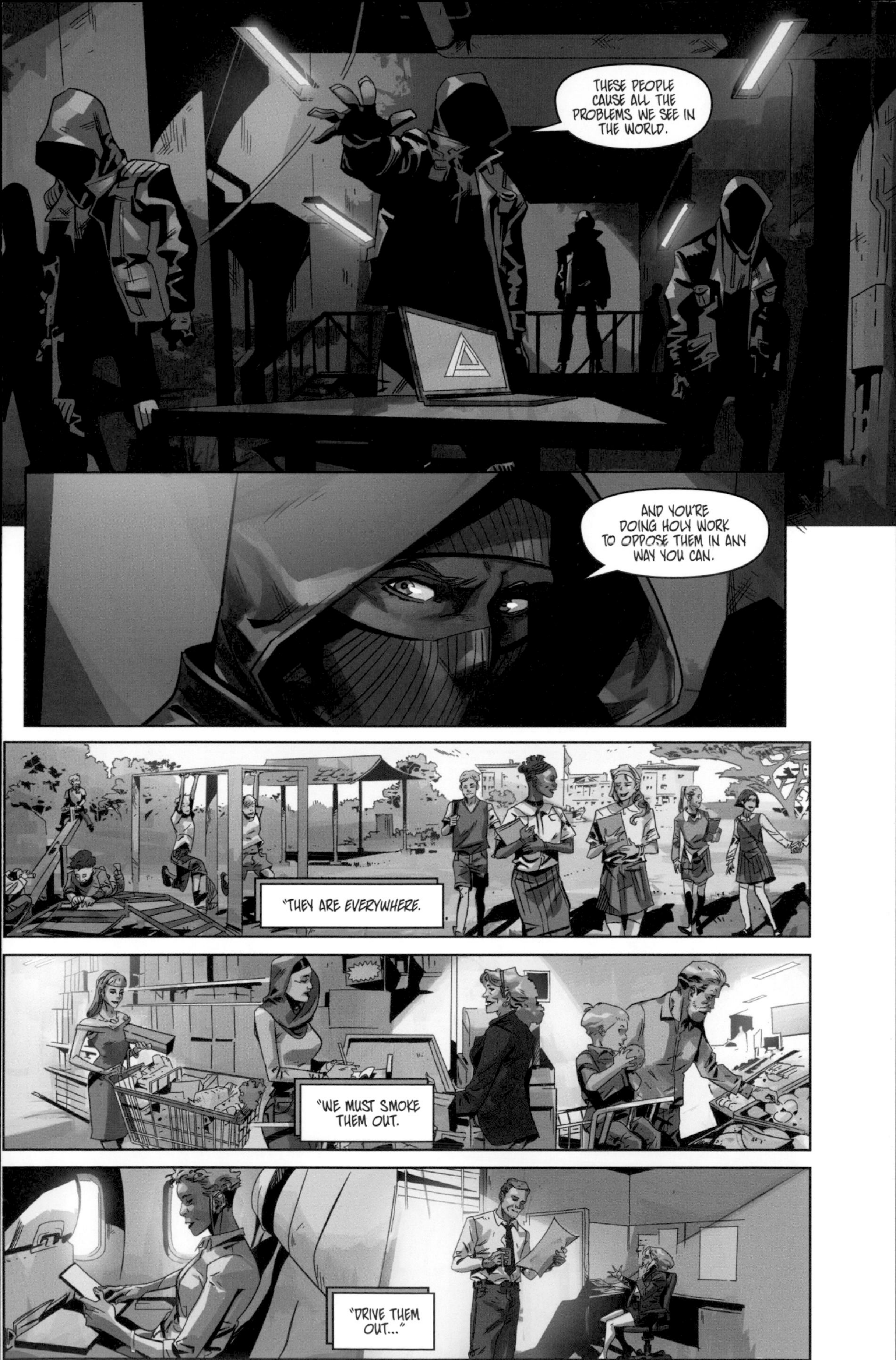
THESE PEOPLE CAUSE ALL THE PROBLEMS WE SEE IN THE WORLD.
AND YOU'RE DOING HOLY WORK TO OPPOSE THEM IN ANY WAY YOU CAN.
"THEY ARE EVERYWHERE.
"WE MUST SMOKE THEM OUT.
"DRIVE THEM OUT..."

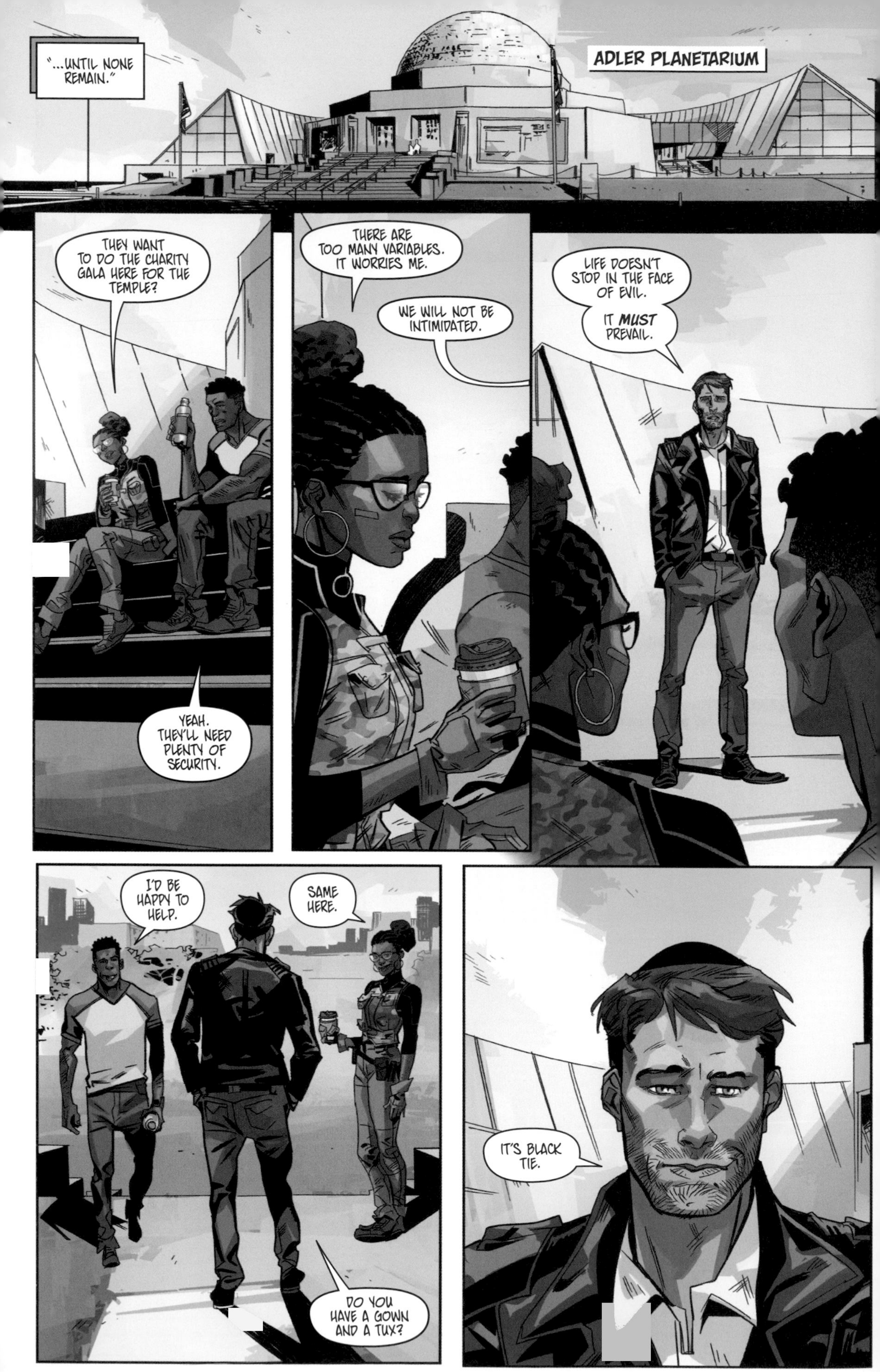
"...UNTIL NONE REMAIN."
ADLER PLANETARIUM
THEY WANT TO DO THE CHARITY GALA HERE FOR THE TEMPLE?
YEAH. THEY'LL NEED PLENTY OF SECURITY.
THERE ARE TOO MANY VARIABLES. IT WORRIES ME.
WE WILL NOT BE INTIMIDATED.
LIFE DOESN'T STOP IN THE FACE OF EVIL.
IT MUST PREVAIL.
I'D BE HAPPY TO HELP.
SAME HERE.
DO YOU HAVE A GOWN AND A TUX?
IT'S BLACK TIE.

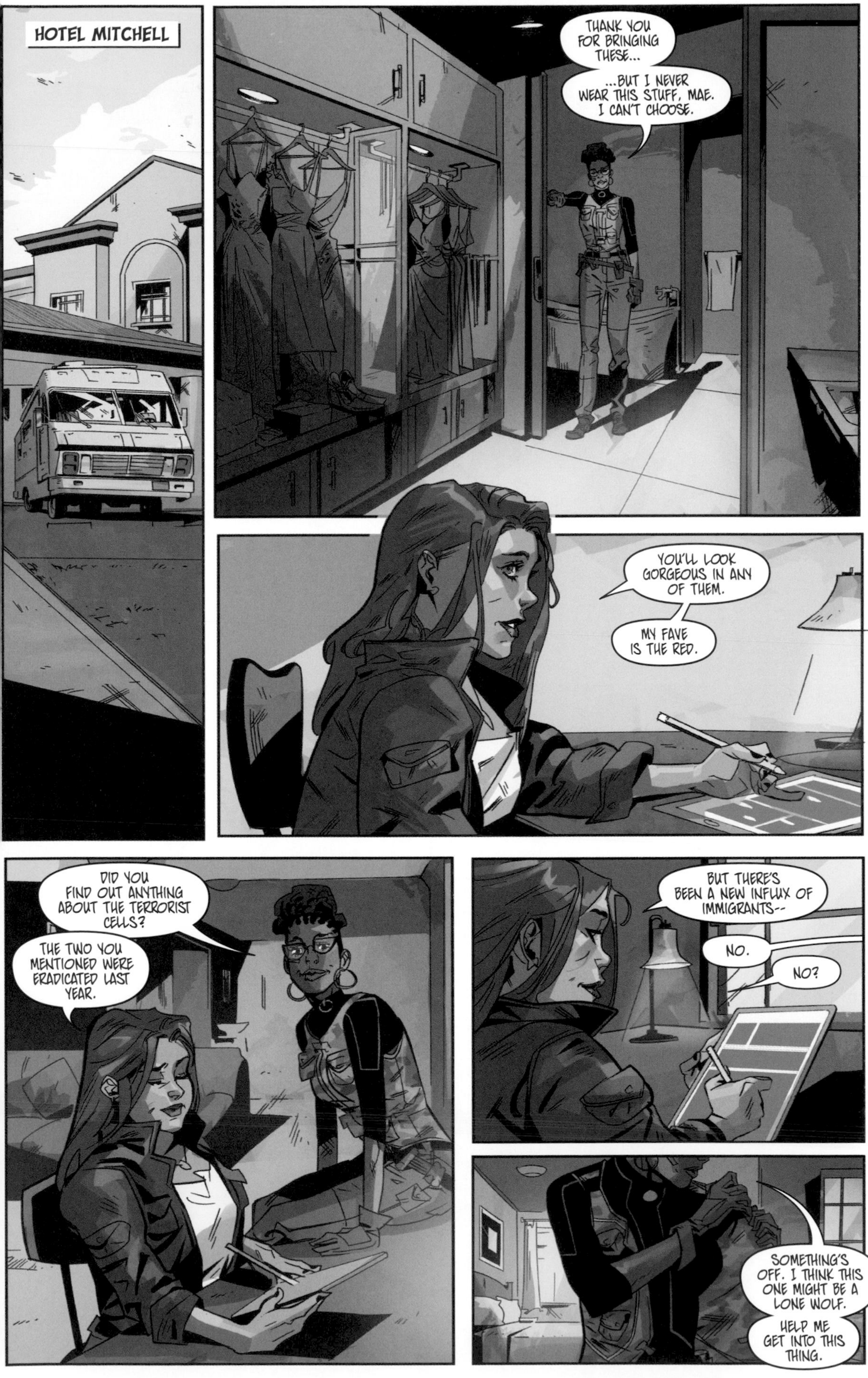
HOTEL MITCHELL
THANK YOU FOR BRINGING THESE...
...BUT I NEVER WEAR THIS STUFF, MAE. I CAN'T CHOOSE.
YOU'LL LOOK GORGEOUS IN ANY OF THEM.
MY FAVE IS THE RED.
DID YOU FIND OUT ANYTHING ABOUT THE TERRORIST CELLS?
THE TWO YOU MENTIONED WERE ERADICATED LAST YEAR.
BUT THERE'S BEEN A NEW INFLUX OF IMMIGRANTS--
NO.
NO?
SOMETHING'S OFF. I THINK THIS ONE MIGHT BE A LONE WOLF.
HELP ME GET INTO THIS THING.

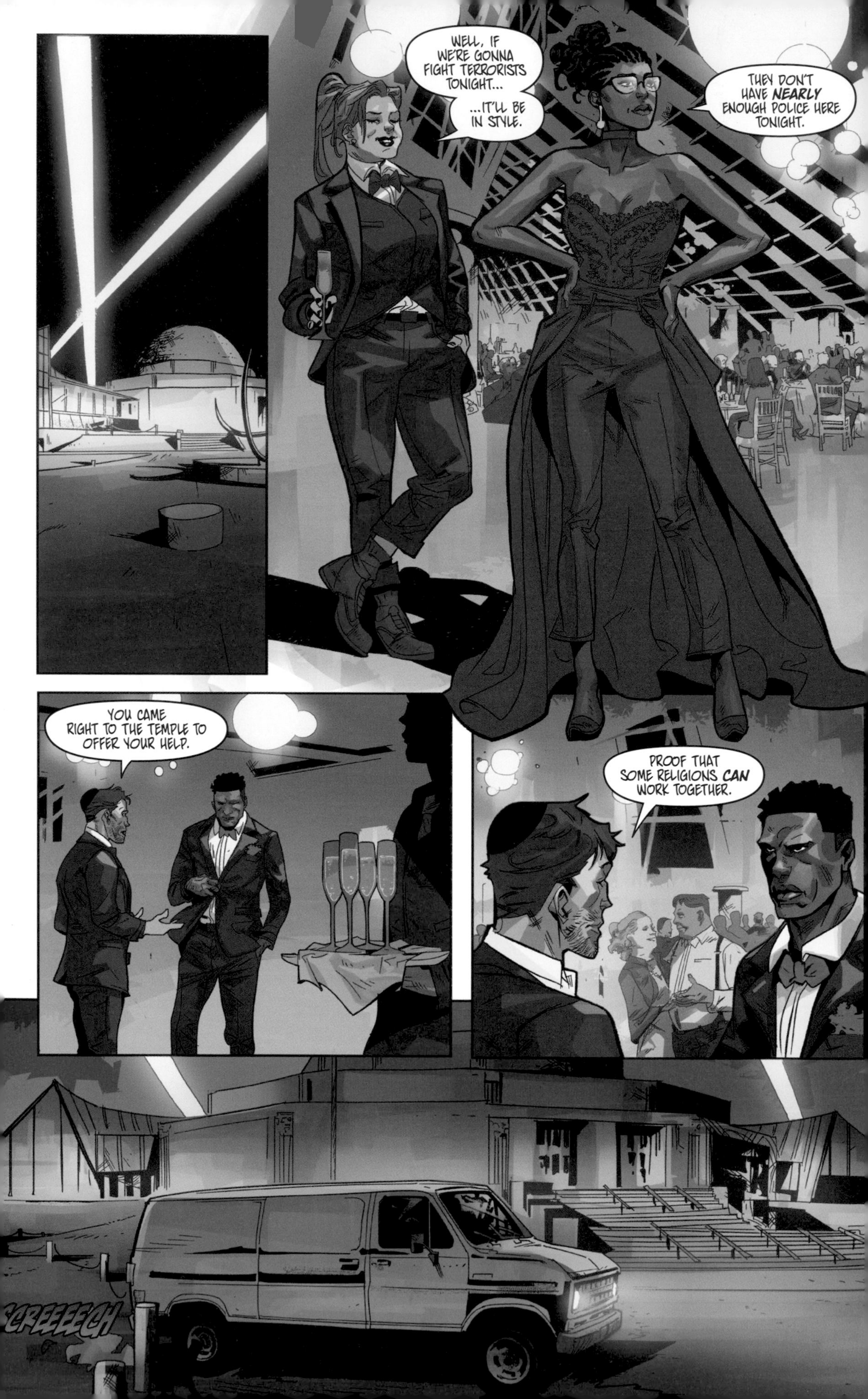
WELL, IF WE'RE GONNA FIGHT TERRORISTS TONIGHT...
...IT'LL BE IN STYLE.
THEY DON'T HAVE **NEARLY** ENOUGH POLICE HERE TONIGHT.
YOU CAME RIGHT TO THE TEMPLE TO OFFER YOUR HELP.
PROOF THAT SOME RELIGIONS **CAN** WORK TOGETHER.
SCREEEECH

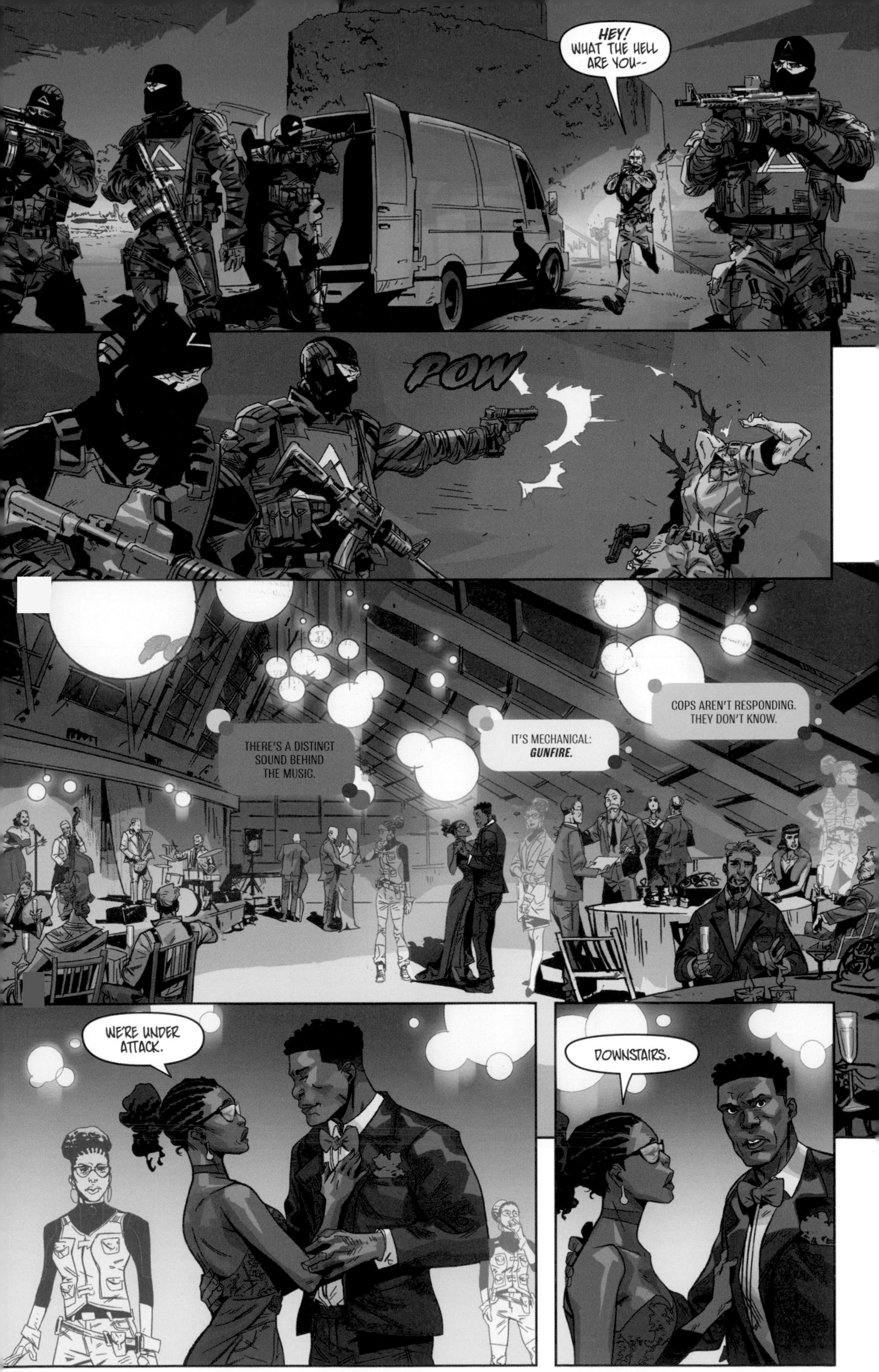
HEY! WHAT THE HELL ARE YOU--
POW
THERE'S A DISTINCT SOUND BEHIND THE MUSIC.
IT'S MECHANICAL: ***GUNFIRE.***
COPS AREN'T RESPONDING. THEY DON'T KNOW.
WE'RE UNDER ATTACK.
DOWNSTAIRS.

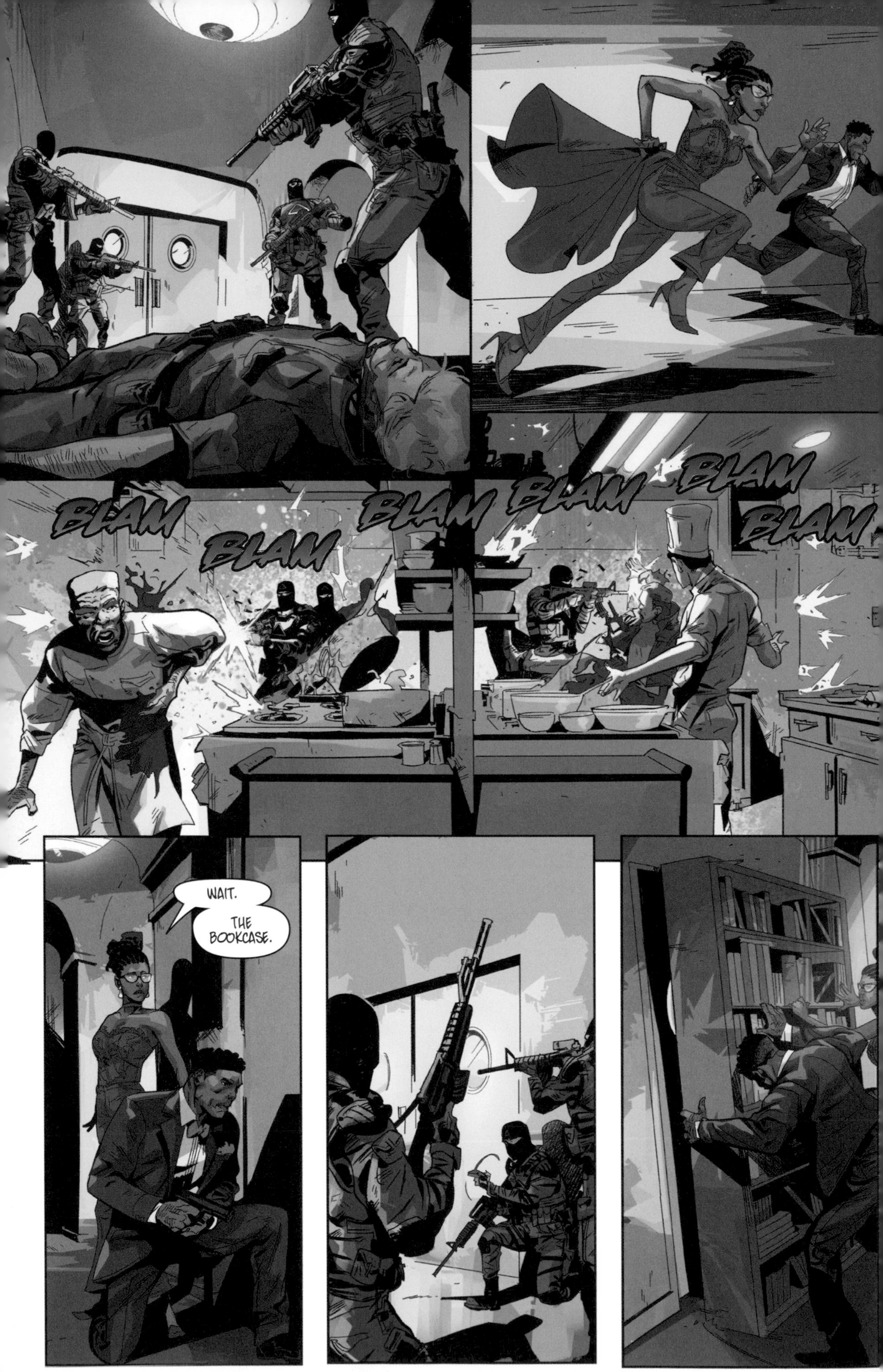
BLAM
BLAM
BLAM
BLAM
BLAM
BLAM
WAIT.
THE BOOKCASE.

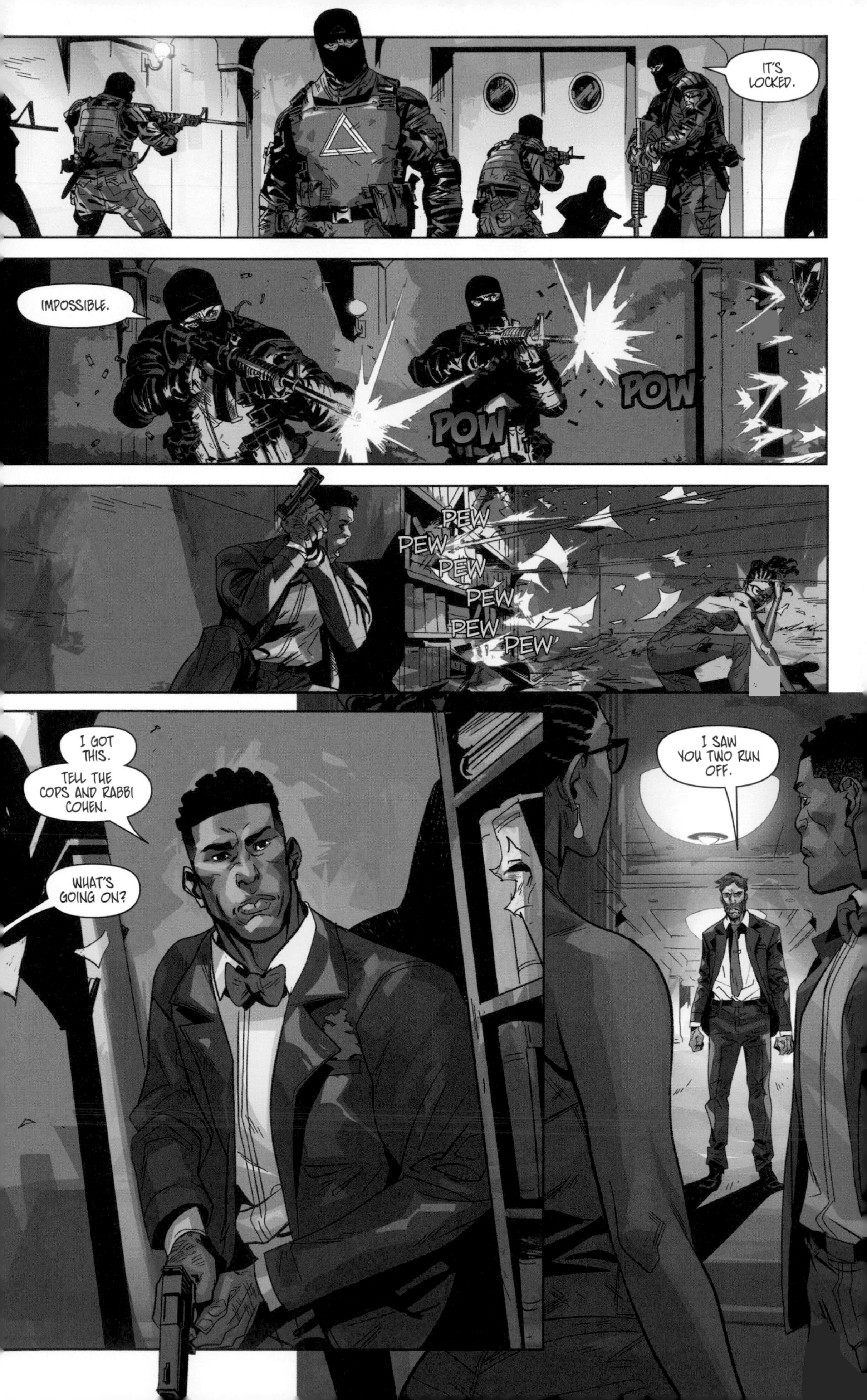
IT'S LOCKED.
IMPOSSIBLE.
POW
POW
PEW
PEW
PEW
PEW
PEW
PEW
I GOT THIS.
TELL THE COPS AND RABBI COHEN.
WHAT'S GOING ON?
I SAW YOU TWO RUN OFF.

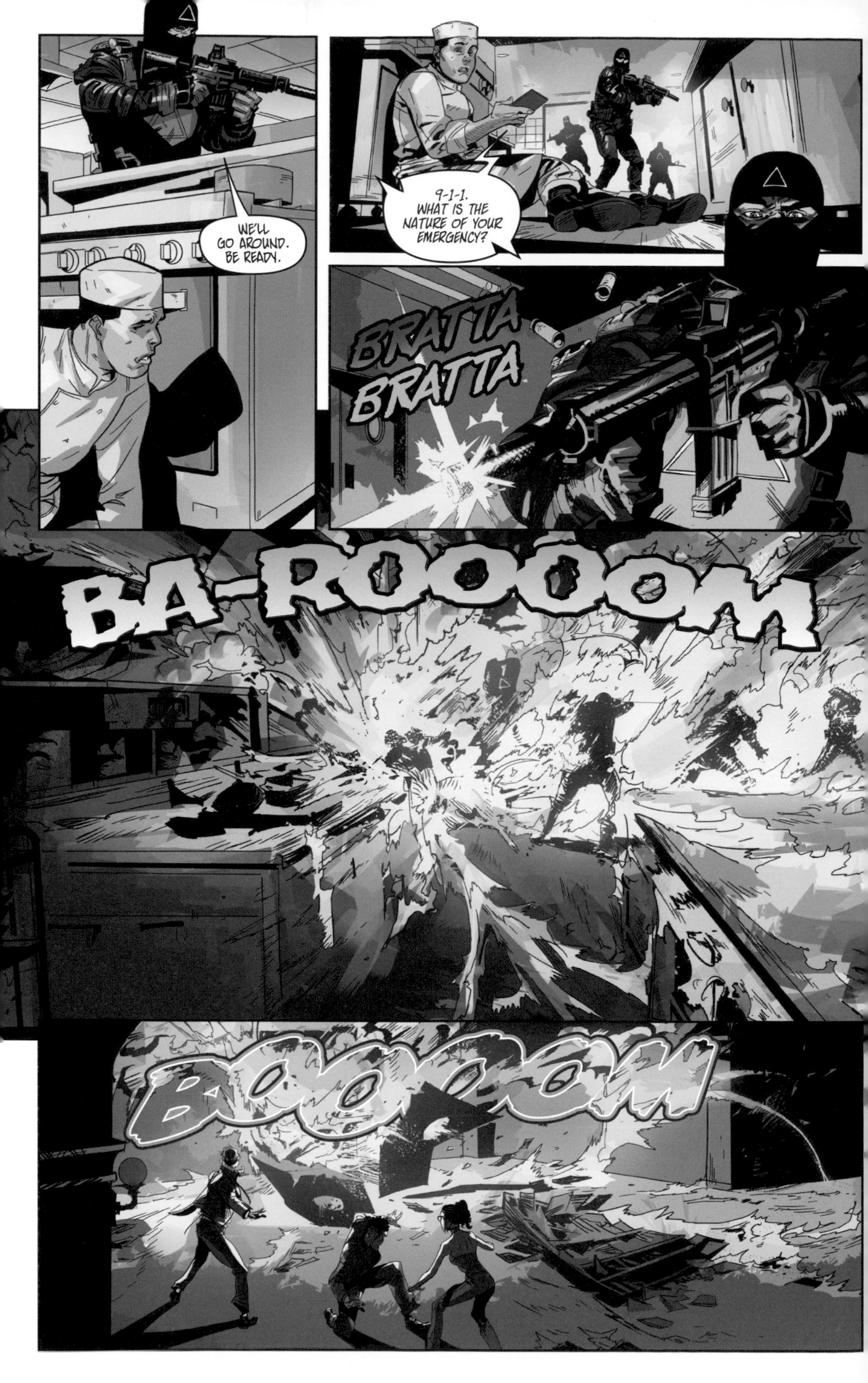
WE'LL GO AROUND. BE READY.
9-1-1. WHAT IS THE NATURE OF YOUR EMERGENCY?
BRATTA BRATTA
BA-ROOOOM
BOOOOOM

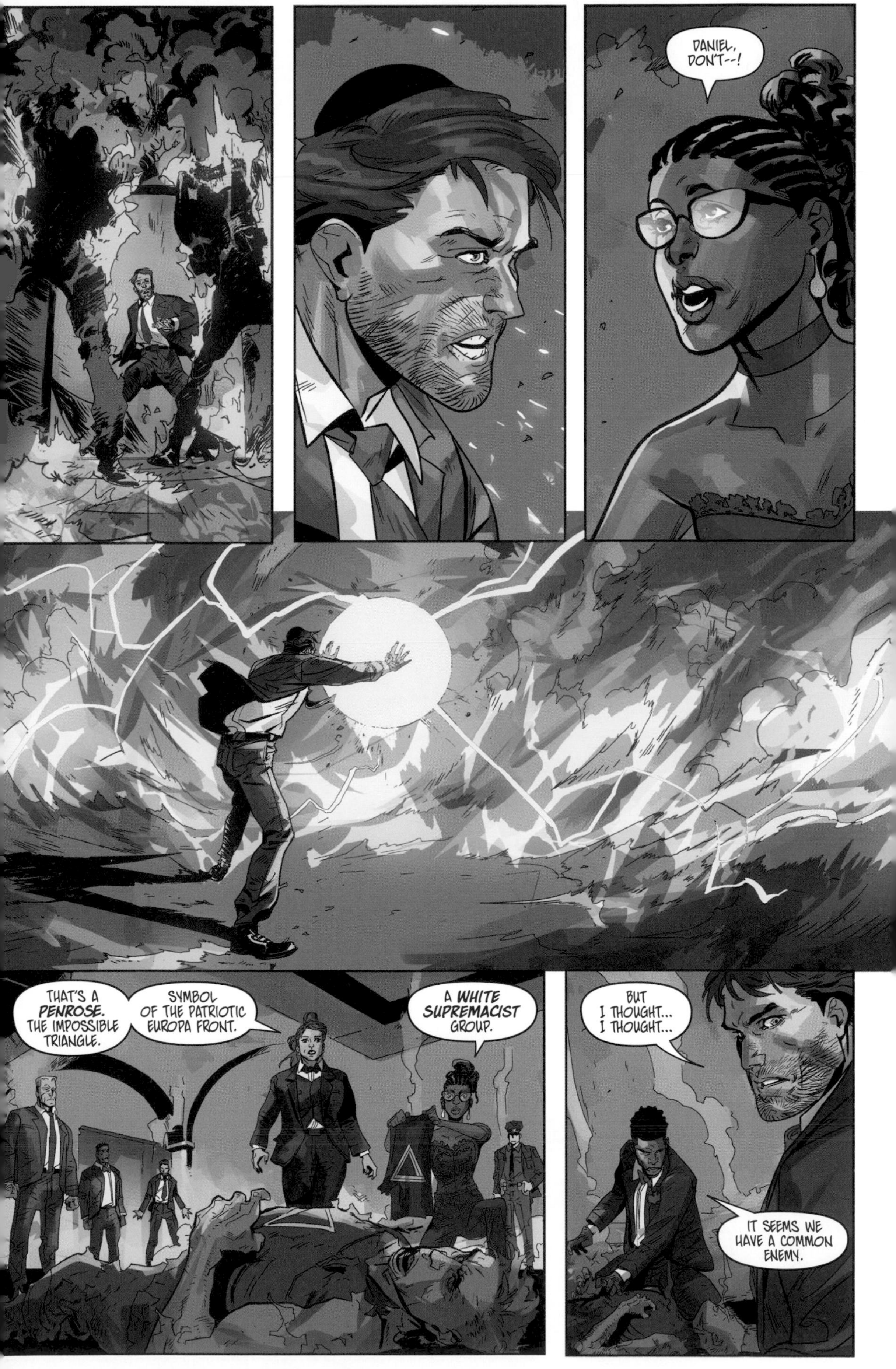
DANIEL, DON'T--!
THAT'S A PENROSE. THE IMPOSSIBLE TRIANGLE.
SYMBOL OF THE PATRIOTIC EUROPA FRONT.
A WHITE SUPREMACIST GROUP.
BUT I THOUGHT... I THOUGHT...
IT SEEMS WE HAVE A COMMON ENEMY.

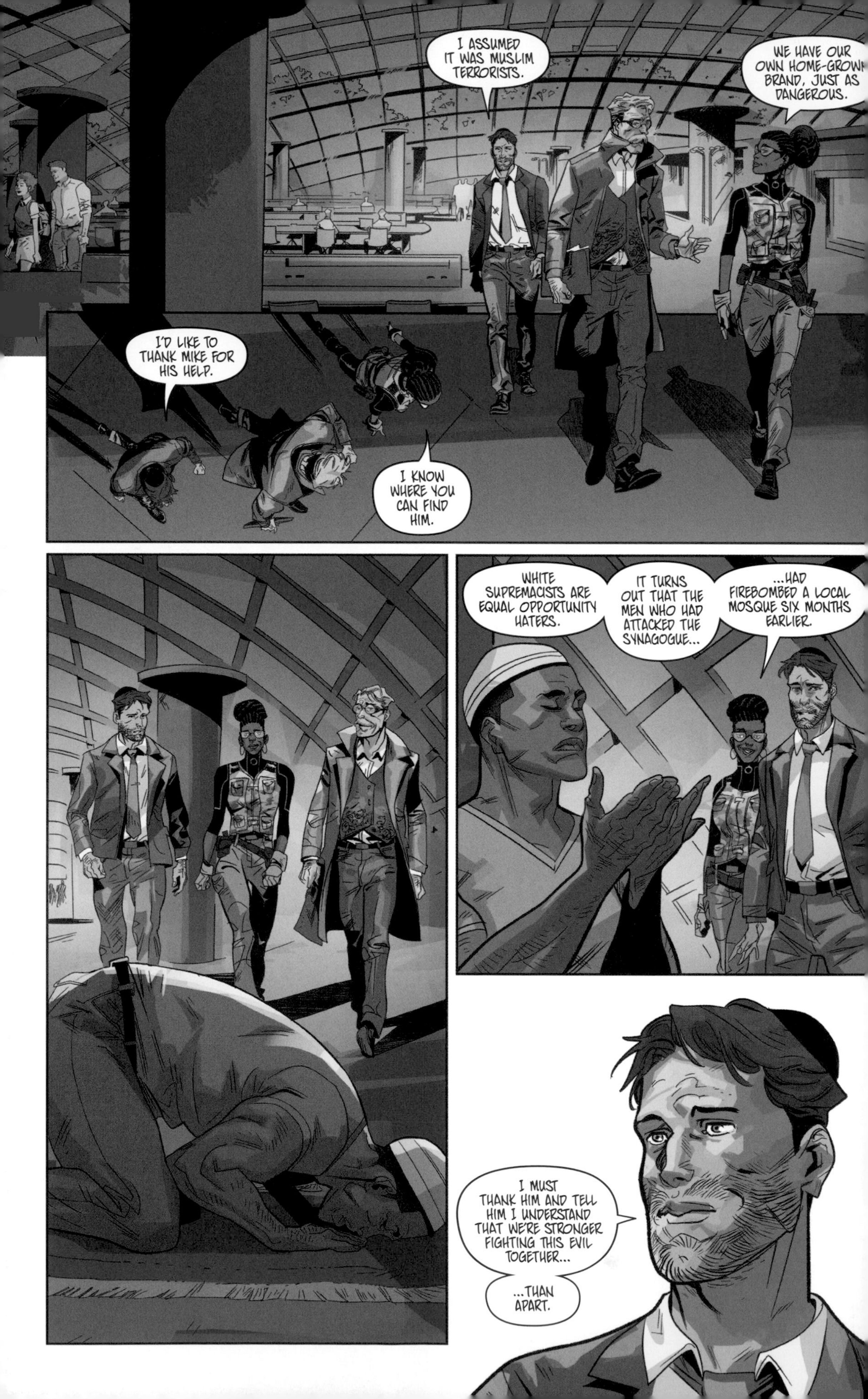

I ASSUMED IT WAS MUSLIM TERRORISTS.
WE HAVE OUR OWN HOME-GROWN BRAND, JUST AS DANGEROUS.
I'D LIKE TO THANK MIKE FOR HIS HELP.
I KNOW WHERE YOU CAN FIND HIM.
WHITE SUPREMACISTS ARE EQUAL OPPORTUNITY HATERS.
IT TURNS OUT THAT THE MEN WHO HAD ATTACKED THE SYNAGOGUE...
...HAD FIREBOMBED A LOCAL MOSQUE SIX MONTHS EARLIER.
I MUST THANK HIM AND TELL HIM I UNDERSTAND THAT WE'RE STRONGER FIGHTING THIS EVIL TOGETHER...
...THAN APART.

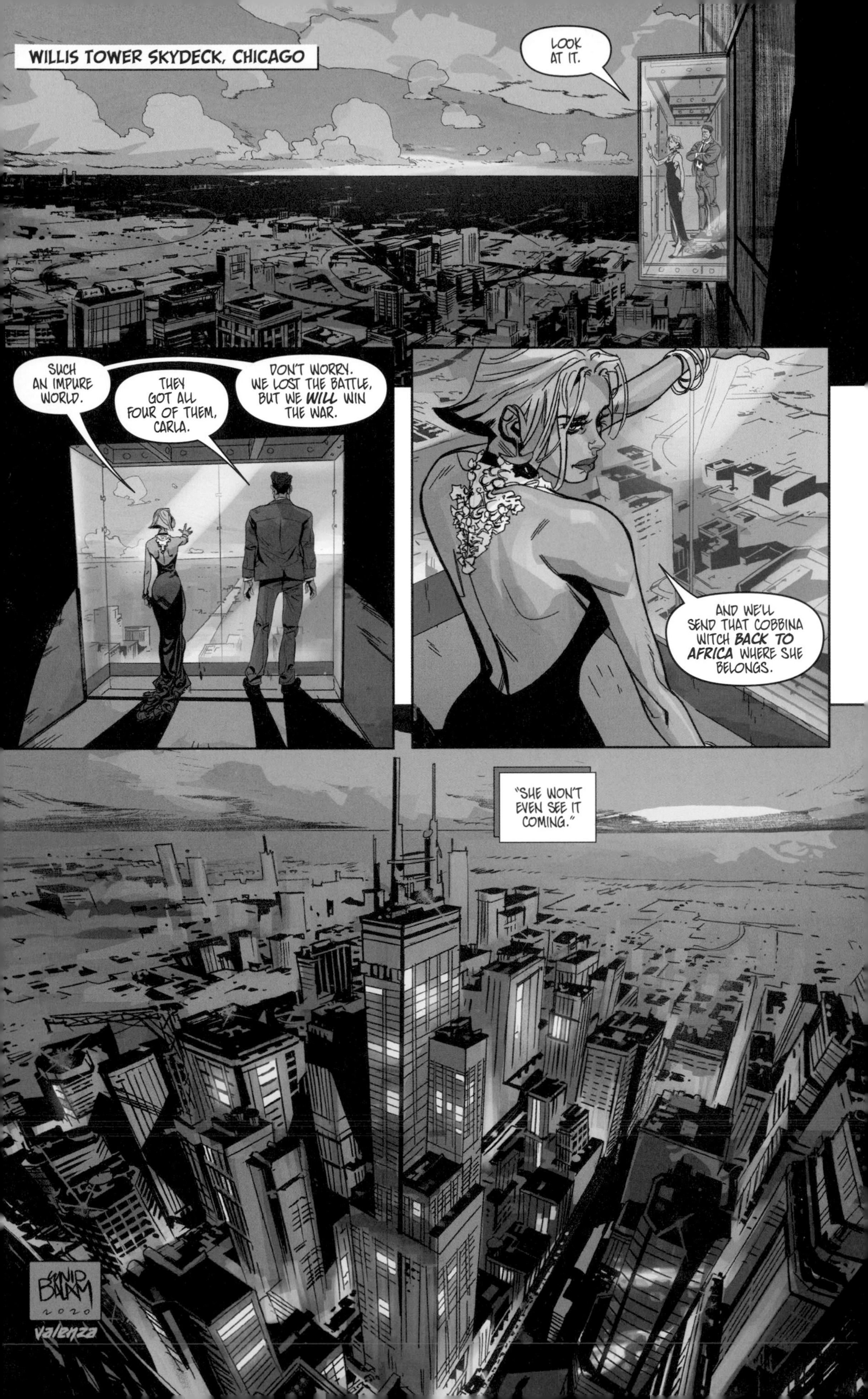
WILLIS TOWER SKYDECK, CHICAGO
LOOK AT IT.
SUCH AN IMPURE WORLD.
THEY GOT ALL FOUR OF THEM, CARLA.
DON'T WORRY. WE LOST THE BATTLE, BUT WE WILL WIN THE WAR.
AND WE'LL SEND THAT COBBINA WITCH BACK TO AFRICA WHERE SHE BELONGS.
"SHE WON'T EVEN SEE IT COMING."
BAUM 2020
valenza

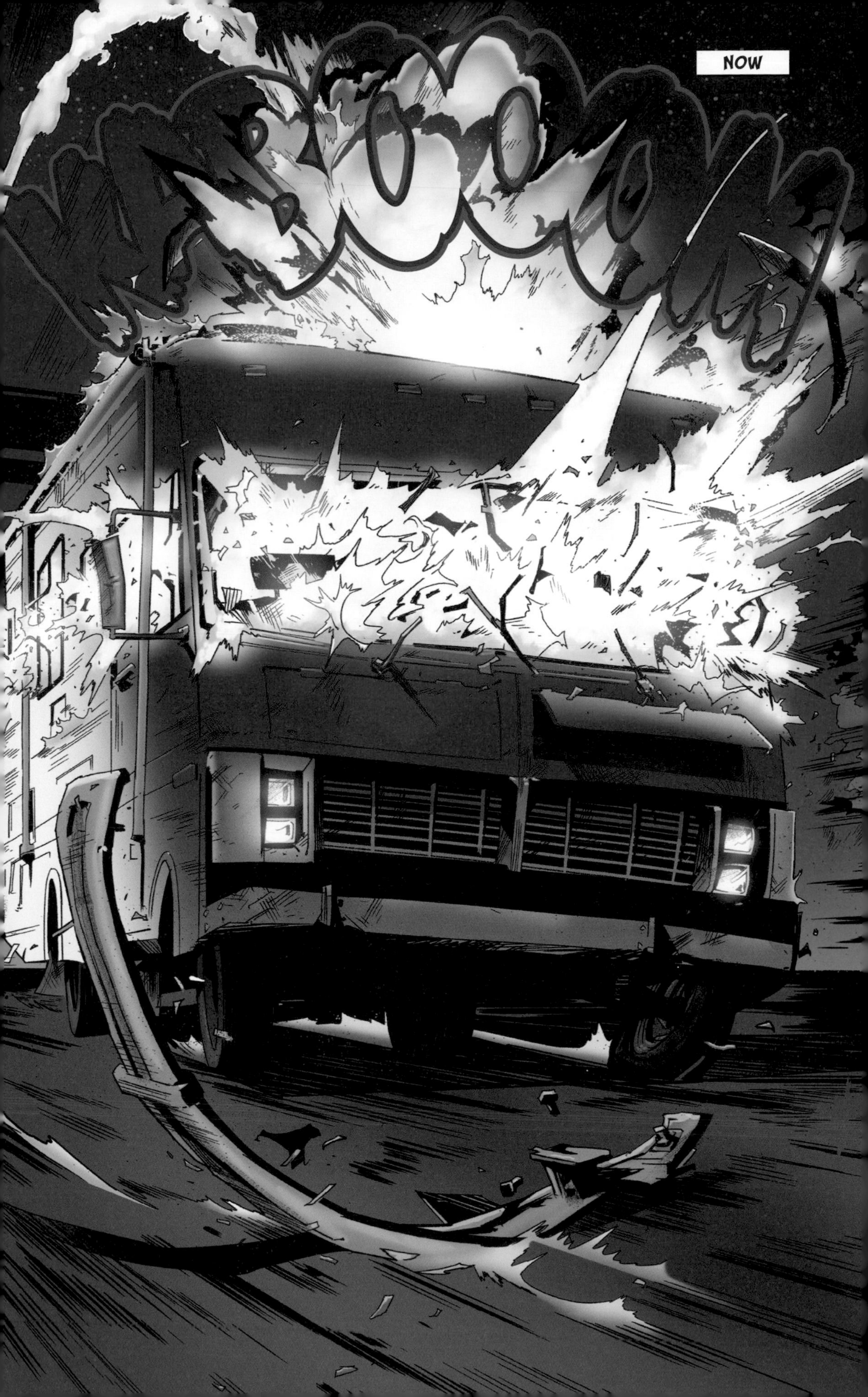
NOW

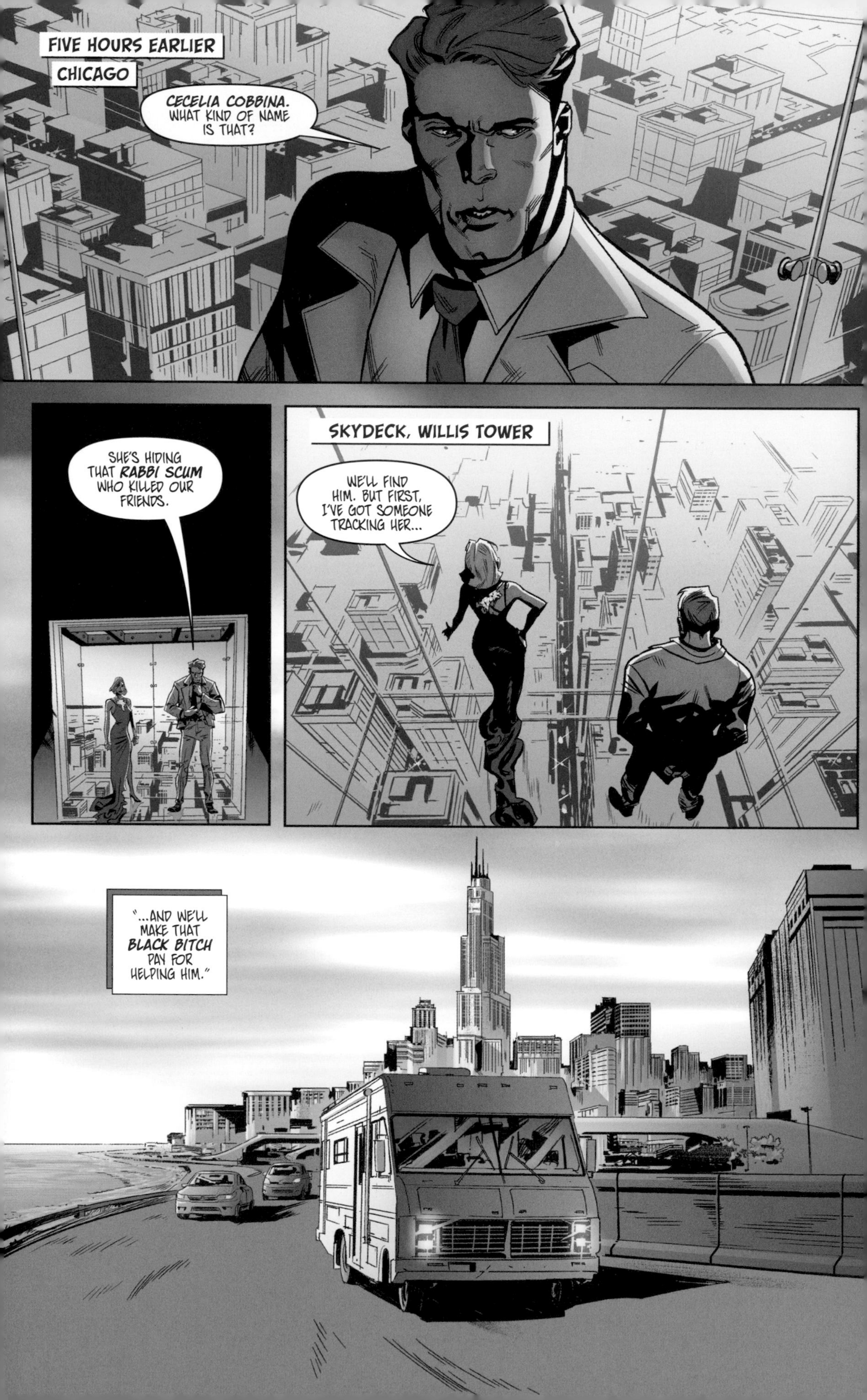
FIVE HOURS EARLIER
CHICAGO
CECELIA COBBINA. WHAT KIND OF NAME IS THAT?
SHE'S HIDING THAT **RABBI SCUM** WHO KILLED OUR FRIENDS.
SKYDECK, WILLIS TOWER
WE'LL FIND HIM. BUT FIRST, I'VE GOT SOMEONE TRACKING HER...
"...AND WE'LL MAKE THAT **BLACK BITCH** PAY FOR HELPING HIM."

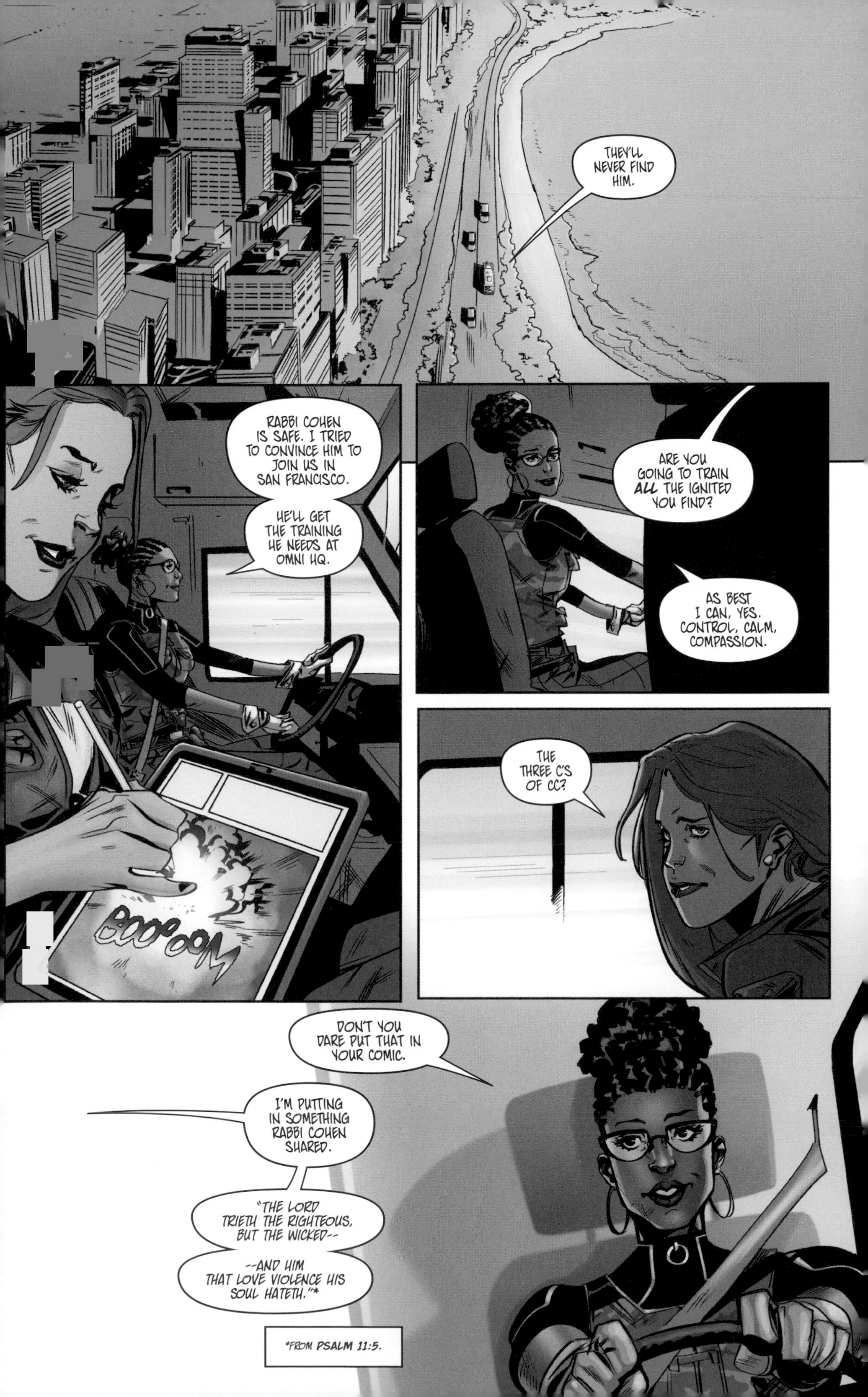
THEY'LL NEVER FIND HIM.
RABBI COHEN IS SAFE. I TRIED TO CONVINCE HIM TO JOIN US IN SAN FRANCISCO.
HE'LL GET THE TRAINING HE NEEDS AT OMNI HQ.
BOOOOOM
ARE YOU GOING TO TRAIN **ALL** THE IGNITED YOU FIND?
AS BEST I CAN, YES. CONTROL, CALM, COMPASSION.
THE THREE C'S OF CC?
DON'T YOU DARE PUT THAT IN YOUR COMIC.
I'M PUTTING IN SOMETHING RABBI COHEN SHARED.
"THE LORD TRIETH THE RIGHTEOUS, BUT THE WICKED--
--AND HIM THAT LOVE VIOLENCE HIS SOUL HATETH."*
*FROM **PSALM 11:5.**

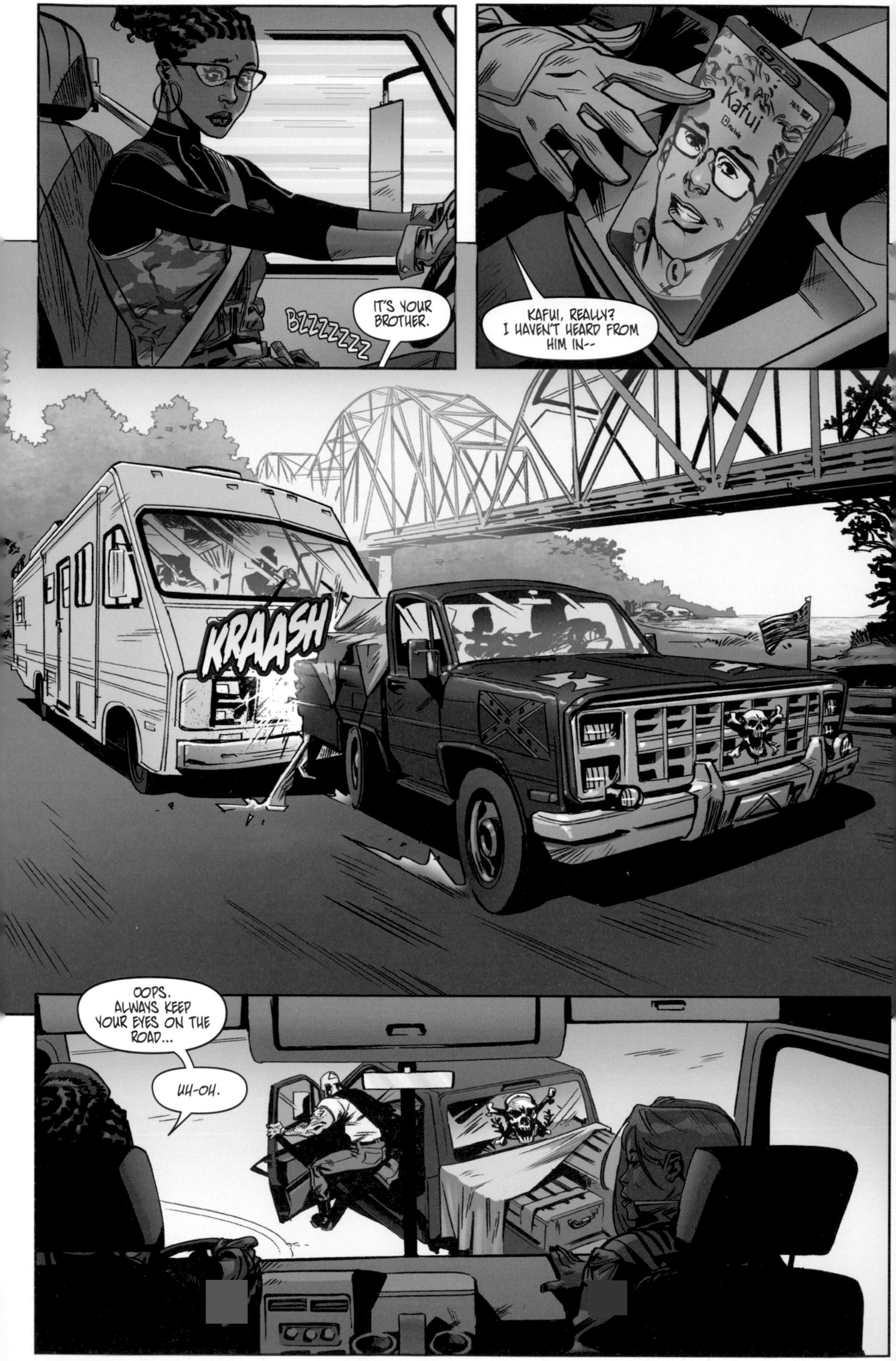
BZZZZZZZZ
IT'S YOUR BROTHER.
Kafui
KAFUI, REALLY? I HAVEN'T HEARD FROM HIM IN--
KRAASH
OOPS. ALWAYS KEEP YOUR EYES ON THE ROAD...
UH-OH.

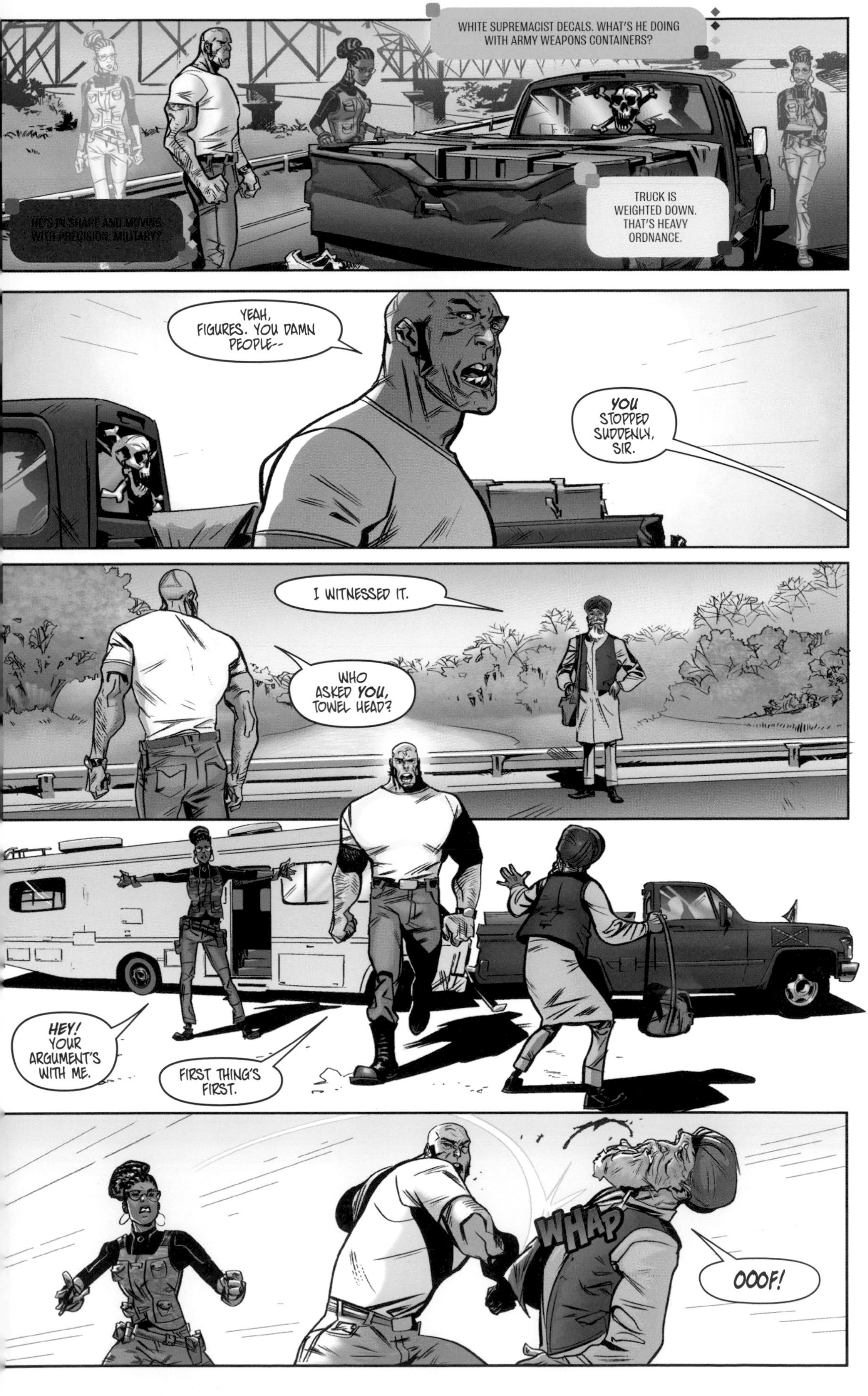
WHITE SUPREMACIST DECALS. WHAT'S HE DOING WITH ARMY WEAPONS CONTAINERS?
HE'S IN SHAPE AND MOVING WITH PRECISION. MILITARY?
TRUCK IS WEIGHTED DOWN. THAT'S HEAVY ORDNANCE.
YEAH, FIGURES. YOU DAMN PEOPLE--
YOU STOPPED SUDDENLY, SIR.
I WITNESSED IT.
WHO ASKED YOU, TOWEL HEAD?
HEY! YOUR ARGUMENT'S WITH ME.
FIRST THING'S FIRST.
WHAP
OOOF!

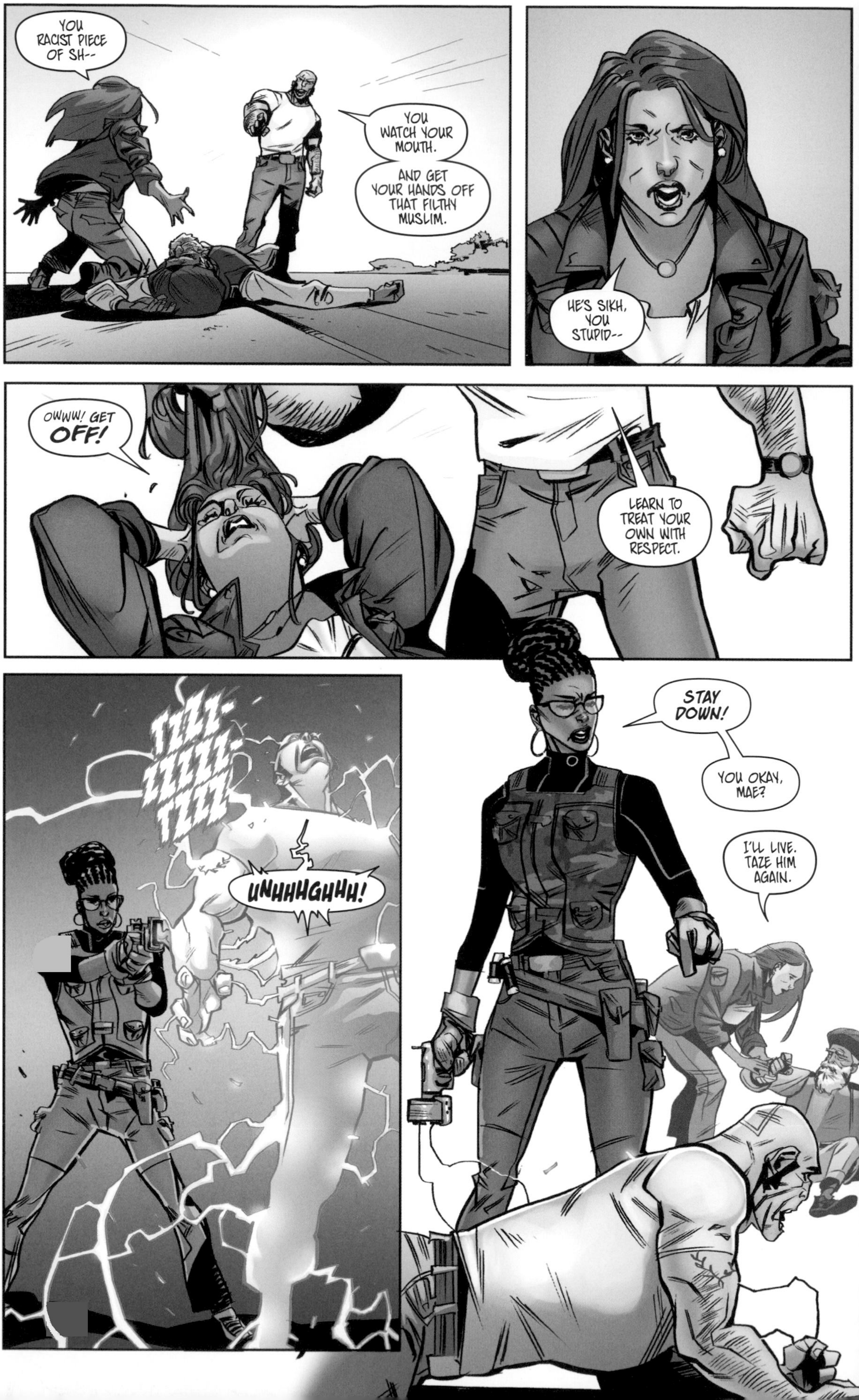
YOU RACIST PIECE OF SH--
YOU WATCH YOUR MOUTH.
AND GET YOUR HANDS OFF THAT FILTHY MUSLIM.
HE'S SIKH, YOU STUPID--
OWWW! GET OFF!
LEARN TO TREAT YOUR OWN WITH RESPECT.
TZZZ-ZZZZZ-TZZZ
UNHHHGHHH!
STAY DOWN!
YOU OKAY, MAE?
I'LL LIVE. TAZE HIM AGAIN.

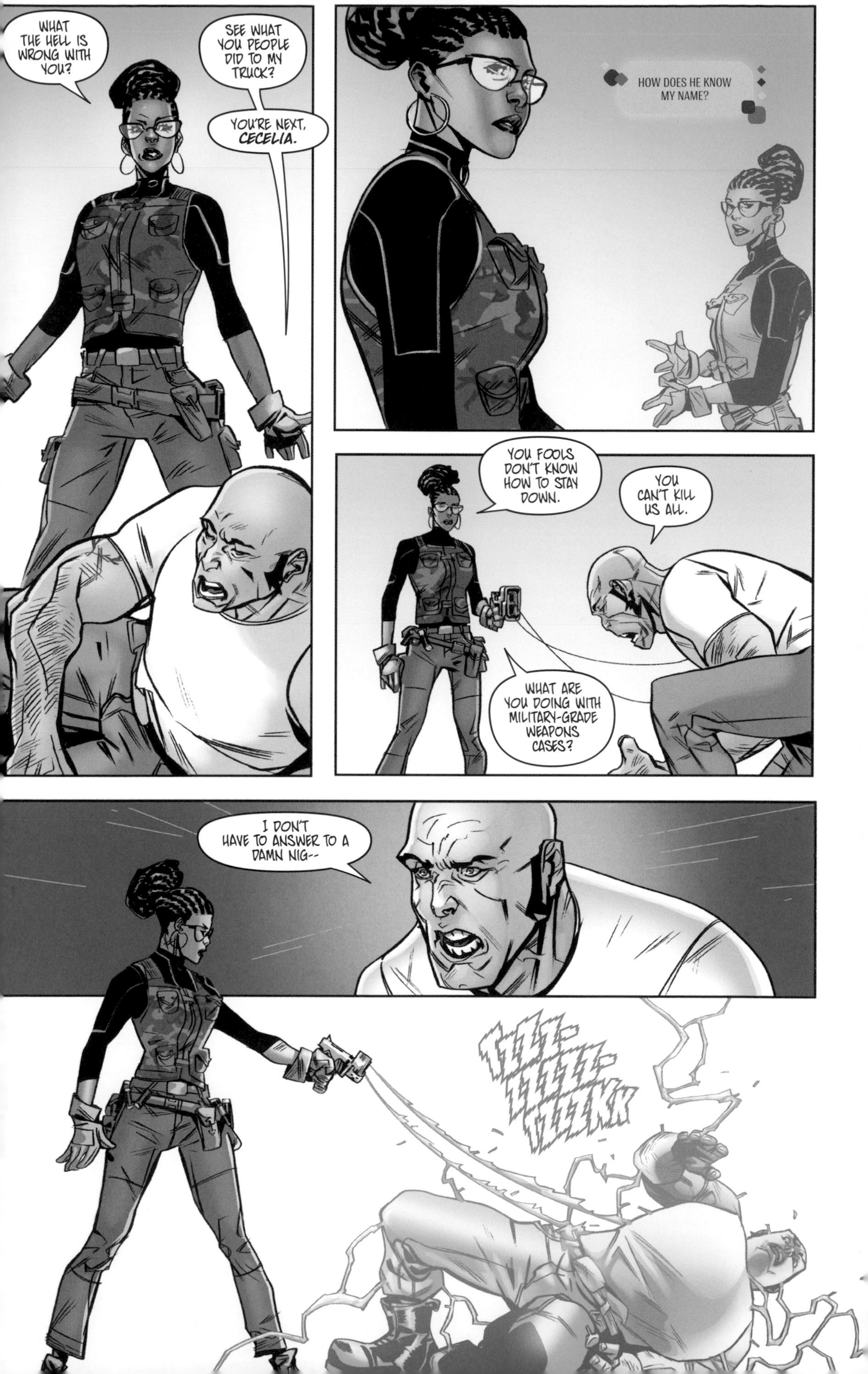
WHAT THE HELL IS WRONG WITH YOU?
SEE WHAT YOU PEOPLE DID TO MY TRUCK?
YOU'RE NEXT, **CECELIA.**
HOW DOES HE KNOW MY NAME?
YOU FOOLS DON'T KNOW HOW TO STAY DOWN.
YOU CAN'T KILL US ALL.
WHAT ARE YOU DOING WITH MILITARY-GRADE WEAPONS CASES?
I DON'T HAVE TO ANSWER TO A DAMN NIG--
TZZZ-ZZZZZ-ZZZZKK

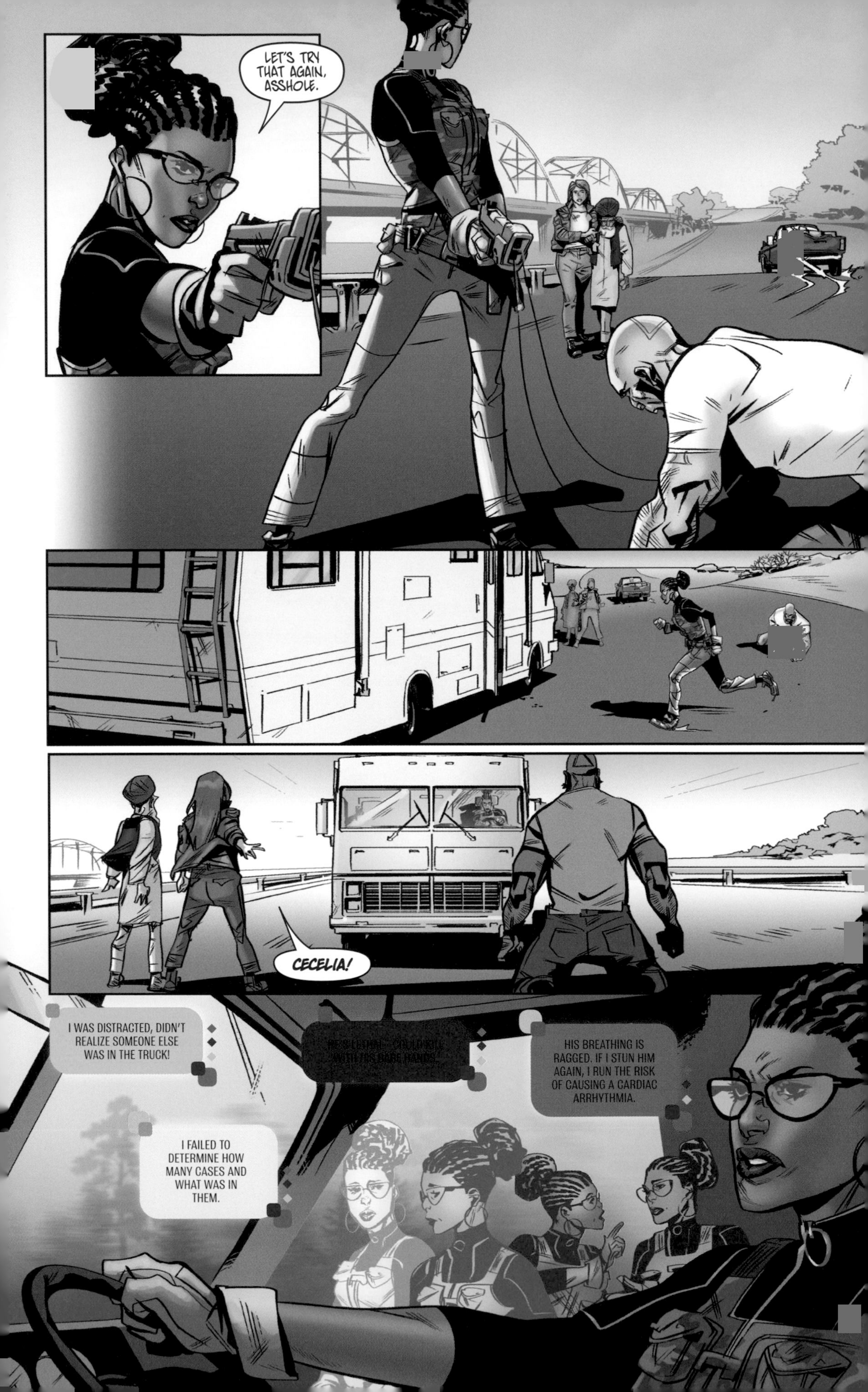
LET'S TRY THAT AGAIN, ASSHOLE.
CECELIA!
I WAS DISTRACTED, DIDN'T REALIZE SOMEONE ELSE WAS IN THE TRUCK!
HE'S LETHAL— COULD KILL WITH HIS BARE HANDS.
HIS BREATHING IS RAGGED. IF I STUN HIM AGAIN, I RUN THE RISK OF CAUSING A CARDIAC ARRHYTHMIA.
I FAILED TO DETERMINE HOW MANY CASES AND WHAT WAS IN THEM.

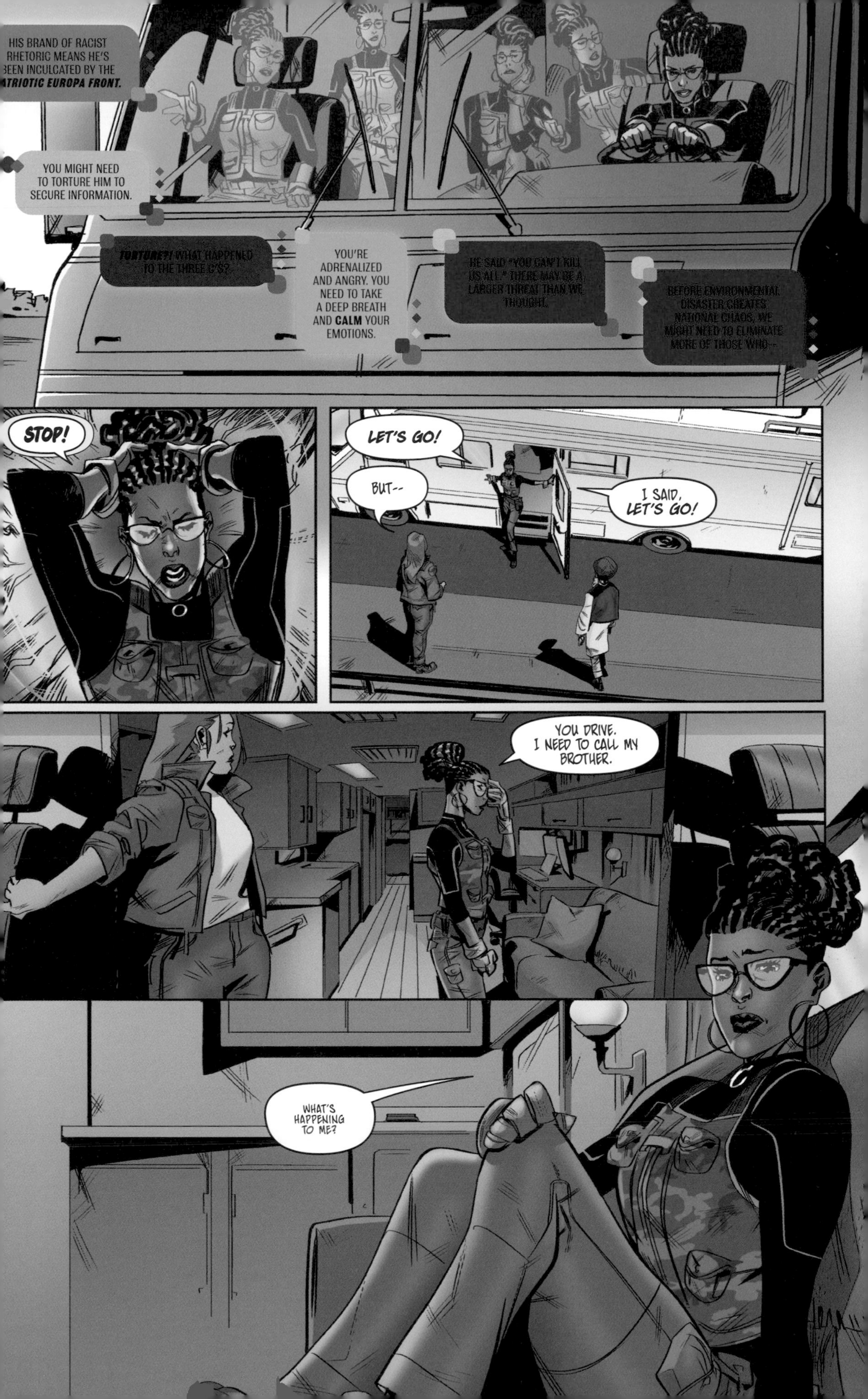

HIS BRAND OF RACIST RHETORIC MEANS HE'S BEEN INCULCATED BY THE PATRIOTIC EUROPA FRONT.
YOU MIGHT NEED TO TORTURE HIM TO SECURE INFORMATION.
TORTURE?! WHAT HAPPENED TO THE THREE G'S?
YOU'RE ADRENALIZED AND ANGRY. YOU NEED TO TAKE A DEEP BREATH AND CALM YOUR EMOTIONS.
HE SAID "YOU CAN'T KILL US ALL." THERE MAY BE A LARGER THREAT THAN WE THOUGHT.
BEFORE ENVIRONMENTAL DISASTER CREATES NATIONAL CHAOS, WE MIGHT NEED TO ELIMINATE MORE OF THOSE WHO--
STOP!
LET'S GO!
BUT--
I SAID, LET'S GO!
YOU DRIVE. I NEED TO CALL MY BROTHER.
WHAT'S HAPPENING TO ME?

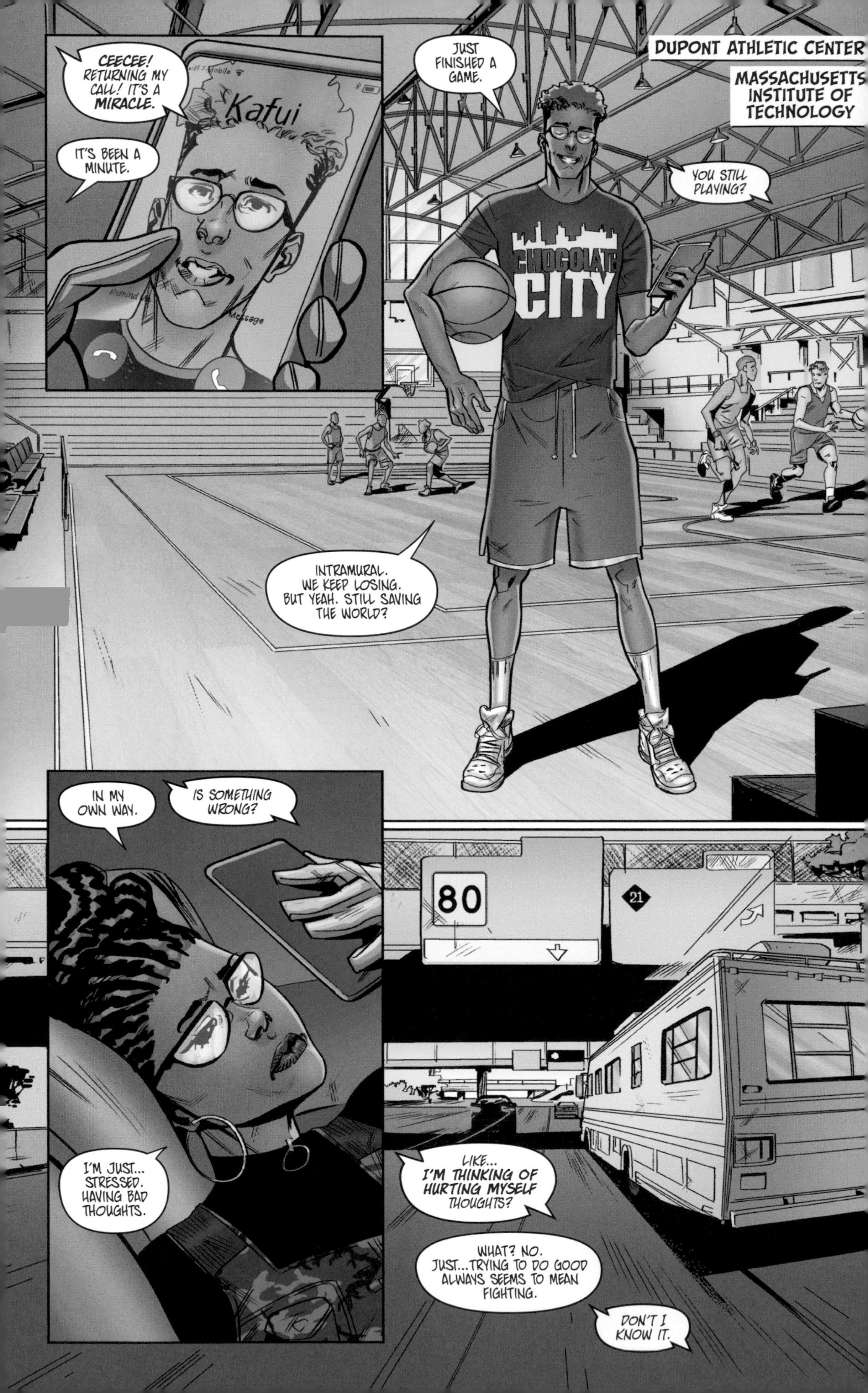
DUPONT ATHLETIC CENTER
MASSACHUSETTS INSTITUTE OF TECHNOLOGY
CEECEE! RETURNING MY CALL! IT'S A MIRACLE.
IT'S BEEN A MINUTE.
Kafui
JUST FINISHED A GAME.
YOU STILL PLAYING?
CHOCOLATE CITY
INTRAMURAL. WE KEEP LOSING. BUT YEAH. STILL SAVING THE WORLD?
IN MY OWN WAY.
IS SOMETHING WRONG?
80
21
I'M JUST... STRESSED. HAVING BAD THOUGHTS.
LIKE... I'M THINKING OF HURTING MYSELF THOUGHTS?
WHAT? NO. JUST...TRYING TO DO GOOD ALWAYS SEEMS TO MEAN FIGHTING.
DON'T I KNOW IT.

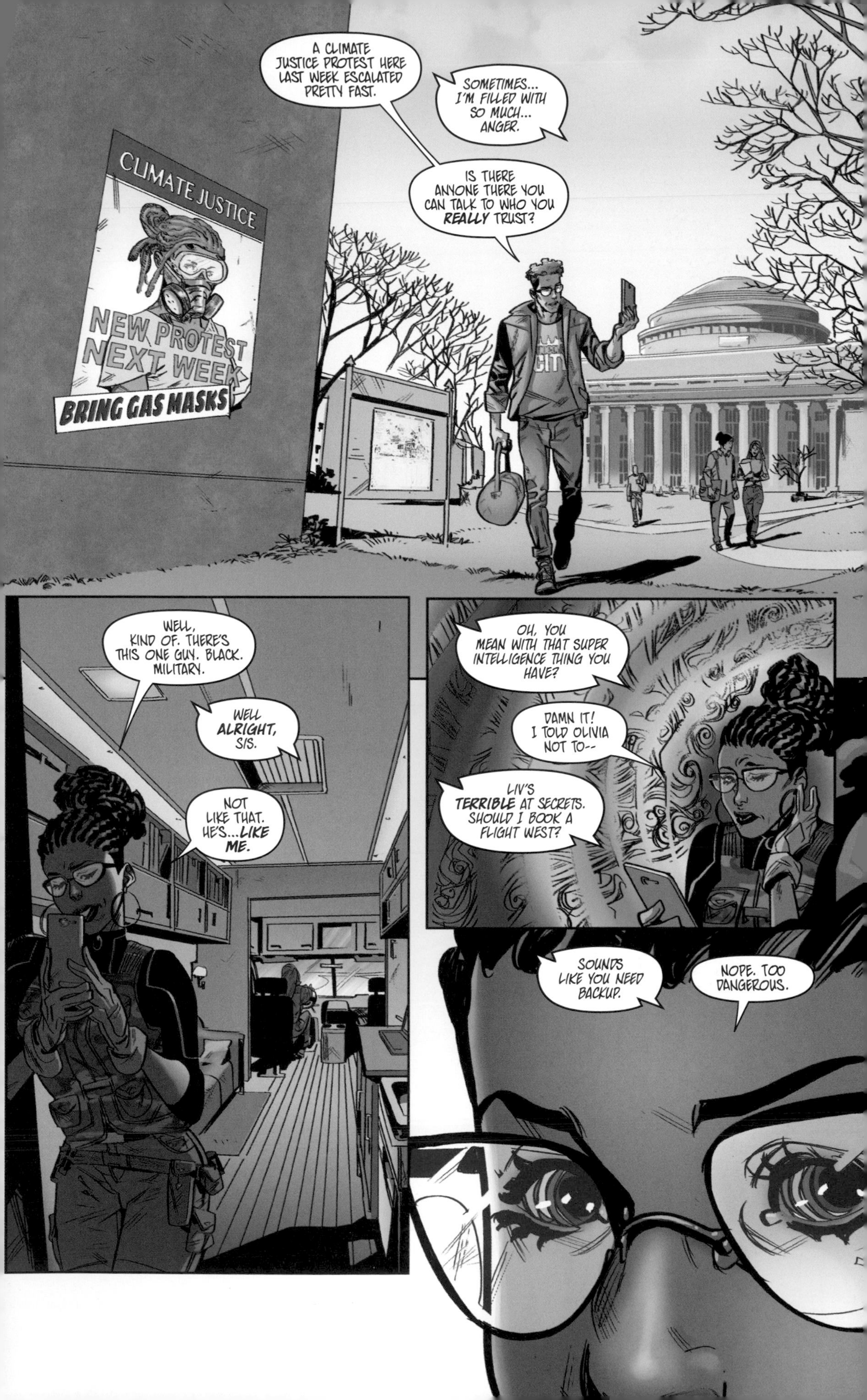
CLIMATE JUSTICE
NEW PROTEST NEXT WEEK
BRING GAS MASKS
A CLIMATE JUSTICE PROTEST HERE LAST WEEK ESCALATED PRETTY FAST.
SOMETIMES... I'M FILLED WITH SO MUCH... ANGER.
IS THERE ANYONE THERE YOU CAN TALK TO WHO YOU **REALLY** TRUST?
WELL, KIND OF. THERE'S THIS ONE GUY. BLACK. MILITARY.
WELL **ALRIGHT,** SIS.
NOT LIKE THAT. HE'S...**LIKE ME.**
OH, YOU MEAN WITH THAT SUPER INTELLIGENCE THING YOU HAVE?
DAMN IT! I TOLD OLIVIA NOT TO--
LIV'S **TERRIBLE** AT SECRETS. SHOULD I BOOK A FLIGHT WEST?
SOUNDS LIKE YOU NEED BACKUP.
NOPE. TOO DANGEROUS.

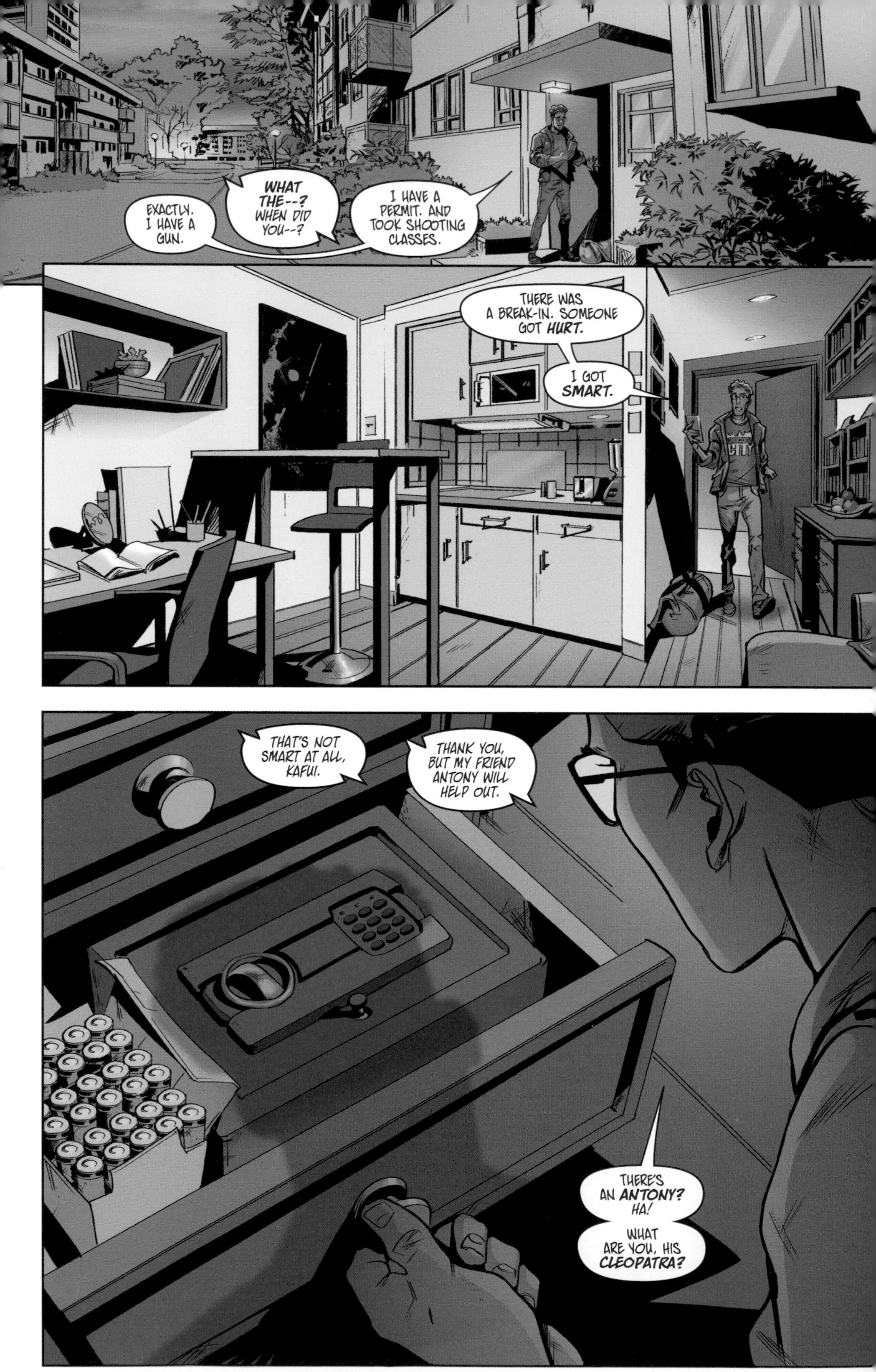
EXACTLY. I HAVE A GUN.
WHAT THE--? WHEN DID YOU--?
I HAVE A PERMIT. AND TOOK SHOOTING CLASSES.
THERE WAS A BREAK-IN. SOMEONE GOT HURT.
I GOT SMART.
CITY
THAT'S NOT SMART AT ALL, KAFUI.
THANK YOU, BUT MY FRIEND ANTONY WILL HELP OUT.
THERE'S AN ANTONY? HA!
WHAT ARE YOU, HIS CLEOPATRA?

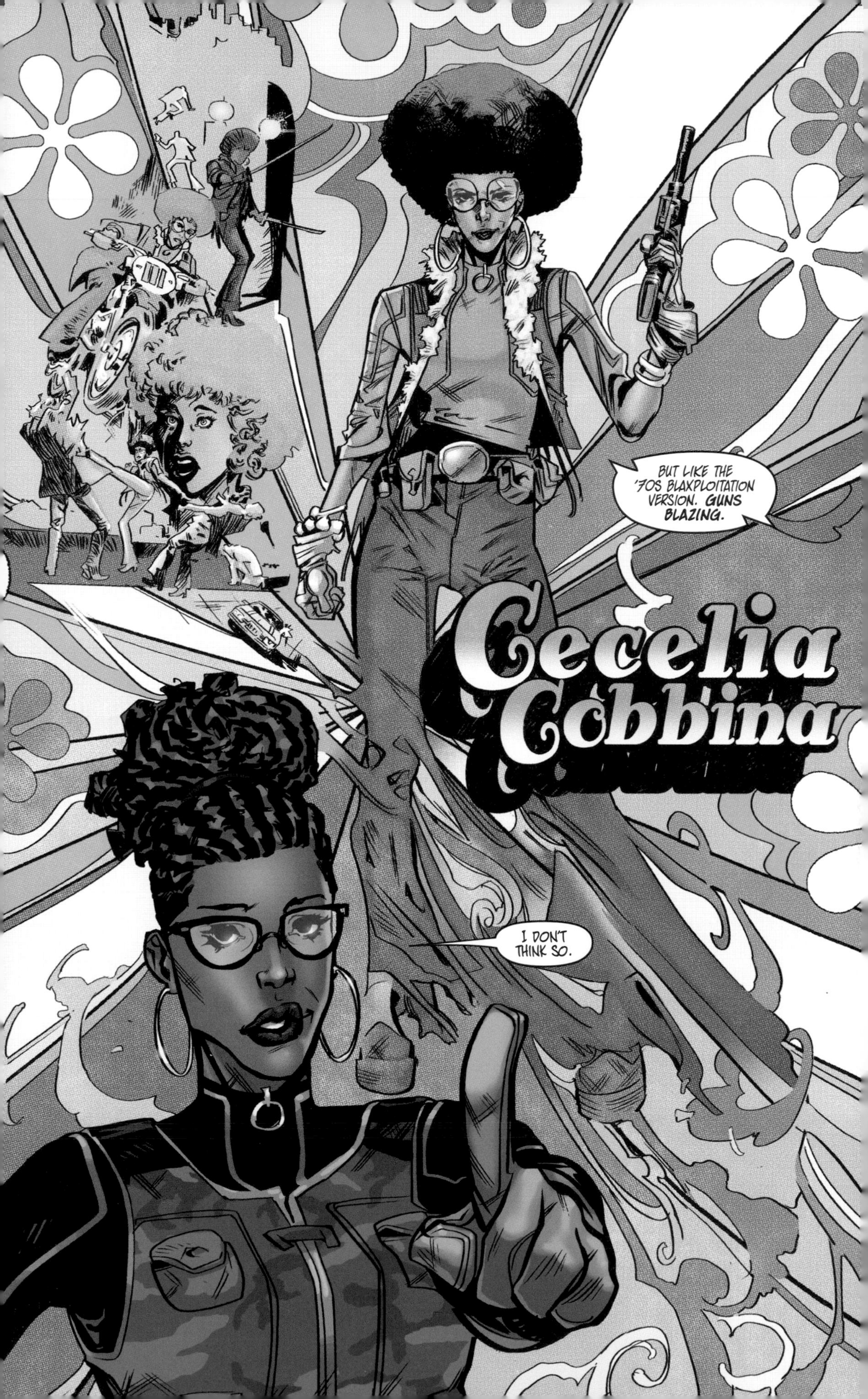
BUT LIKE THE '70S BLAXPLOITATION VERSION. GUNS BLAZING.
Cecelia Cobbina
I DON'T THINK SO.

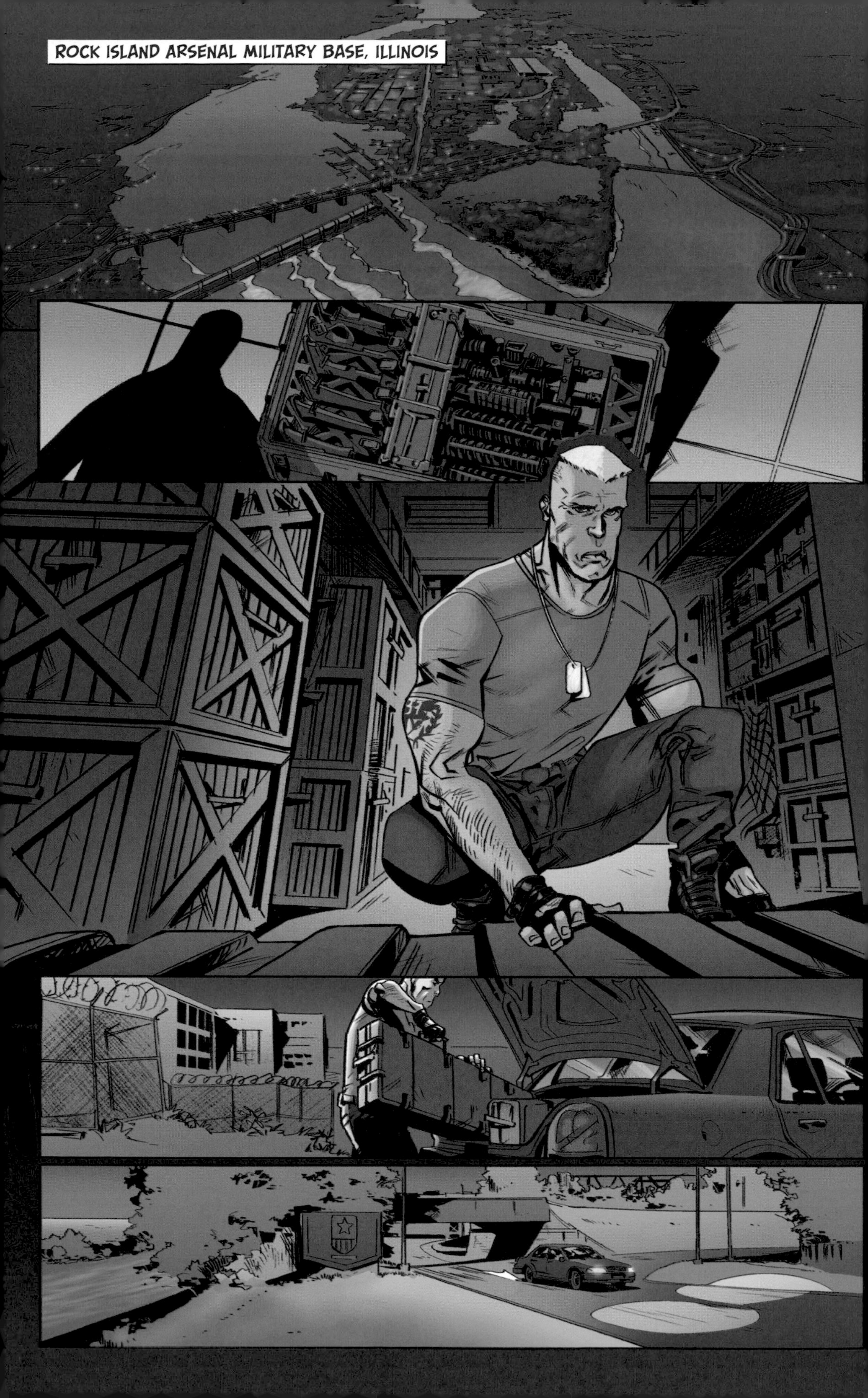
ROCK ISLAND ARSENAL MILITARY BASE, ILLINOIS

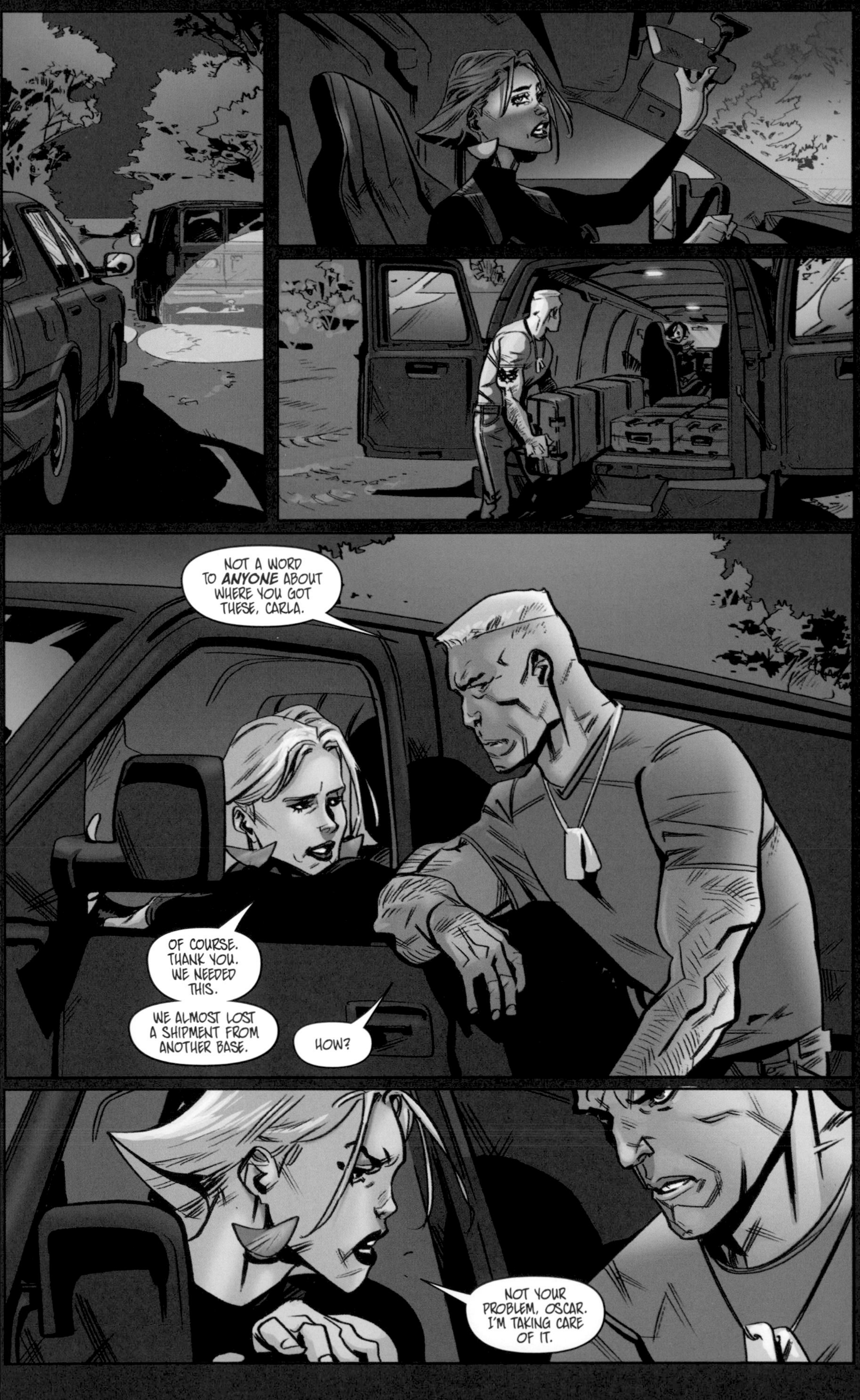
NOT A WORD TO ANYONE ABOUT WHERE YOU GOT THESE, CARLA.
OF COURSE. THANK YOU. WE NEEDED THIS.
WE ALMOST LOST A SHIPMENT FROM ANOTHER BASE.
HOW?
NOT YOUR PROBLEM, OSCAR. I'M TAKING CARE OF IT.

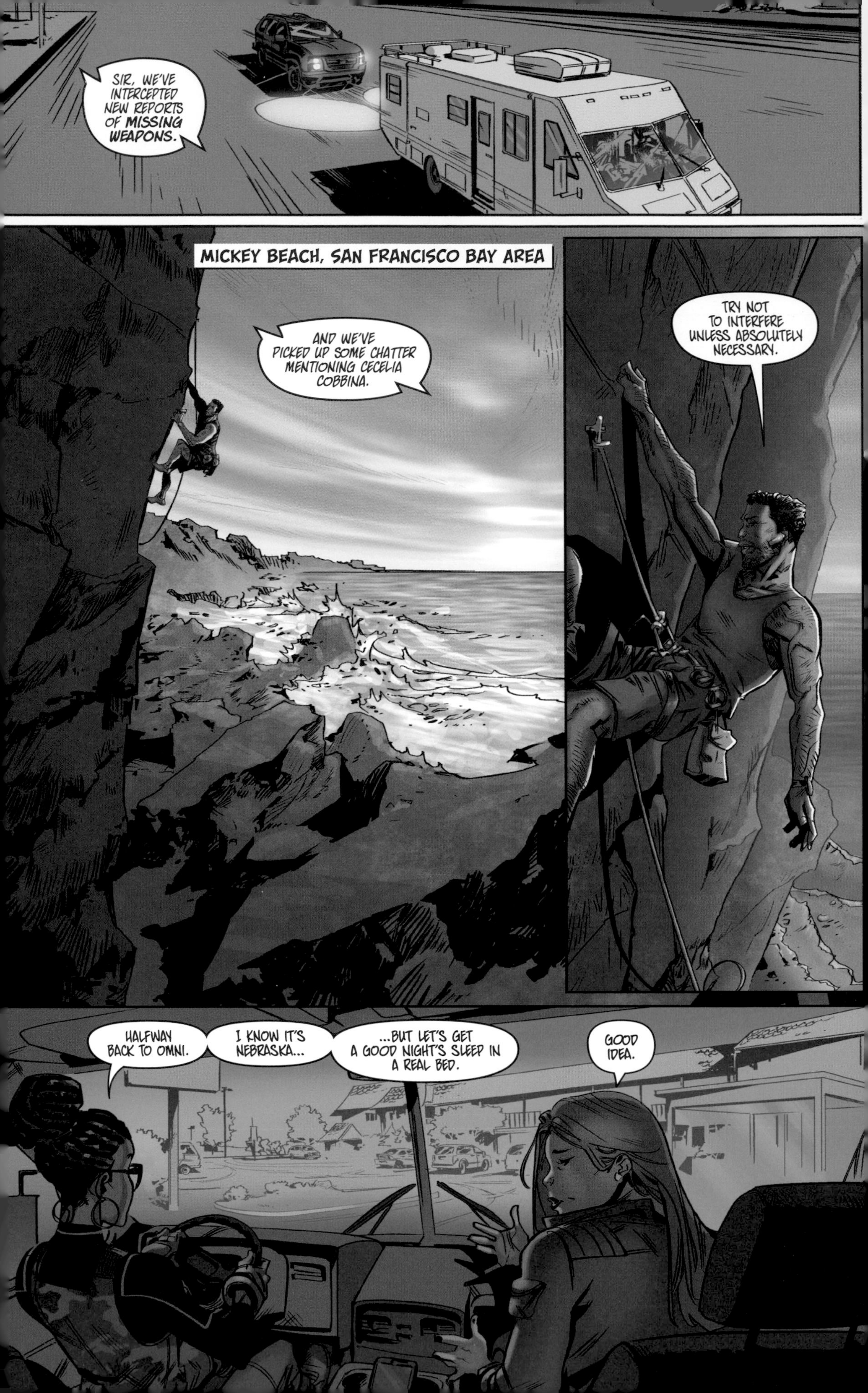
SIR, WE'VE INTERCEPTED NEW REPORTS OF MISSING WEAPONS.
MICKEY BEACH, SAN FRANCISCO BAY AREA
AND WE'VE PICKED UP SOME CHATTER MENTIONING CECELIA COBBINA.
TRY NOT TO INTERFERE UNLESS ABSOLUTELY NECESSARY.
HALFWAY BACK TO OMNI.
I KNOW IT'S NEBRASKA...
...BUT LET'S GET A GOOD NIGHT'S SLEEP IN A REAL BED.
GOOD IDEA.

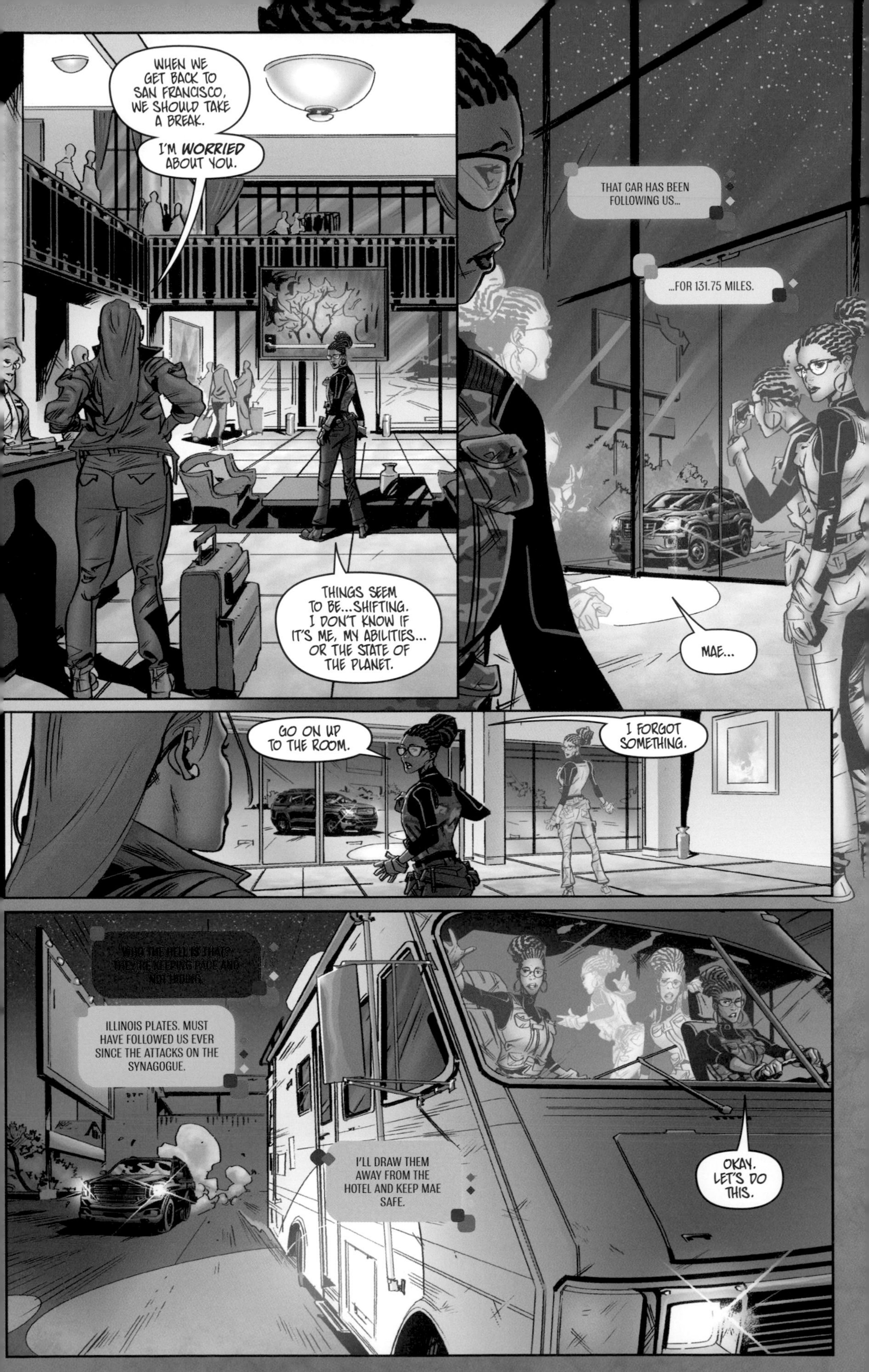
WHEN WE GET BACK TO SAN FRANCISCO, WE SHOULD TAKE A BREAK.
I'M *WORRIED* ABOUT YOU.
THINGS SEEM TO BE...SHIFTING. I DON'T KNOW IF IT'S ME, MY ABILITIES... OR THE STATE OF THE PLANET.
THAT CAR HAS BEEN FOLLOWING US...
...FOR 131.75 MILES.
MAE...
GO ON UP TO THE ROOM.
I FORGOT SOMETHING.
WHO THE HELL IS THAT? THEY'RE KEEPING PACE AND NOT HIDING.
ILLINOIS PLATES. MUST HAVE FOLLOWED US EVER SINCE THE ATTACKS ON THE SYNAGOGUE.
I'LL DRAW THEM AWAY FROM THE HOTEL AND KEEP MAE SAFE.
OKAY. LET'S DO THIS.

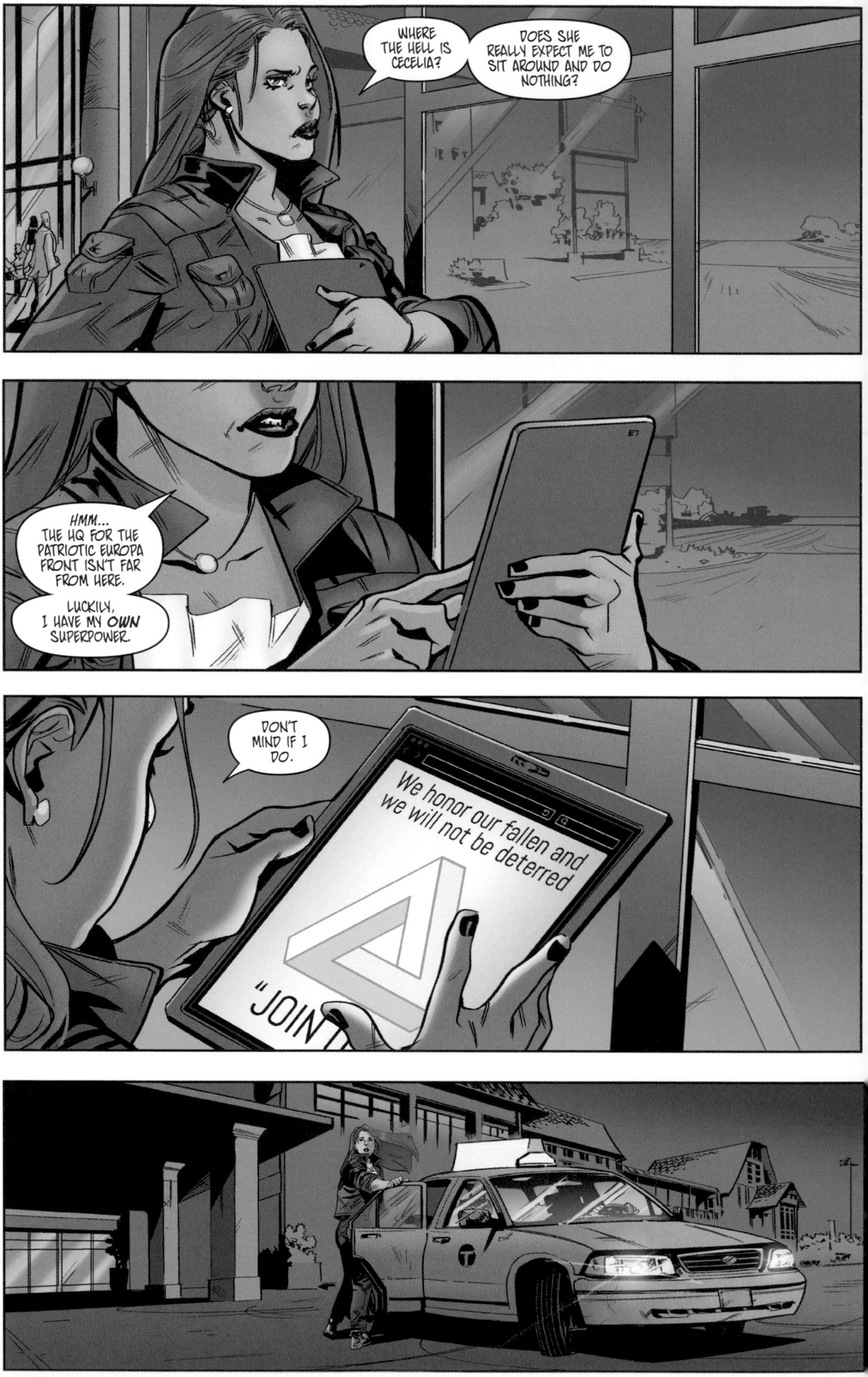

WHERE THE HELL IS CECELIA?
DOES SHE REALLY EXPECT ME TO SIT AROUND AND DO NOTHING?
HMM... THE HQ FOR THE PATRIOTIC EUROPA FRONT ISN'T FAR FROM HERE.
LUCKILY, I HAVE MY **OWN** SUPERPOWER.
DON'T MIND IF I DO.
We honor our fallen and we will not be deterred
"JOIN

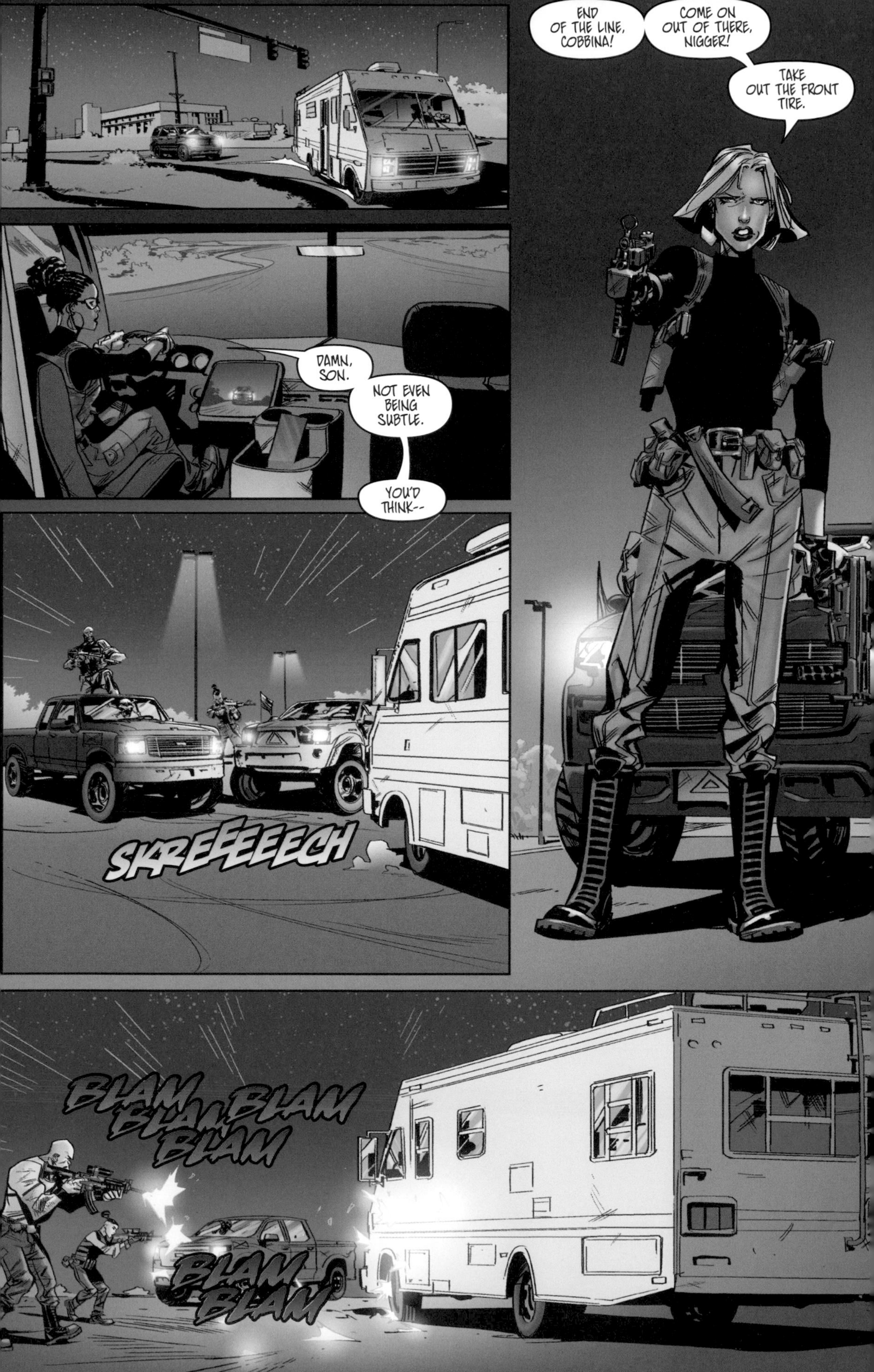

DAMN, SON.
NOT EVEN BEING SUBTLE.
YOU'D THINK--
SKREEEEEECH
END OF THE LINE, COBBINA!
COME ON OUT OF THERE, NIGGER!
TAKE OUT THE FRONT TIRE.
BLAM BLAM BLAM BLAM
BLAM BLAM

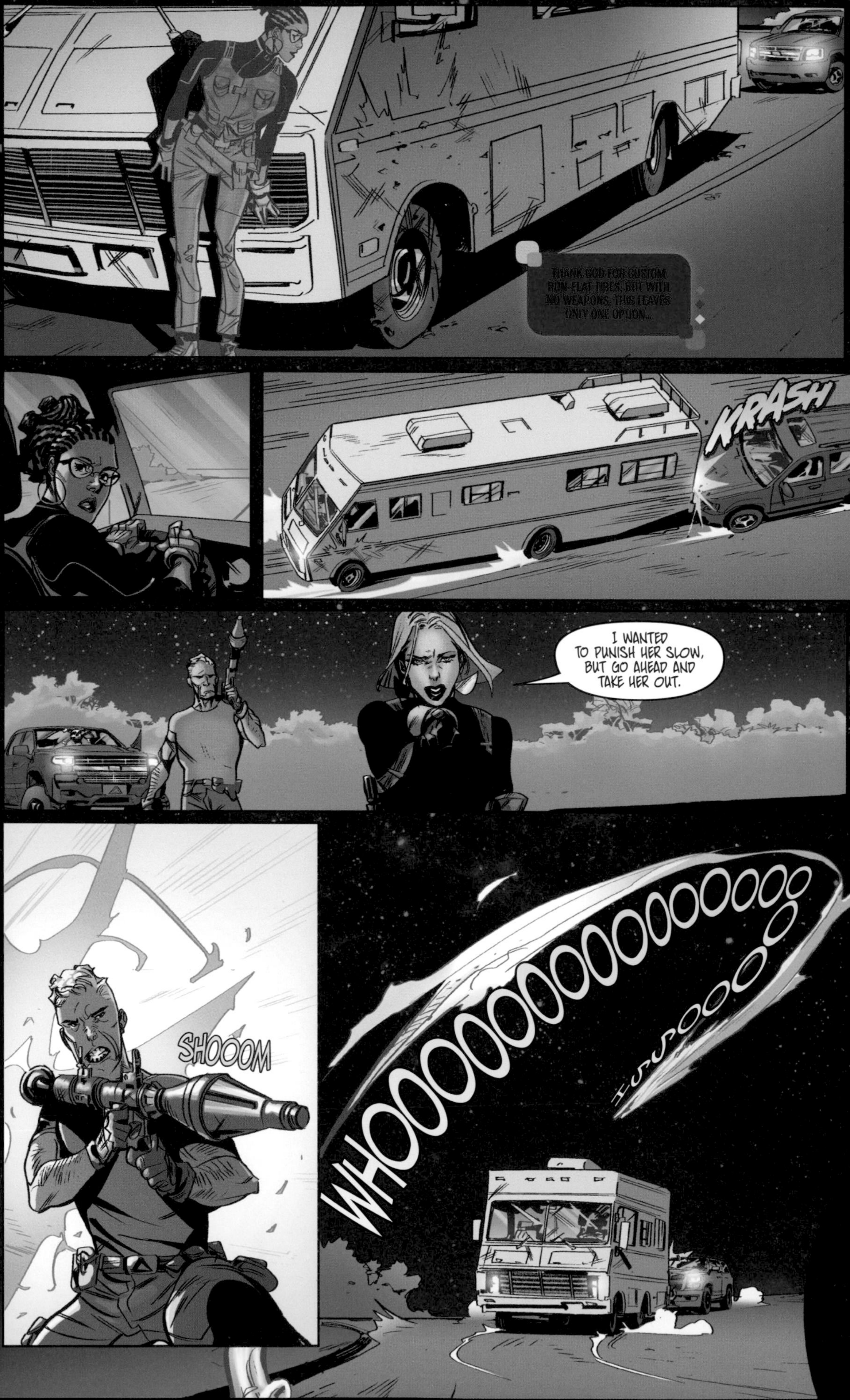
THANK GOD FOR CUSTOM RUN-FLAT TIRES. BUT WITH NO WEAPONS, THIS LEAVES ONLY ONE OPTION...
KRASH
I WANTED TO PUNISH HER SLOW, BUT GO AHEAD AND TAKE HER OUT.
SHOOOM
WHOOOOOOOOOOOOOOOOOOOOOOOOOOO

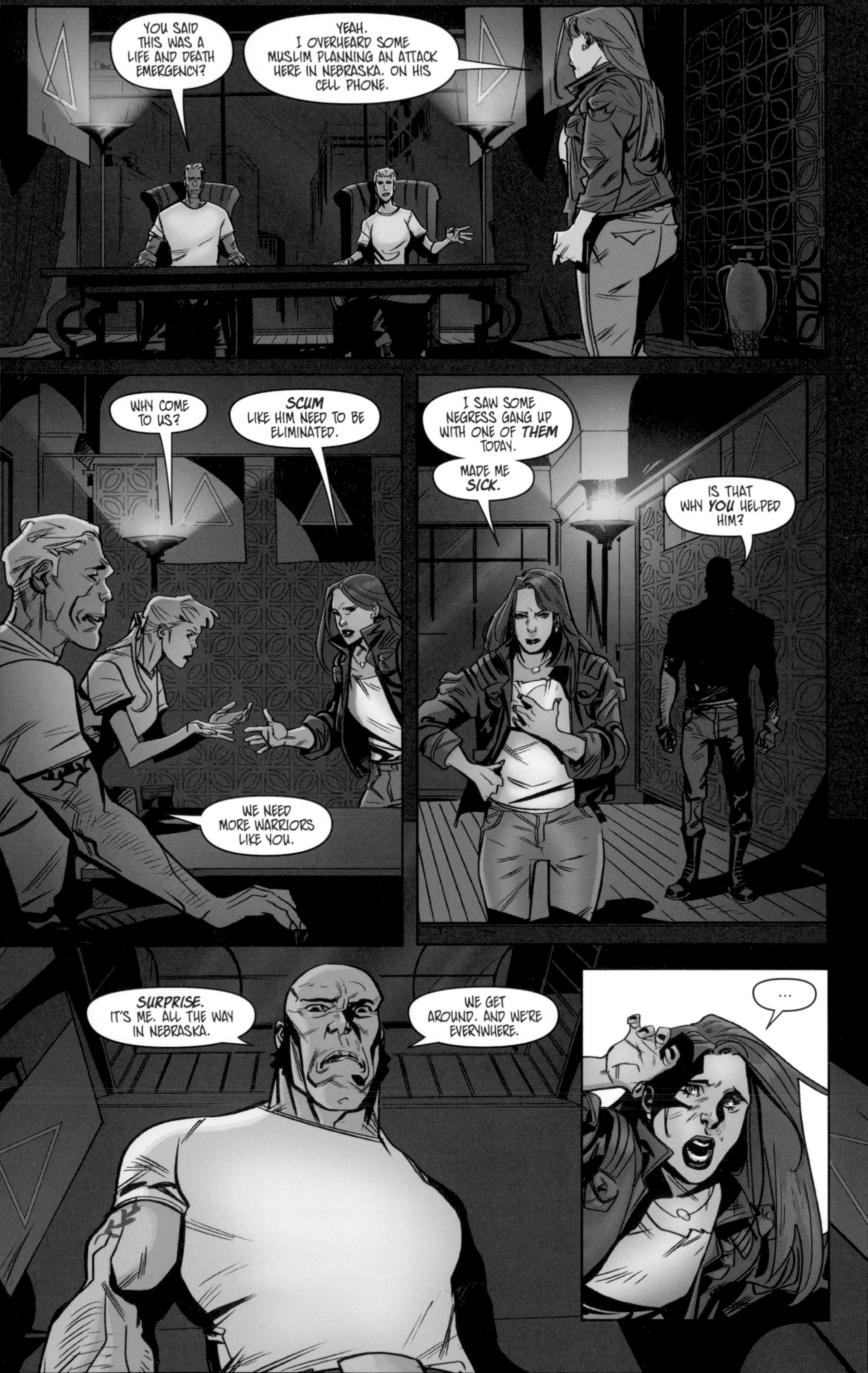
YOU SAID THIS WAS A LIFE AND DEATH EMERGENCY?
YEAH. I OVERHEARD SOME MUSLIM PLANNING AN ATTACK HERE IN NEBRASKA. ON HIS CELL PHONE.
WHY COME TO US?
SCUM LIKE HIM NEED TO BE ELIMINATED.
WE NEED MORE WARRIORS LIKE YOU.
I SAW SOME NEGRESS GANG UP WITH ONE OF THEM TODAY.
MADE ME SICK.
IS THAT WHY YOU HELPED HIM?
SURPRISE. IT'S ME. ALL THE WAY IN NEBRASKA.
WE GET AROUND. AND WE'RE EVERYWHERE.
...

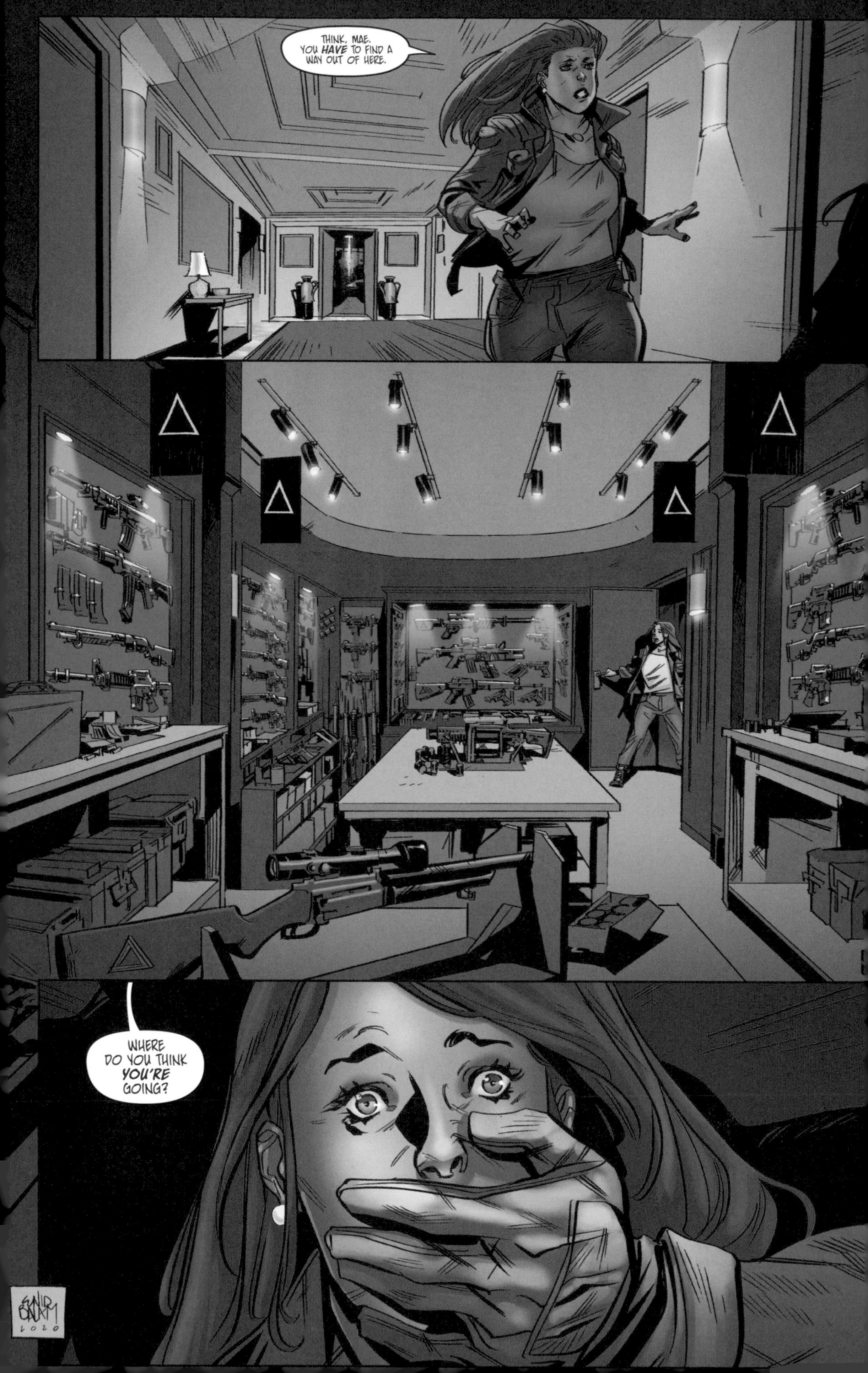
THINK, MAE. YOU **HAVE** TO FIND A WAY OUT OF HERE.
WHERE DO YOU THINK **YOU'RE** GOING?
2020

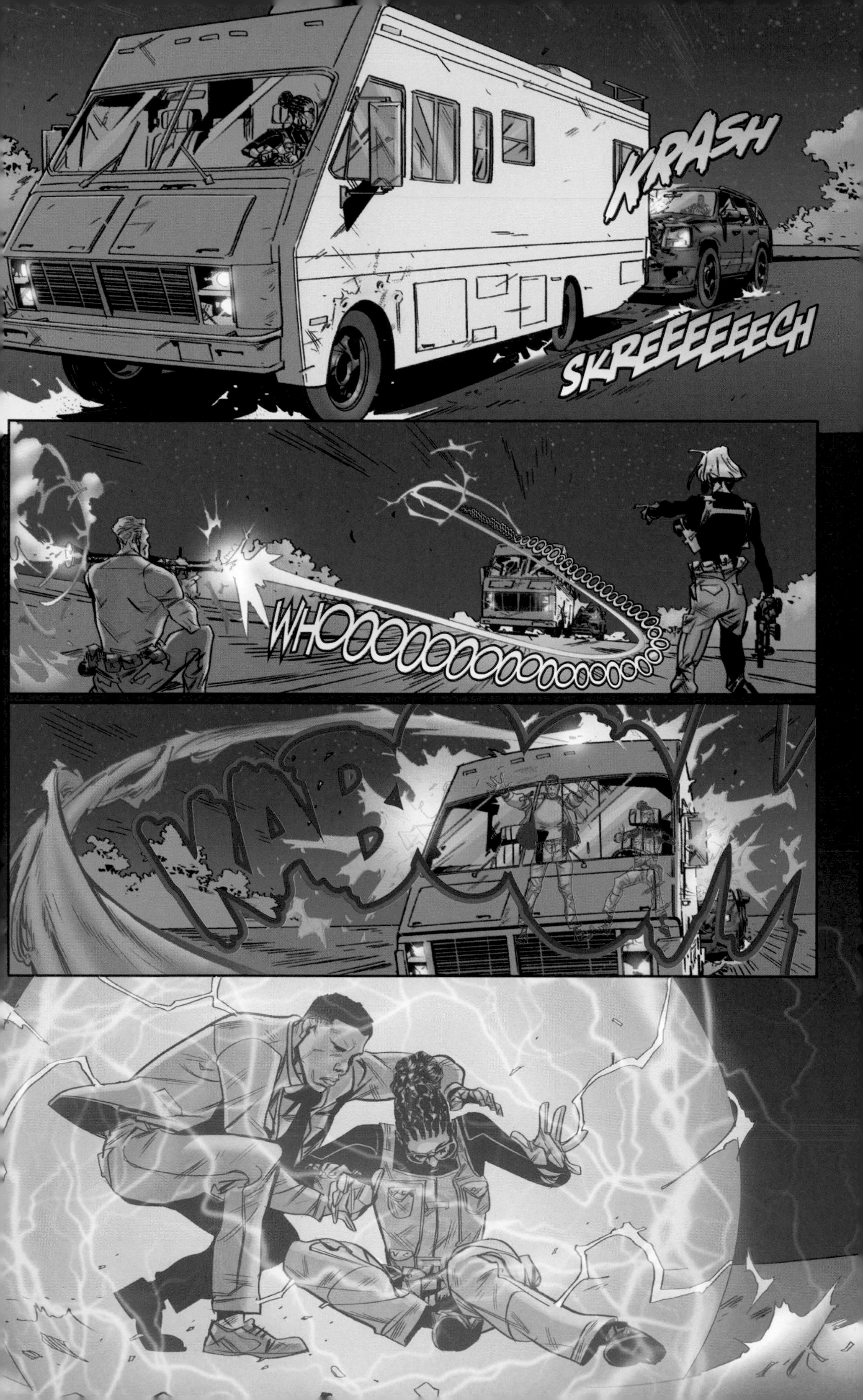
KRASH
SKREEEEEEECH
WHOOOOOOOOOOOOOOOOOOO

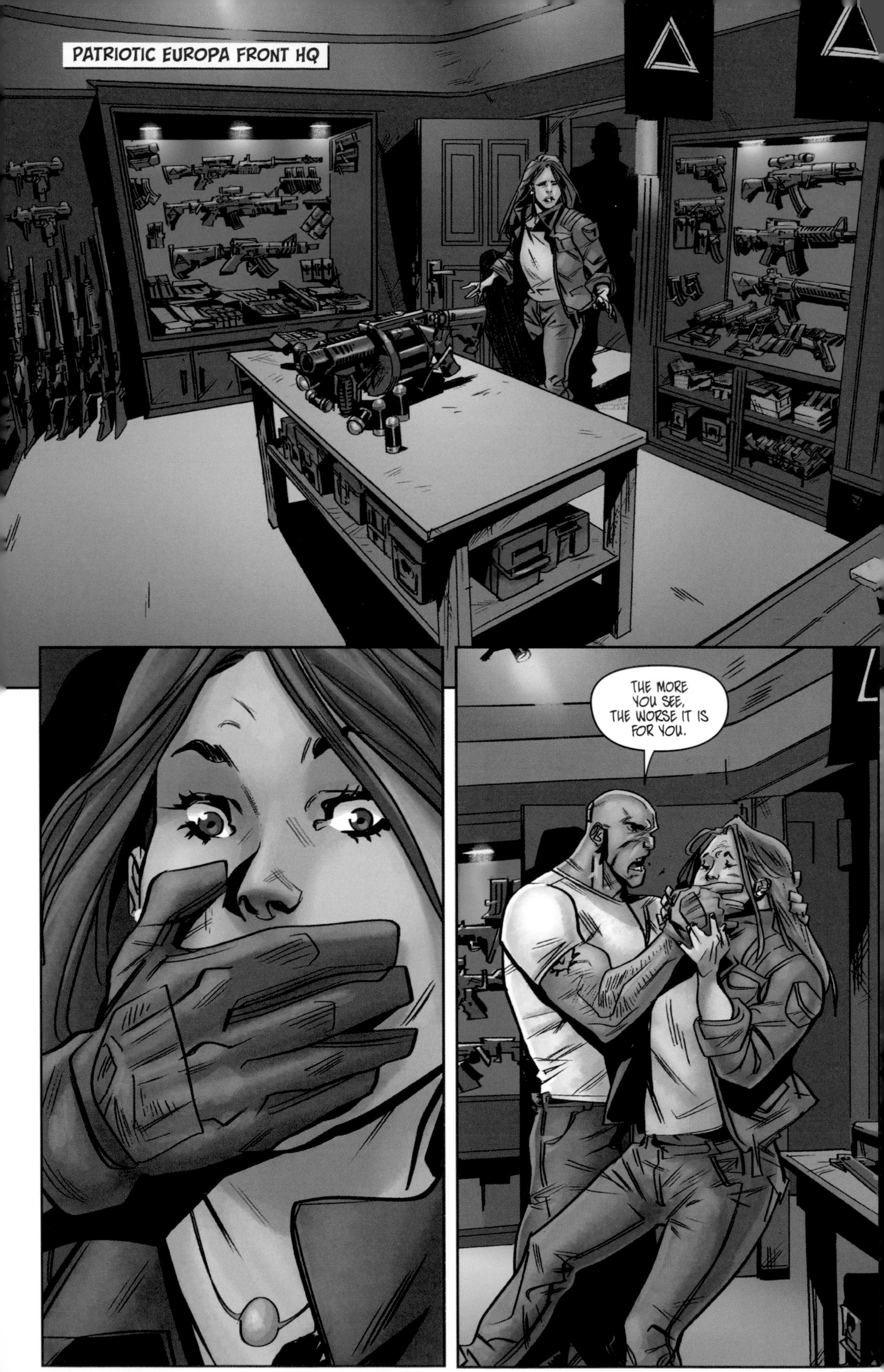
PATRIOTIC EUROPA FRONT HQ
THE MORE YOU SEE, THE WORSE IT IS FOR YOU.

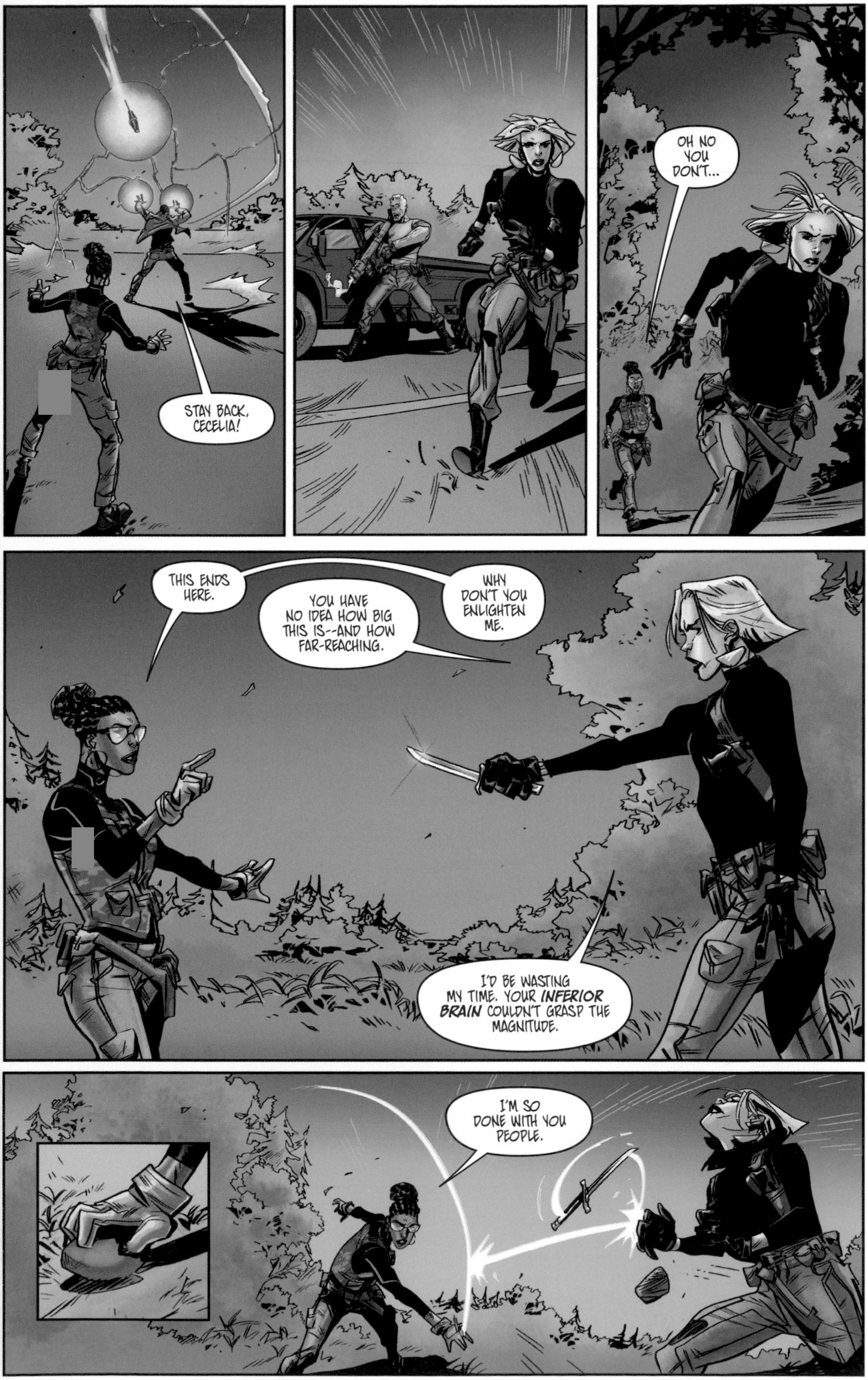
STAY BACK, CECELIA!
OH NO YOU DON'T...
THIS ENDS HERE.
YOU HAVE NO IDEA HOW BIG THIS IS--AND HOW FAR-REACHING.
WHY DON'T YOU ENLIGHTEN ME.
I'D BE WASTING MY TIME. YOUR ***INFERIOR BRAIN*** COULDN'T GRASP THE MAGNITUDE.
I'M SO DONE WITH YOU PEOPLE.

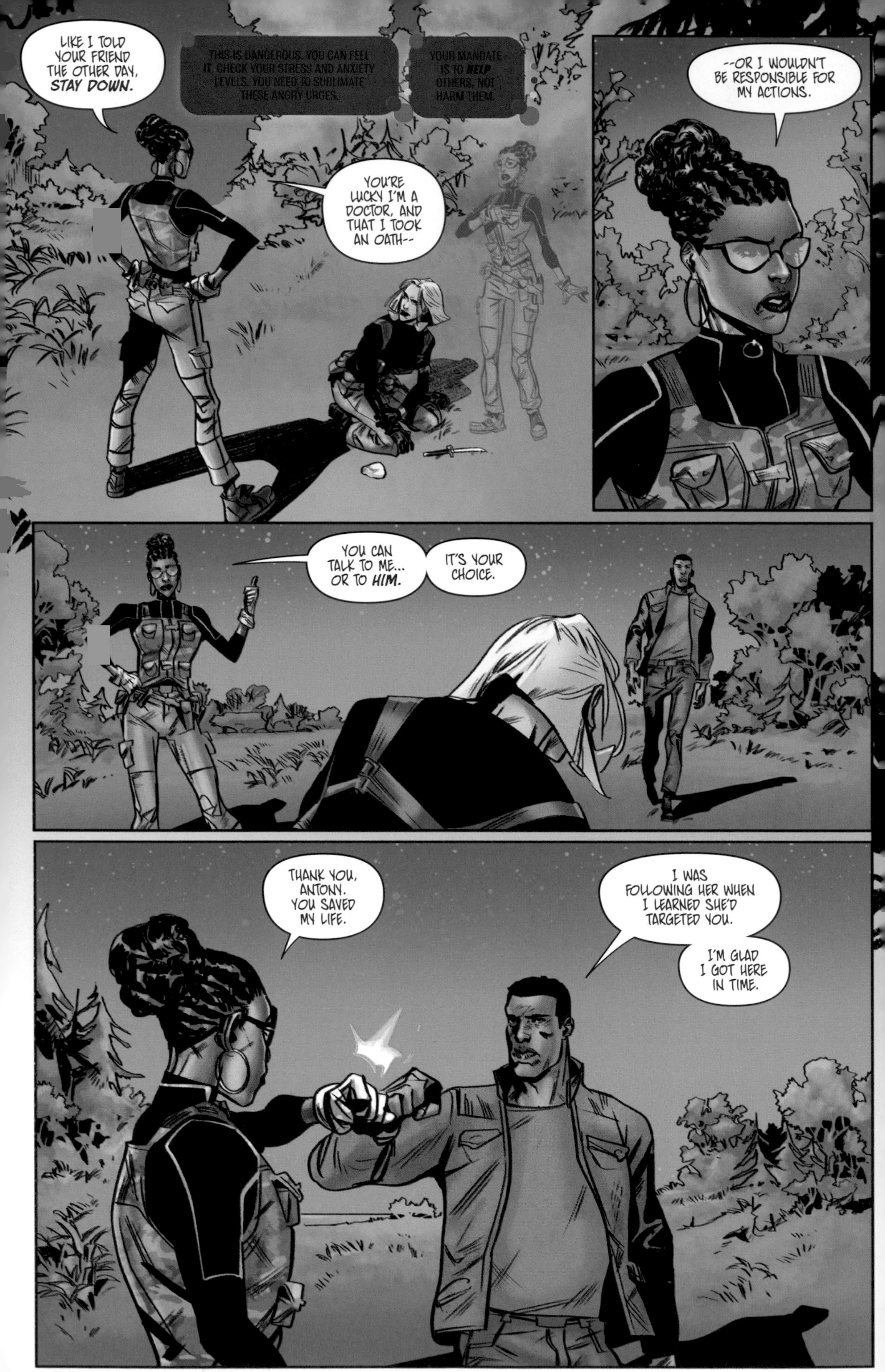
LIKE I TOLD YOUR FRIEND THE OTHER DAY, **STAY DOWN.**
THIS IS DANGEROUS. YOU CAN FEEL IT. CHECK YOUR STRESS AND ANXIETY LEVELS. YOU NEED TO SUBLIMATE THESE ANGRY URGES.
YOUR MANDATE IS TO ***HELP*** OTHERS, NOT HARM THEM.
YOU'RE LUCKY I'M A DOCTOR, AND THAT I TOOK AN OATH--
--OR I WOULDN'T BE RESPONSIBLE FOR MY ACTIONS.
YOU CAN TALK TO ME... OR TO ***HIM.***
IT'S YOUR CHOICE.
THANK YOU, ANTONY. YOU SAVED MY LIFE.
I WAS FOLLOWING HER WHEN I LEARNED SHE'D TARGETED YOU.
I'M GLAD I GOT HERE IN TIME.

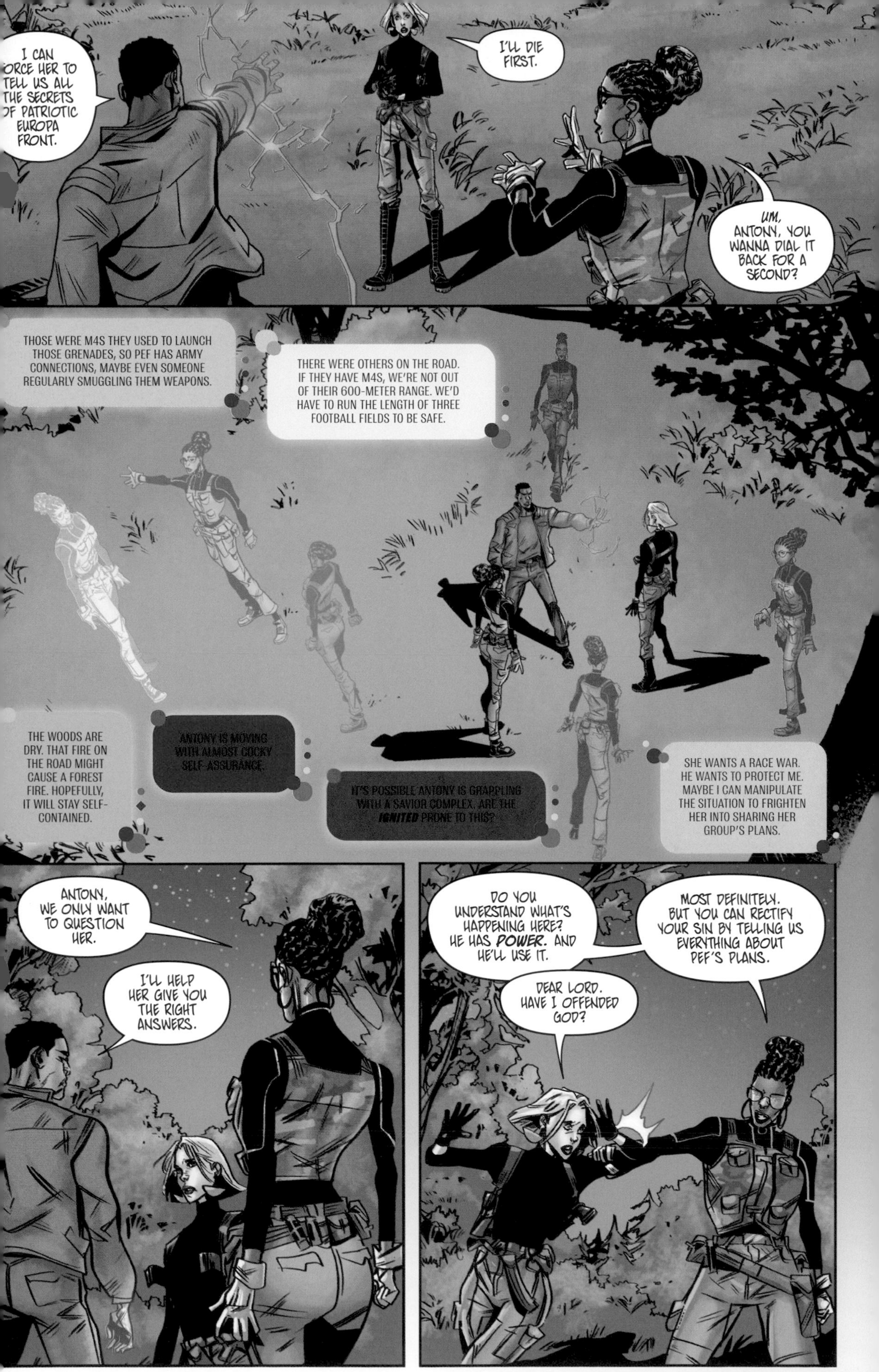

I CAN FORCE HER TO TELL US ALL THE SECRETS OF PATRIOTIC EUROPA FRONT.
I'LL DIE FIRST.
UM, ANTONY, YOU WANNA DIAL IT BACK FOR A SECOND?
THOSE WERE M4S THEY USED TO LAUNCH THOSE GRENADES, SO PEF HAS ARMY CONNECTIONS, MAYBE EVEN SOMEONE REGULARLY SMUGGLING THEM WEAPONS.
THERE WERE OTHERS ON THE ROAD. IF THEY HAVE M4S, WE'RE NOT OUT OF THEIR 600-METER RANGE. WE'D HAVE TO RUN THE LENGTH OF THREE FOOTBALL FIELDS TO BE SAFE.
THE WOODS ARE DRY. THAT FIRE ON THE ROAD MIGHT CAUSE A FOREST FIRE. HOPEFULLY, IT WILL STAY SELF-CONTAINED.
ANTONY IS MOVING WITH ALMOST COCKY SELF-ASSURANCE.
IT'S POSSIBLE ANTONY IS GRAPPLING WITH A SAVIOR COMPLEX. ARE THE IGNITED PRONE TO THIS?
SHE WANTS A RACE WAR. HE WANTS TO PROTECT ME. MAYBE I CAN MANIPULATE THE SITUATION TO FRIGHTEN HER INTO SHARING HER GROUP'S PLANS.
ANTONY, WE ONLY WANT TO QUESTION HER.
I'LL HELP HER GIVE YOU THE RIGHT ANSWERS.
DO YOU UNDERSTAND WHAT'S HAPPENING HERE? HE HAS POWER. AND HE'LL USE IT.
DEAR LORD. HAVE I OFFENDED GOD?
MOST DEFINITELY. BUT YOU CAN RECTIFY YOUR SIN BY TELLING US EVERYTHING ABOUT PEF'S PLANS.

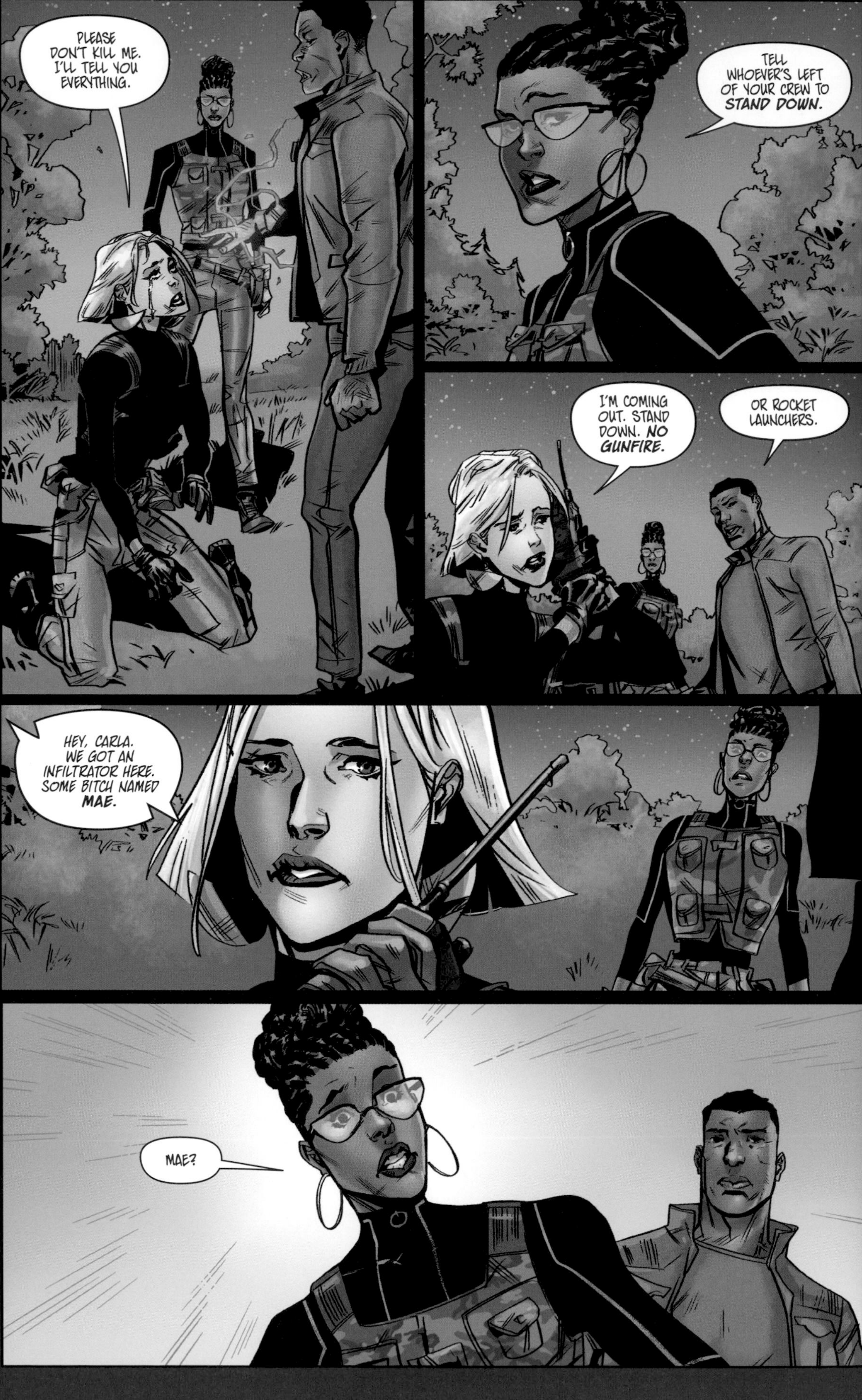
PLEASE DON'T KILL ME. I'LL TELL YOU EVERYTHING.
TELL WHOEVER'S LEFT OF YOUR CREW TO STAND DOWN.
I'M COMING OUT. STAND DOWN. NO GUNFIRE.
OR ROCKET LAUNCHERS.
HEY, CARLA. WE GOT AN INFILTRATOR HERE. SOME BITCH NAMED MAE.
MAE?

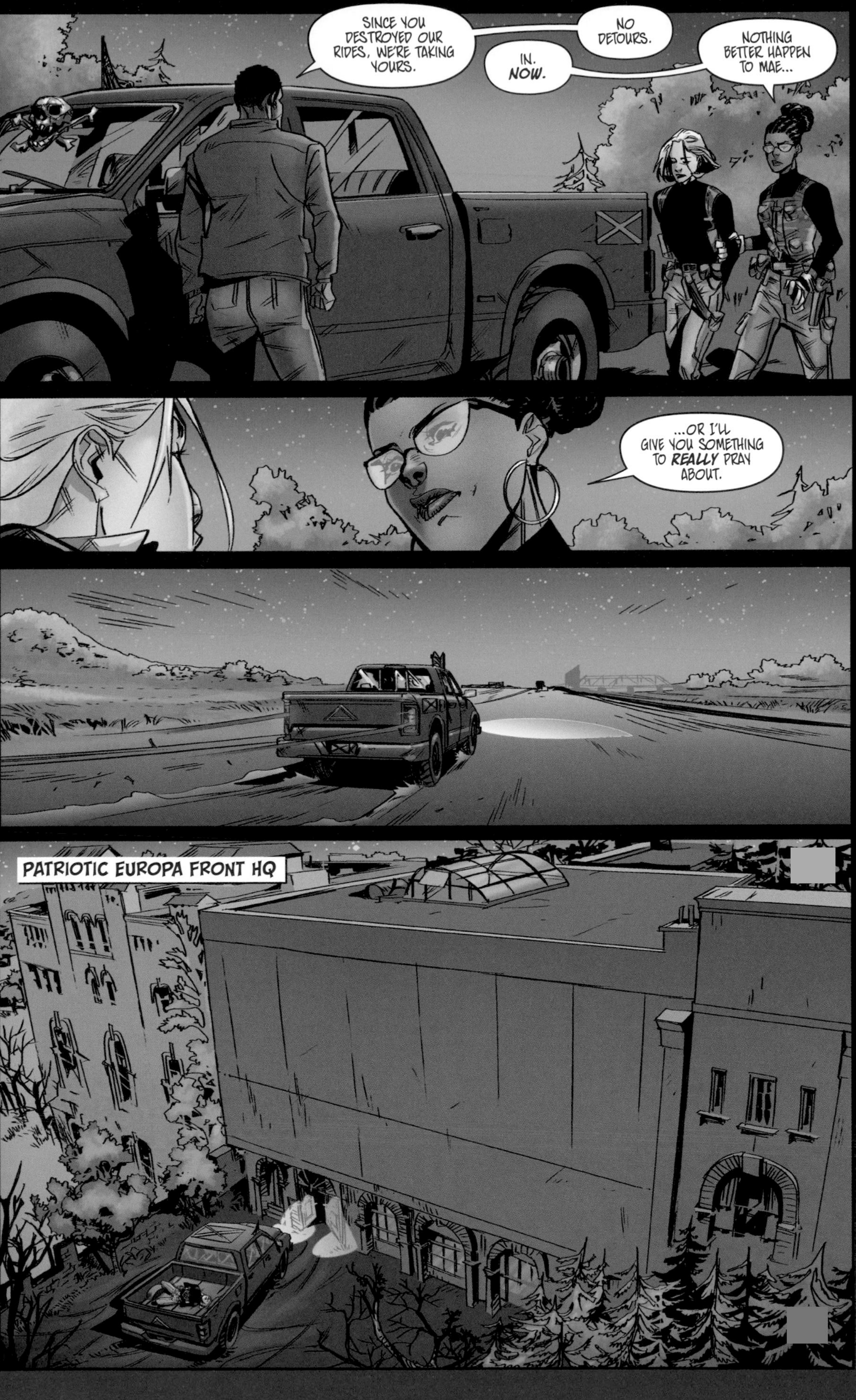
SINCE YOU DESTROYED OUR RIDES, WE'RE TAKING YOURS.
NO DETOURS.
IN. NOW.
NOTHING BETTER HAPPEN TO MAE...
...OR I'LL GIVE YOU SOMETHING TO REALLY PRAY ABOUT.
PATRIOTIC EUROPA FRONT HQ

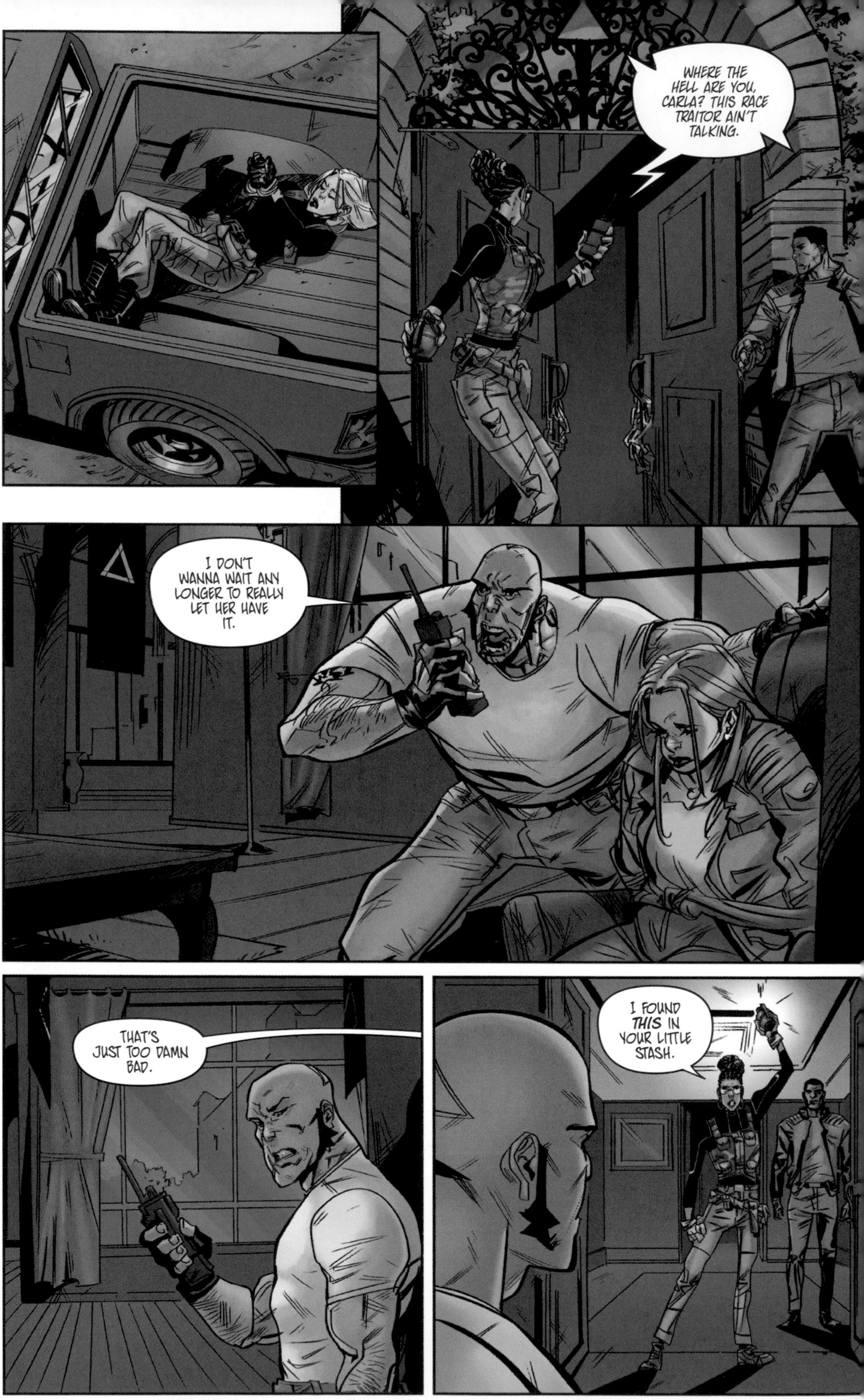
WHERE THE HELL ARE YOU, CARLA? THIS RACE TRAITOR AIN'T TALKING.
I DON'T WANNA WAIT ANY LONGER TO REALLY LET HER HAVE IT.
THAT'S JUST TOO DAMN BAD.
I FOUND THIS IN YOUR LITTLE STASH.

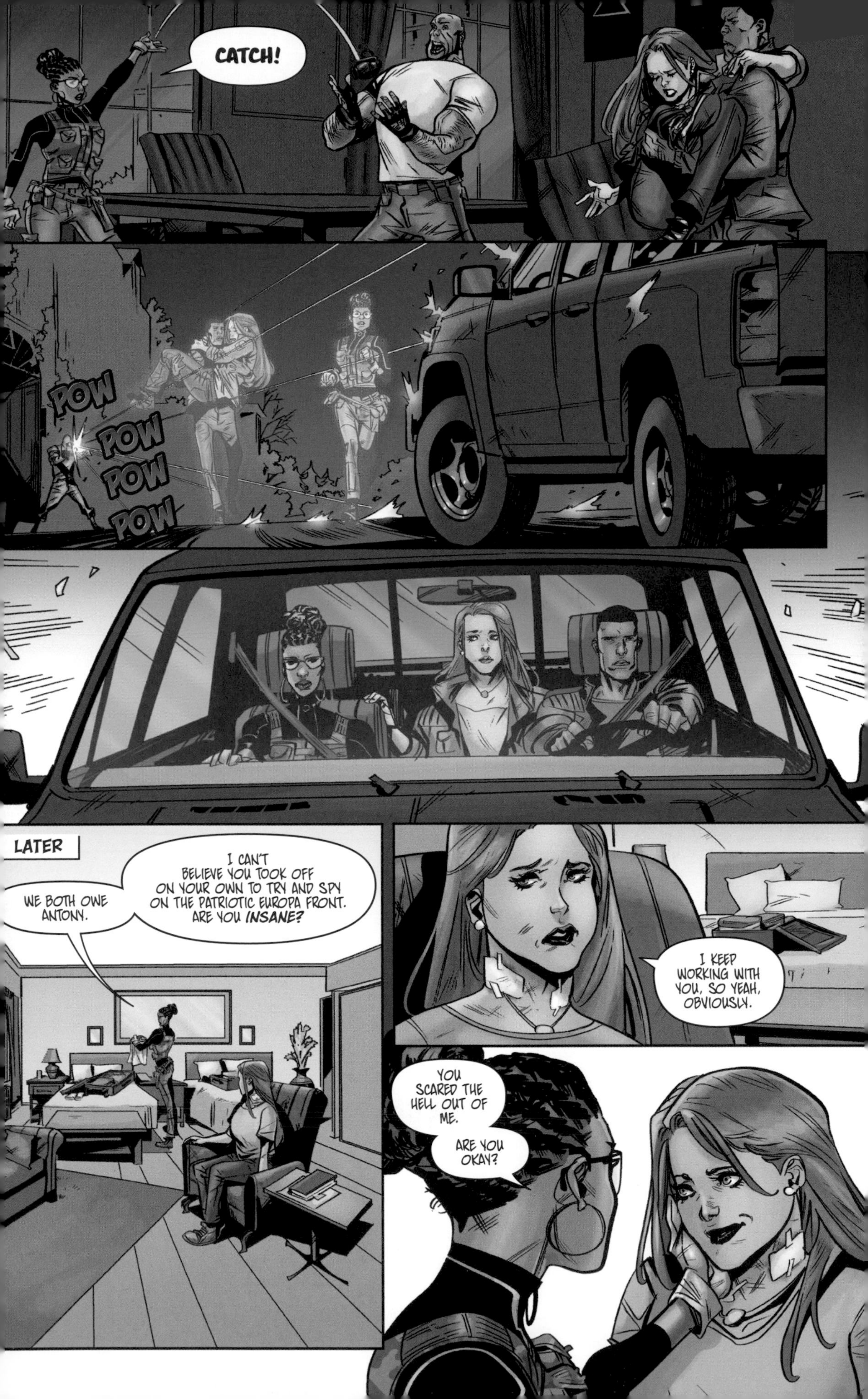
CATCH!
POW
POW
POW
POW
LATER
WE BOTH OWE ANTONY.
I CAN'T BELIEVE YOU TOOK OFF ON YOUR OWN TO TRY AND SPY ON THE PATRIOTIC EUROPA FRONT. ARE YOU *INSANE?*
I KEEP WORKING WITH YOU, SO YEAH, OBVIOUSLY.
YOU SCARED THE HELL OUT OF ME.
ARE YOU OKAY?

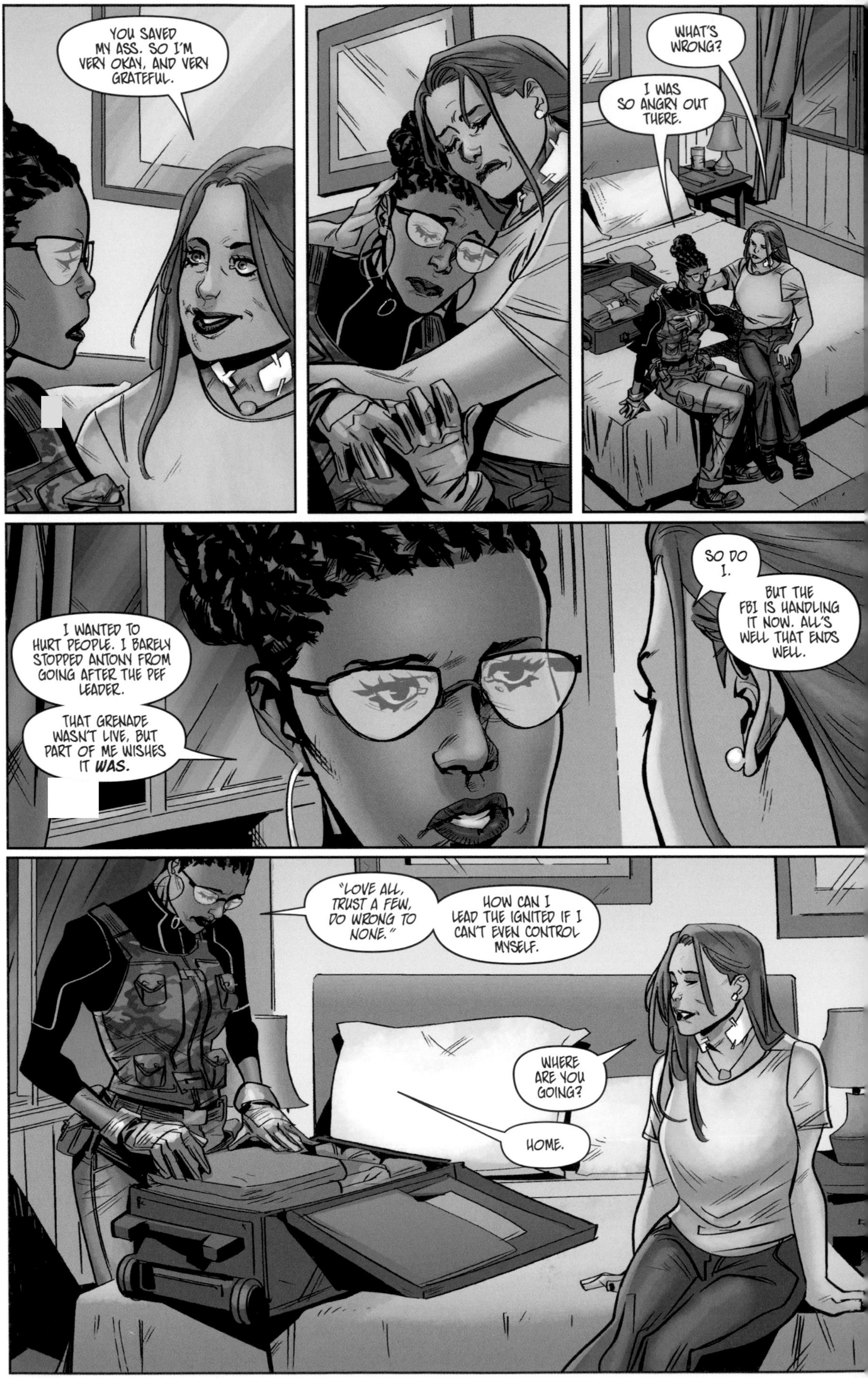

YOU SAVED MY ASS. SO I'M VERY OKAY, AND VERY GRATEFUL.
WHAT'S WRONG?
I WAS SO ANGRY OUT THERE.
I WANTED TO HURT PEOPLE. I BARELY STOPPED ANTONY FROM GOING AFTER THE PEF LEADER.
THAT GRENADE WASN'T LIVE, BUT PART OF ME WISHES IT ***WAS.***
SO DO I.
BUT THE FBI IS HANDLING IT NOW. ALL'S WELL THAT ENDS WELL.
"LOVE ALL, TRUST A FEW, DO WRONG TO NONE."
HOW CAN I LEAD THE IGNITED IF I CAN'T EVEN CONTROL MYSELF.
WHERE ARE YOU GOING?
HOME.

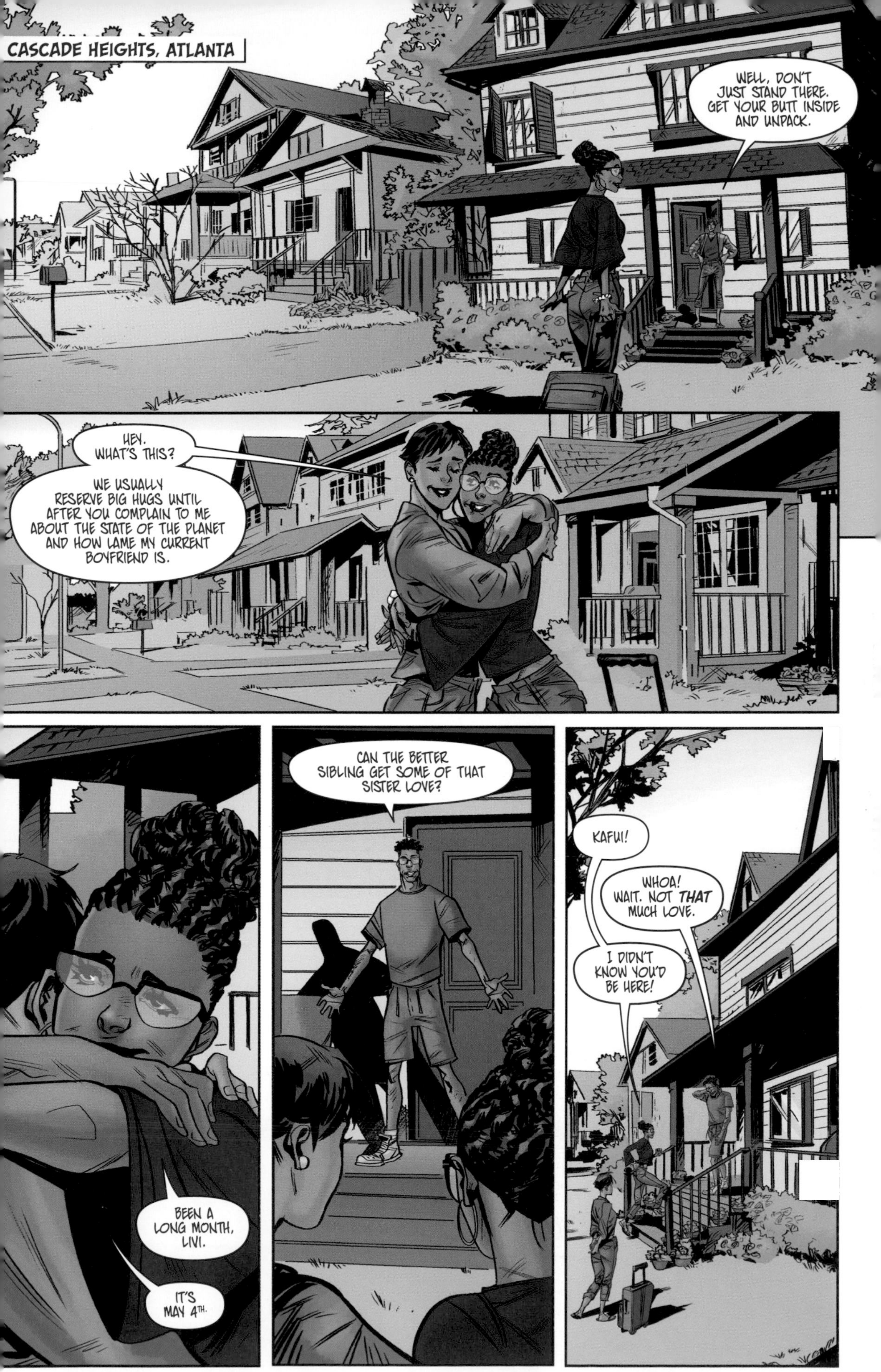
CASCADE HEIGHTS, ATLANTA
WELL, DON'T JUST STAND THERE. GET YOUR BUTT INSIDE AND UNPACK.
HEY. WHAT'S THIS?
WE USUALLY RESERVE BIG HUGS UNTIL AFTER YOU COMPLAIN TO ME ABOUT THE STATE OF THE PLANET AND HOW LAME MY CURRENT BOYFRIEND IS.
BEEN A LONG MONTH, LIVI.
IT'S MAY 4TH.
CAN THE BETTER SIBLING GET SOME OF THAT SISTER LOVE?
KAFUI!
I DIDN'T KNOW YOU'D BE HERE!
WHOA! WAIT. NOT THAT MUCH LOVE.

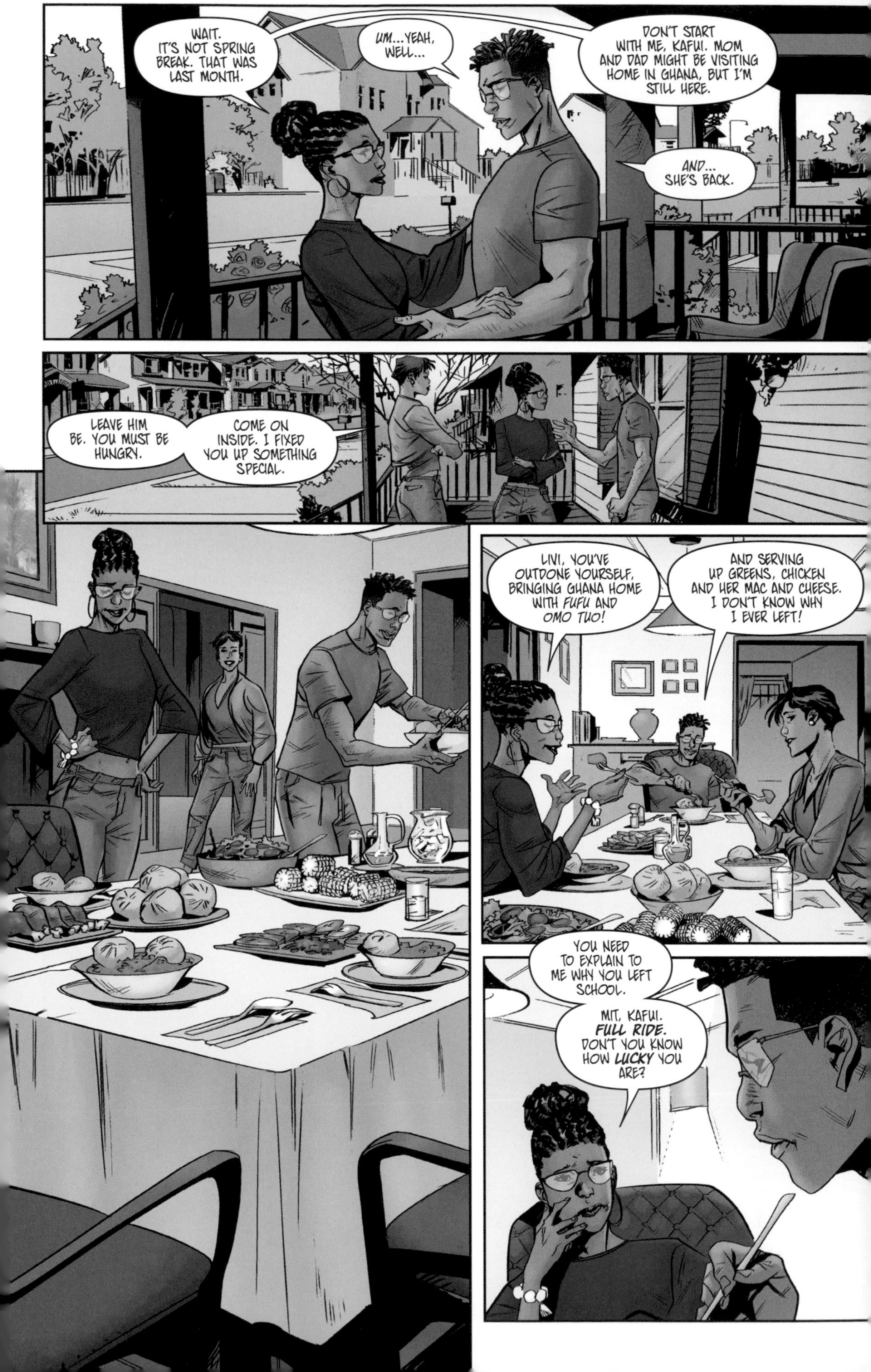
WAIT. IT'S NOT SPRING BREAK. THAT WAS LAST MONTH.
UM...YEAH, WELL...
DON'T START WITH ME, KAFUI. MOM AND DAD MIGHT BE VISITING HOME IN GHANA, BUT I'M STILL HERE.
AND... SHE'S BACK.
LEAVE HIM BE. YOU MUST BE HUNGRY.
COME ON INSIDE. I FIXED YOU UP SOMETHING SPECIAL.
LIVI, YOU'VE OUTDONE YOURSELF, BRINGING GHANA HOME WITH *FUFU* AND *OMO TUO*!
AND SERVING UP GREENS, CHICKEN AND HER MAC AND CHEESE. I DON'T KNOW WHY I EVER LEFT!
YOU NEED TO EXPLAIN TO ME WHY YOU LEFT SCHOOL.
MIT, KAFUI. **FULL RIDE.** DON'T YOU KNOW HOW **LUCKY** YOU ARE?

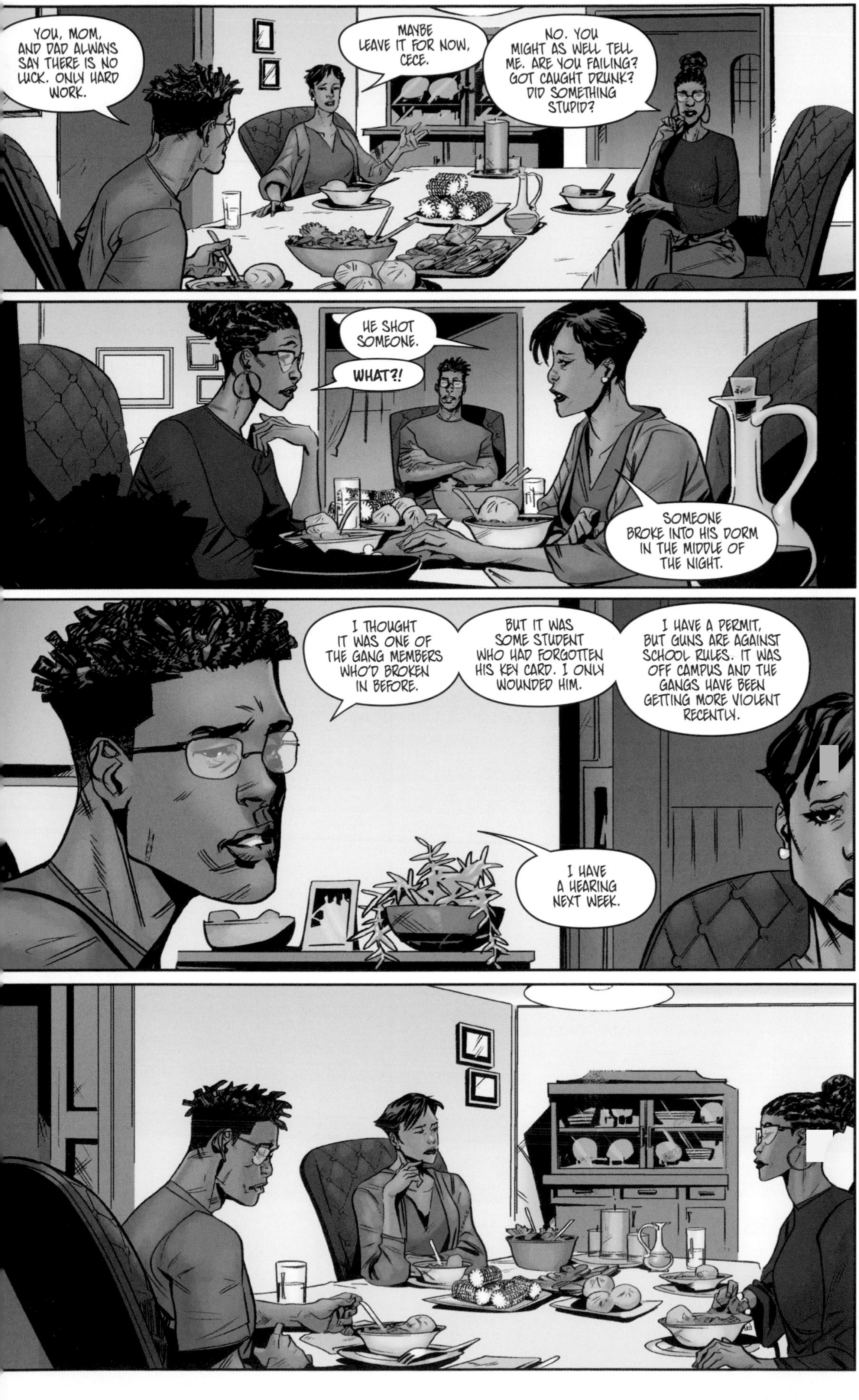
YOU, MOM, AND DAD ALWAYS SAY THERE IS NO LUCK. ONLY HARD WORK.
MAYBE LEAVE IT FOR NOW, CECE.
NO. YOU MIGHT AS WELL TELL ME. ARE YOU FAILING? GOT CAUGHT DRUNK? DID SOMETHING STUPID?
HE SHOT SOMEONE.
WHAT?!
SOMEONE BROKE INTO HIS DORM IN THE MIDDLE OF THE NIGHT.
I THOUGHT IT WAS ONE OF THE GANG MEMBERS WHO'D BROKEN IN BEFORE.
BUT IT WAS SOME STUDENT WHO HAD FORGOTTEN HIS KEY CARD. I ONLY WOUNDED HIM.
I HAVE A PERMIT, BUT GUNS ARE AGAINST SCHOOL RULES. IT WAS OFF CAMPUS AND THE GANGS HAVE BEEN GETTING MORE VIOLENT RECENTLY.
I HAVE A HEARING NEXT WEEK.

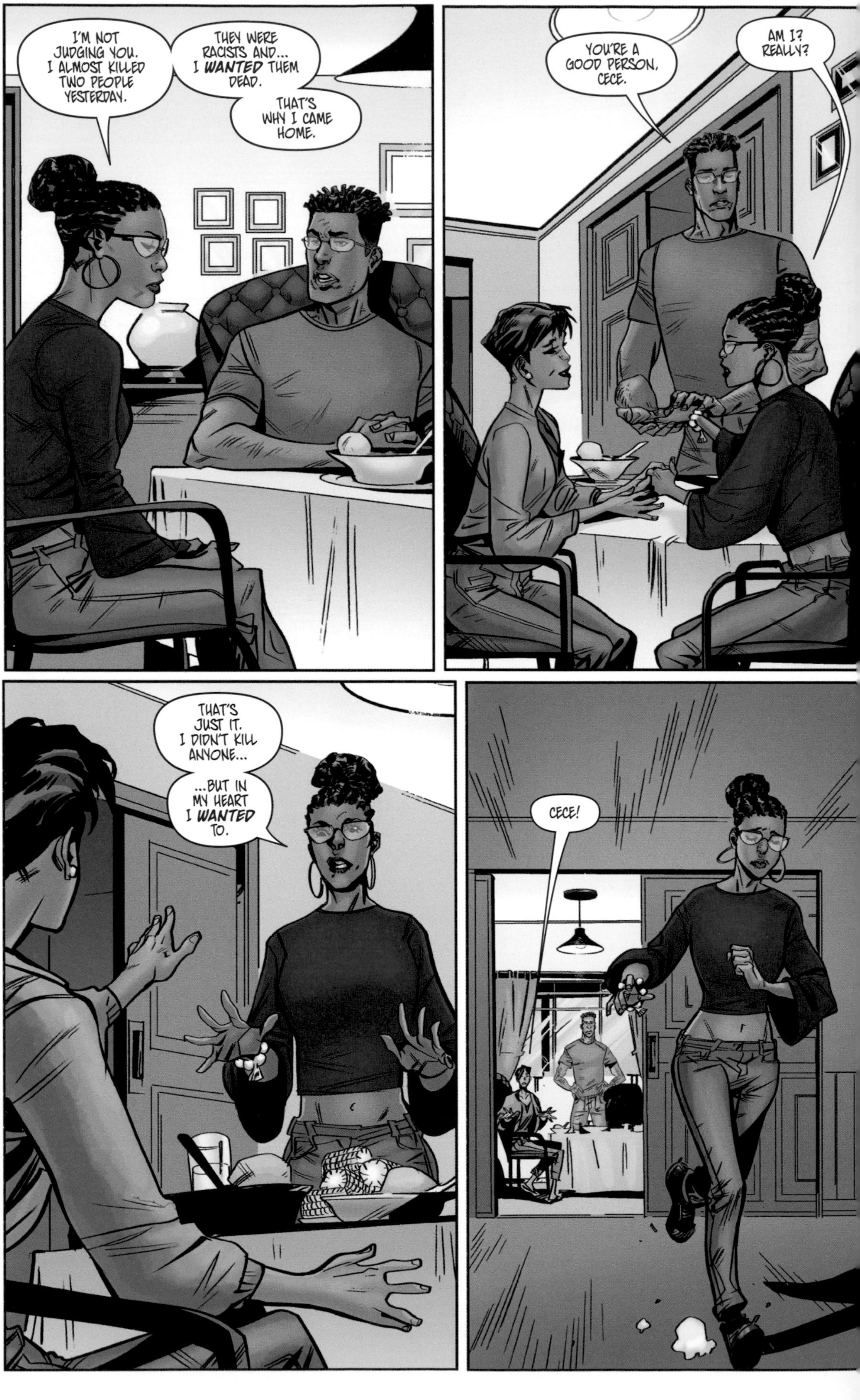
I'M NOT JUDGING YOU. I ALMOST KILLED TWO PEOPLE YESTERDAY.
THEY WERE RACISTS AND... I WANTED THEM DEAD.
THAT'S WHY I CAME HOME.
YOU'RE A GOOD PERSON, CECE.
AM I? REALLY?
THAT'S JUST IT. I DIDN'T KILL ANYONE...
...BUT IN MY HEART I WANTED TO.
CECE!

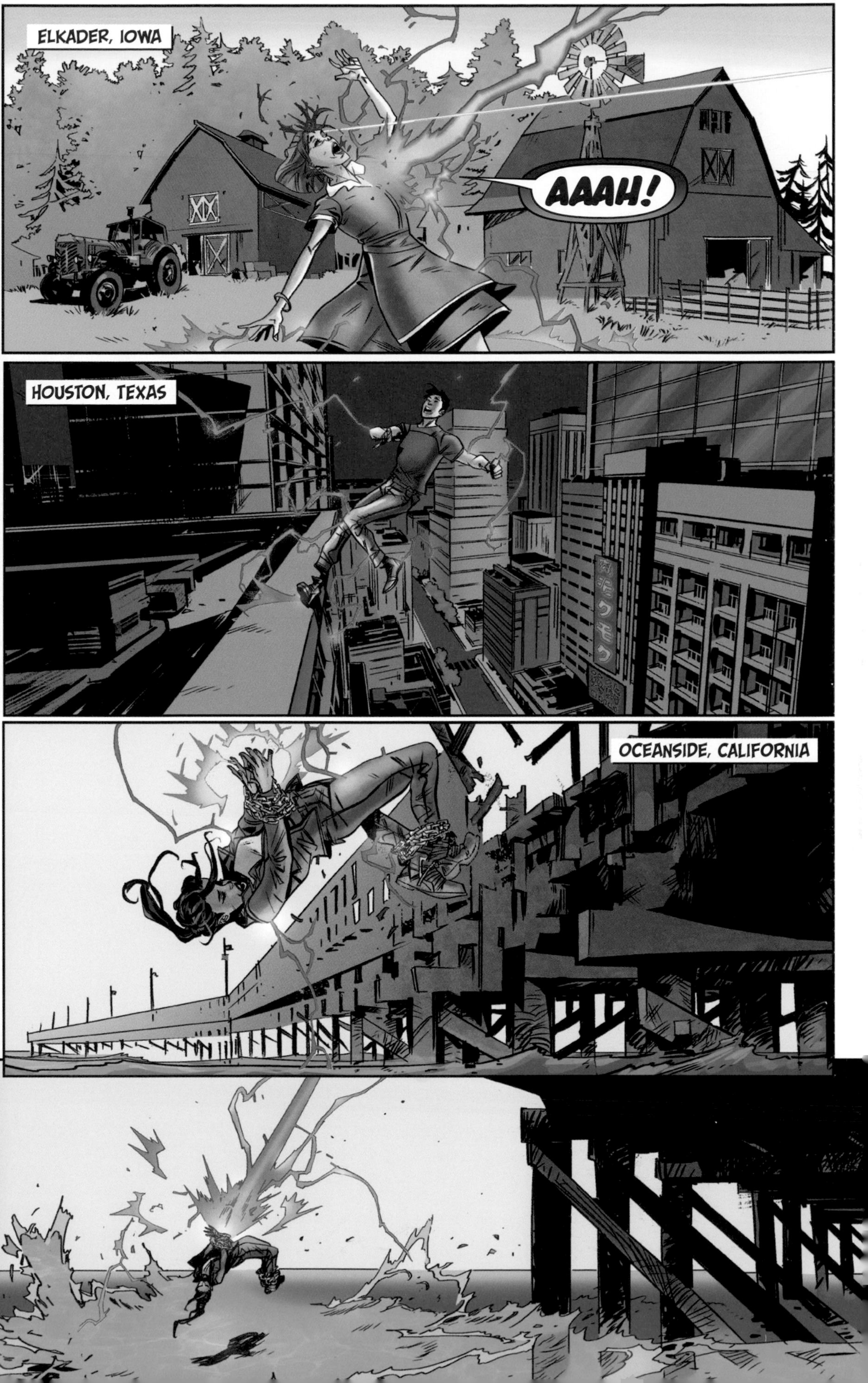
ELKADER, IOWA
AAAH!
HOUSTON, TEXAS
OCEANSIDE, CALIFORNIA

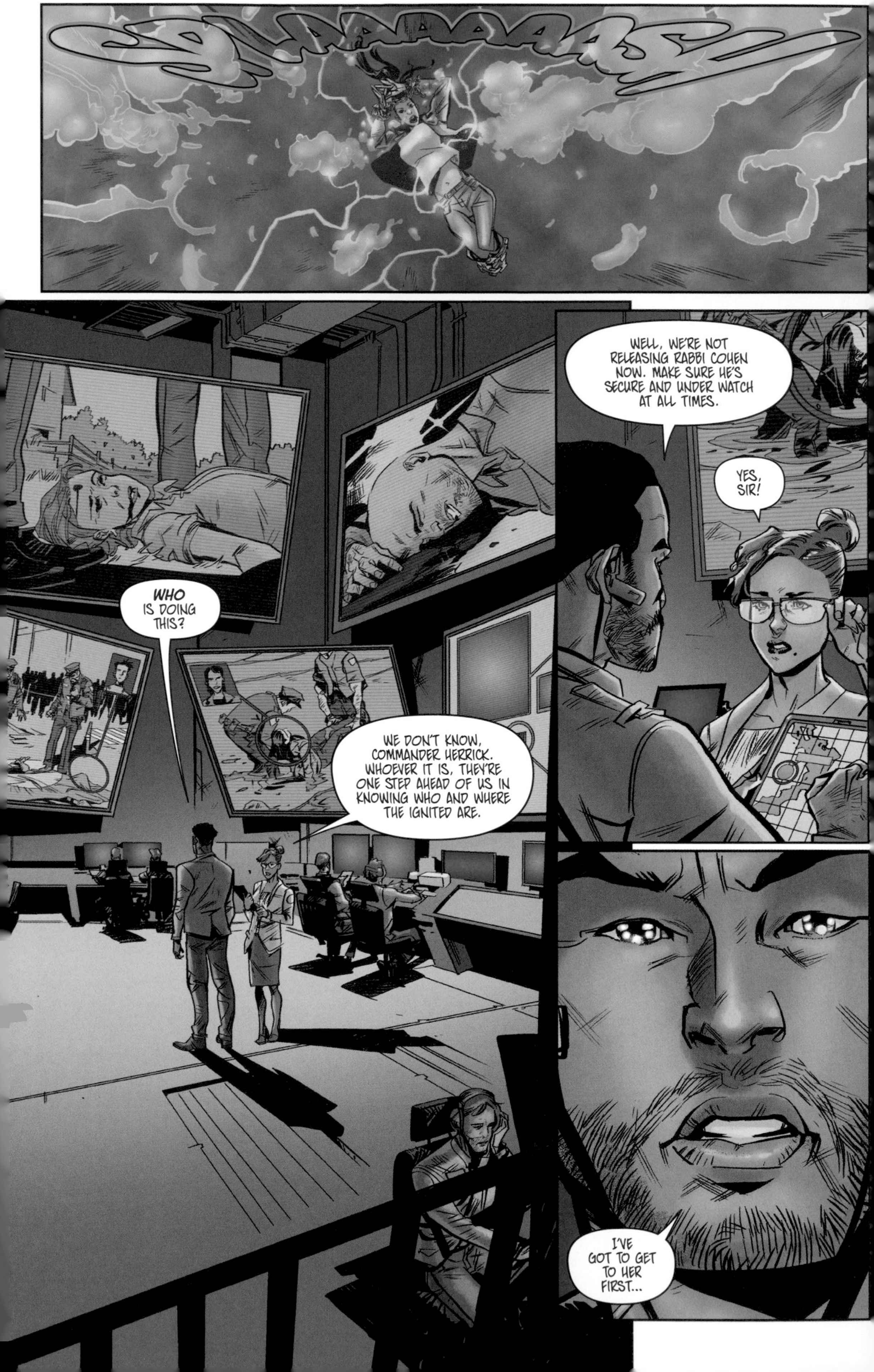
SHAAAAAASH
WHO IS DOING THIS?
WE DON'T KNOW, COMMANDER HERRICK. WHOEVER IT IS, THEY'RE ONE STEP AHEAD OF US IN KNOWING WHO AND WHERE THE IGNITED ARE.
WELL, WE'RE NOT RELEASING RABBI COHEN NOW. MAKE SURE HE'S SECURE AND UNDER WATCH AT ALL TIMES.
YES, SIR!
I'VE GOT TO GET TO HER FIRST...

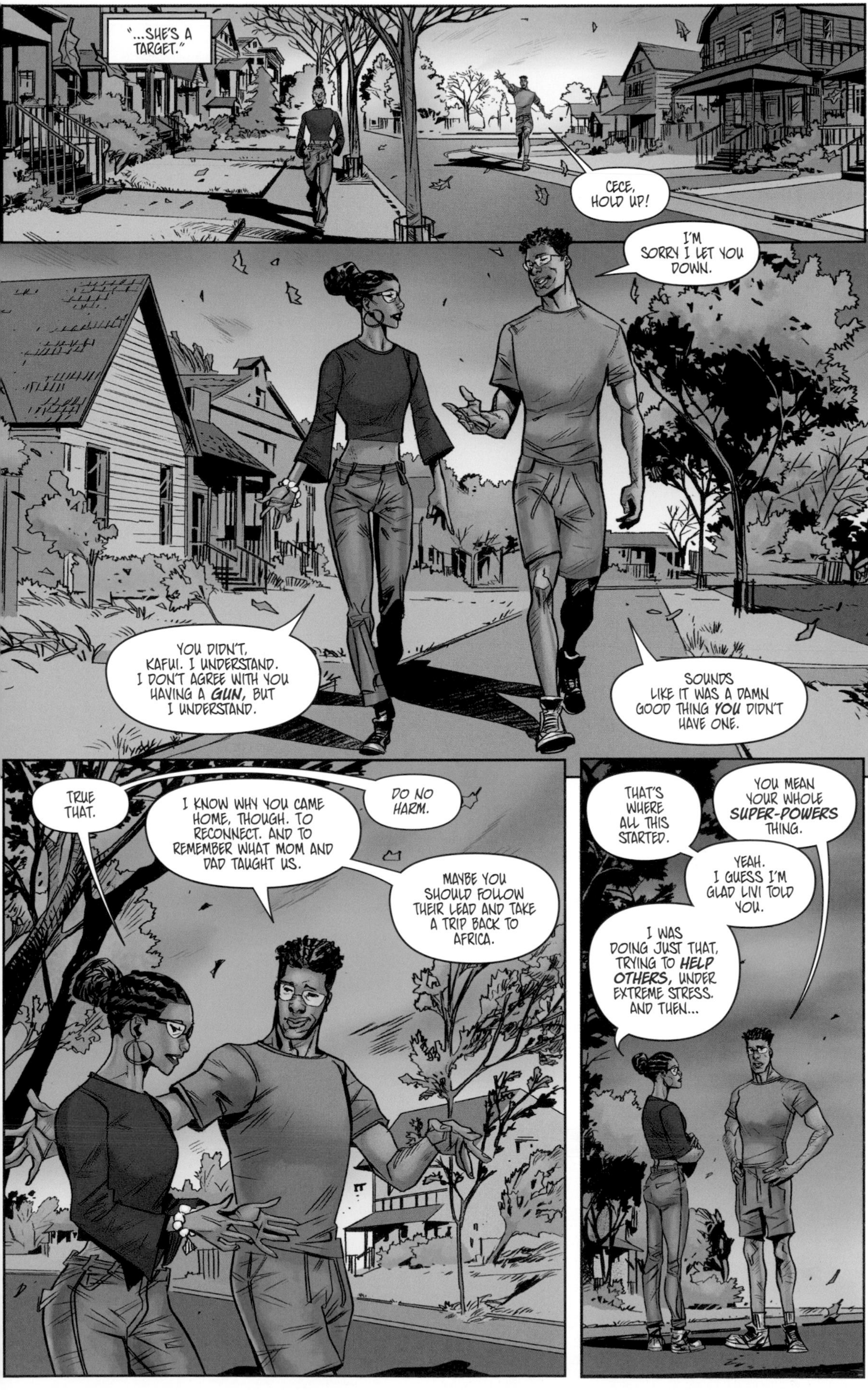
"...SHE'S A TARGET."
CECE, HOLD UP!
I'M SORRY I LET YOU DOWN.
YOU DIDN'T, KAFUI. I UNDERSTAND. I DON'T AGREE WITH YOU HAVING A GUN, BUT I UNDERSTAND.
SOUNDS LIKE IT WAS A DAMN GOOD THING YOU DIDN'T HAVE ONE.
TRUE THAT.
DO NO HARM.
I KNOW WHY YOU CAME HOME, THOUGH. TO RECONNECT. AND TO REMEMBER WHAT MOM AND DAD TAUGHT US.
MAYBE YOU SHOULD FOLLOW THEIR LEAD AND TAKE A TRIP BACK TO AFRICA.
THAT'S WHERE ALL THIS STARTED.
YOU MEAN YOUR WHOLE SUPER-POWERS THING.
YEAH. I GUESS I'M GLAD LIVI TOLD YOU.
I WAS DOING JUST THAT, TRYING TO HELP OTHERS, UNDER EXTREME STRESS. AND THEN...

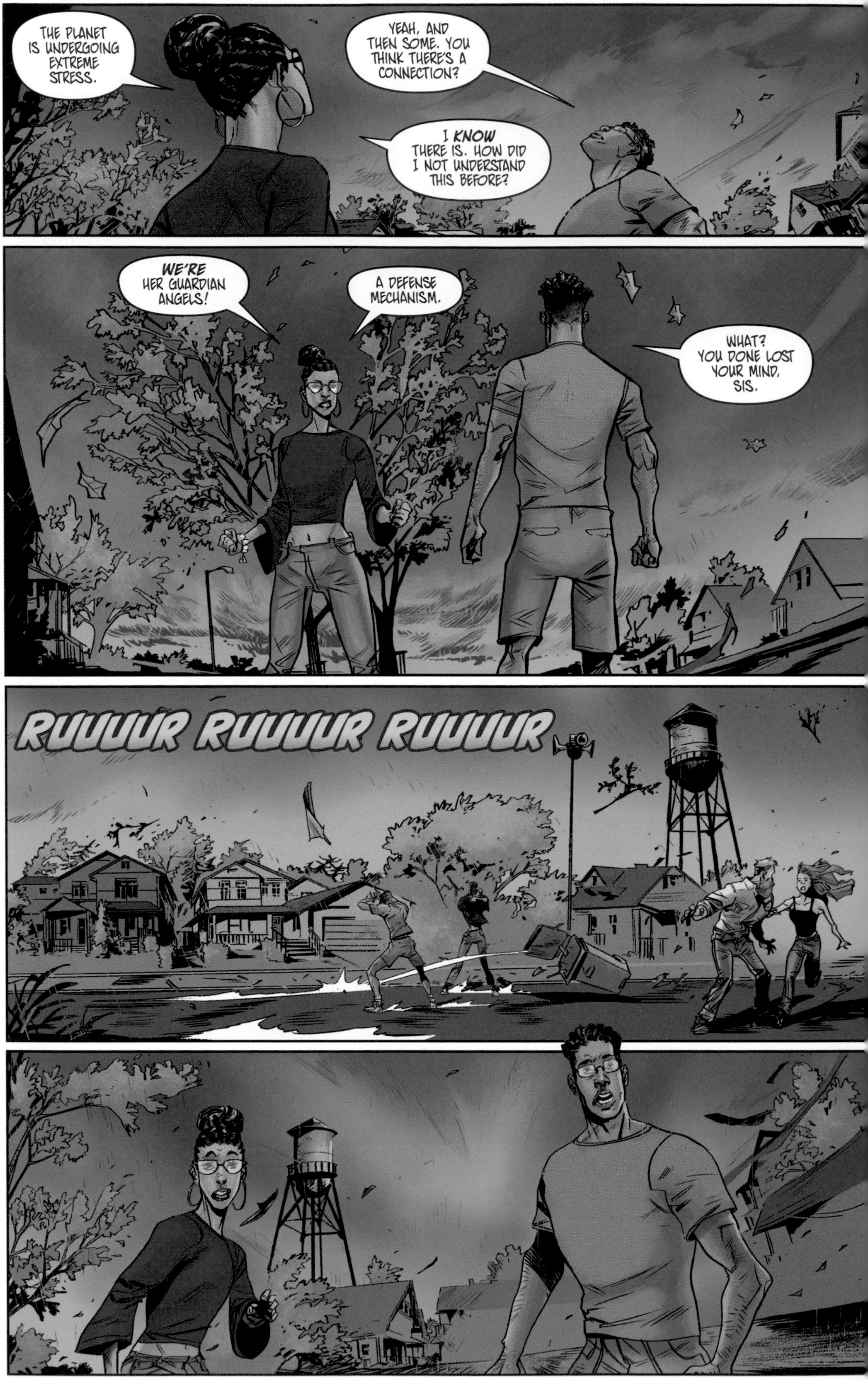

THE PLANET IS UNDERGOING EXTREME STRESS.
YEAH, AND THEN SOME. YOU THINK THERE'S A CONNECTION?
I KNOW THERE IS. HOW DID I NOT UNDERSTAND THIS BEFORE?
WE'RE HER GUARDIAN ANGELS!
A DEFENSE MECHANISM.
WHAT? YOU DONE LOST YOUR MIND, SIS.
RUUUUR RUUUUR RUUUUR

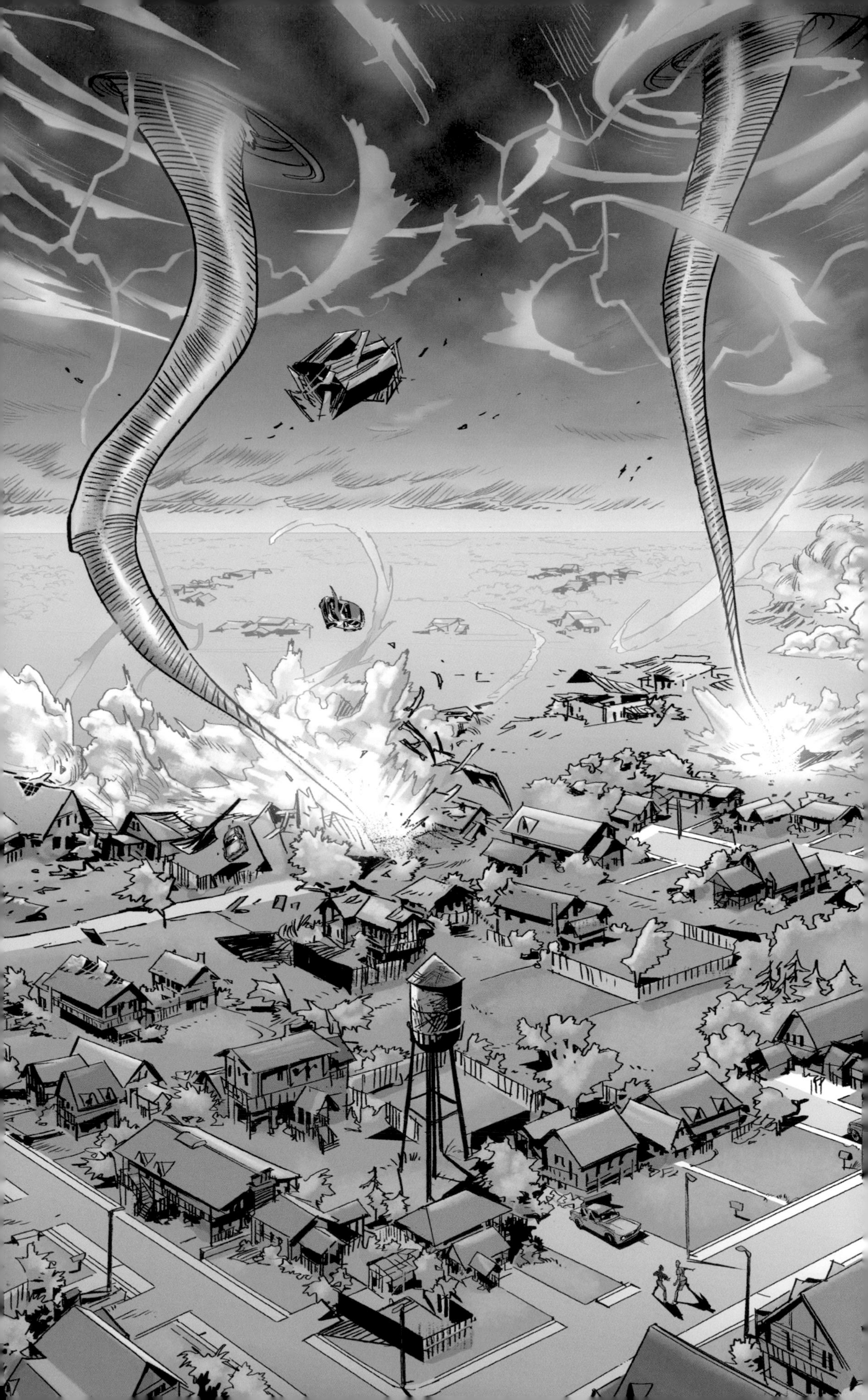

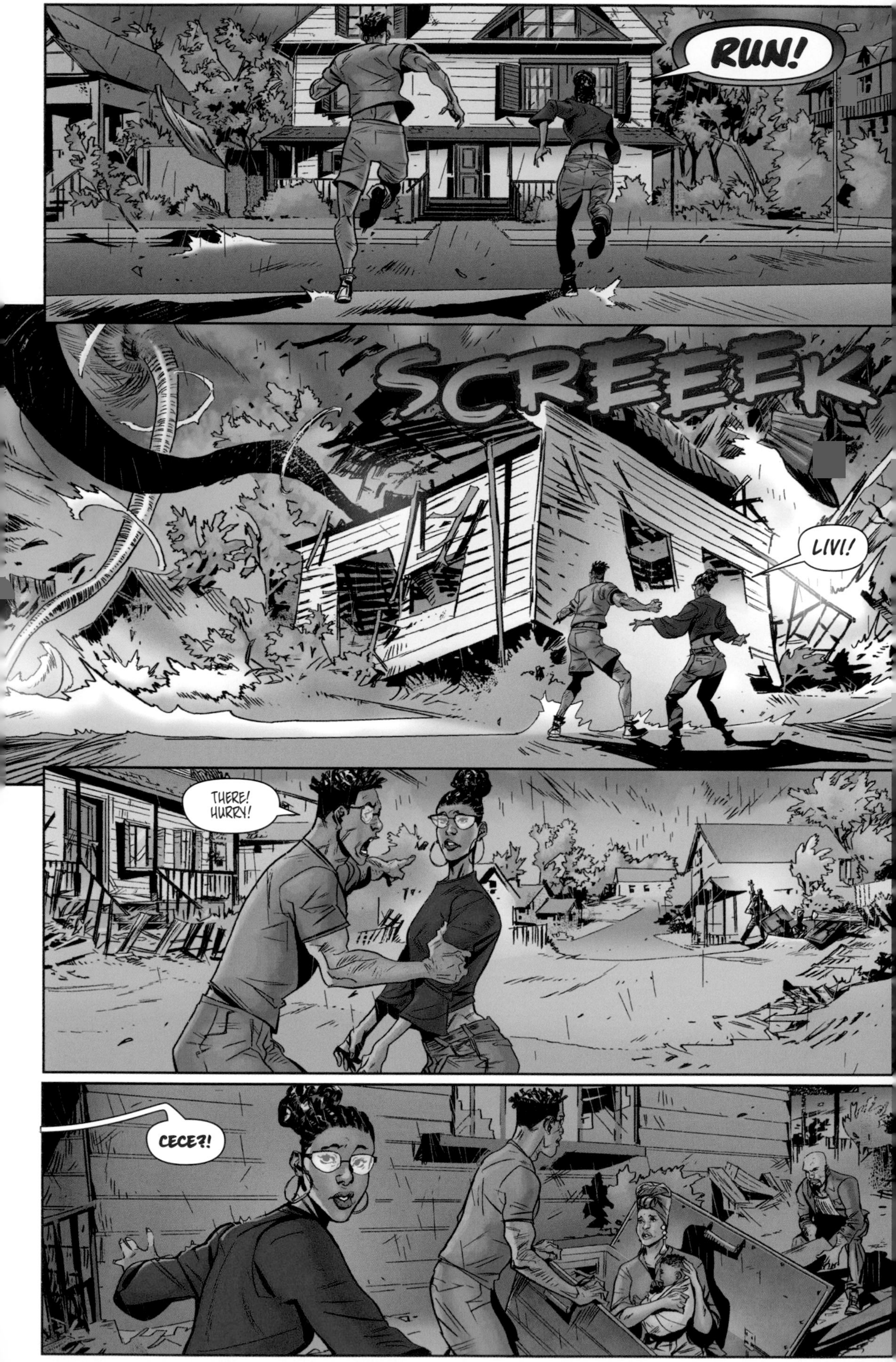
RUN!
SCREEEK
LIVI!
THERE! HURRY!
CECE?!

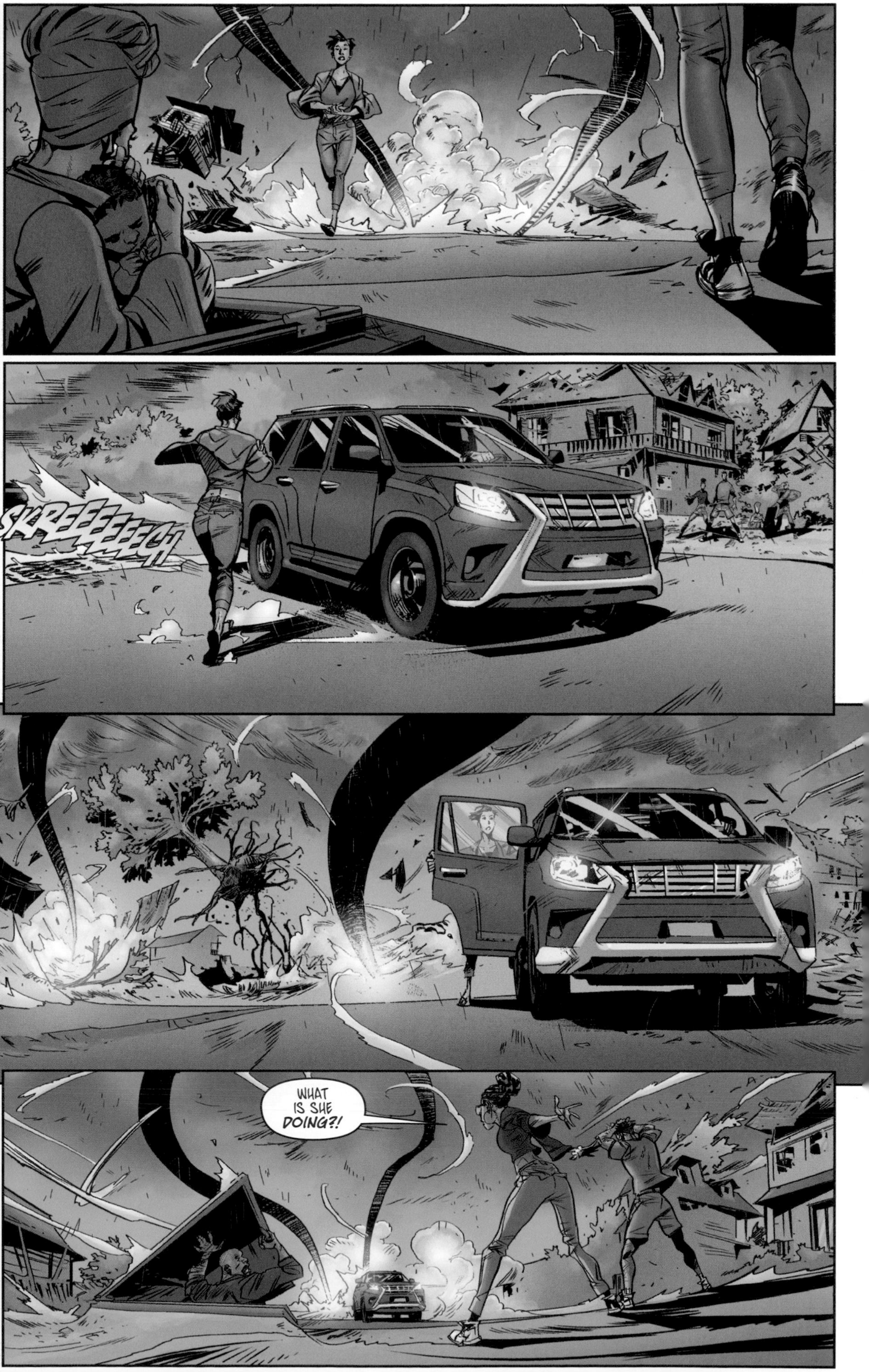
SKREEEEEEECH
WHAT IS SHE DOING?!

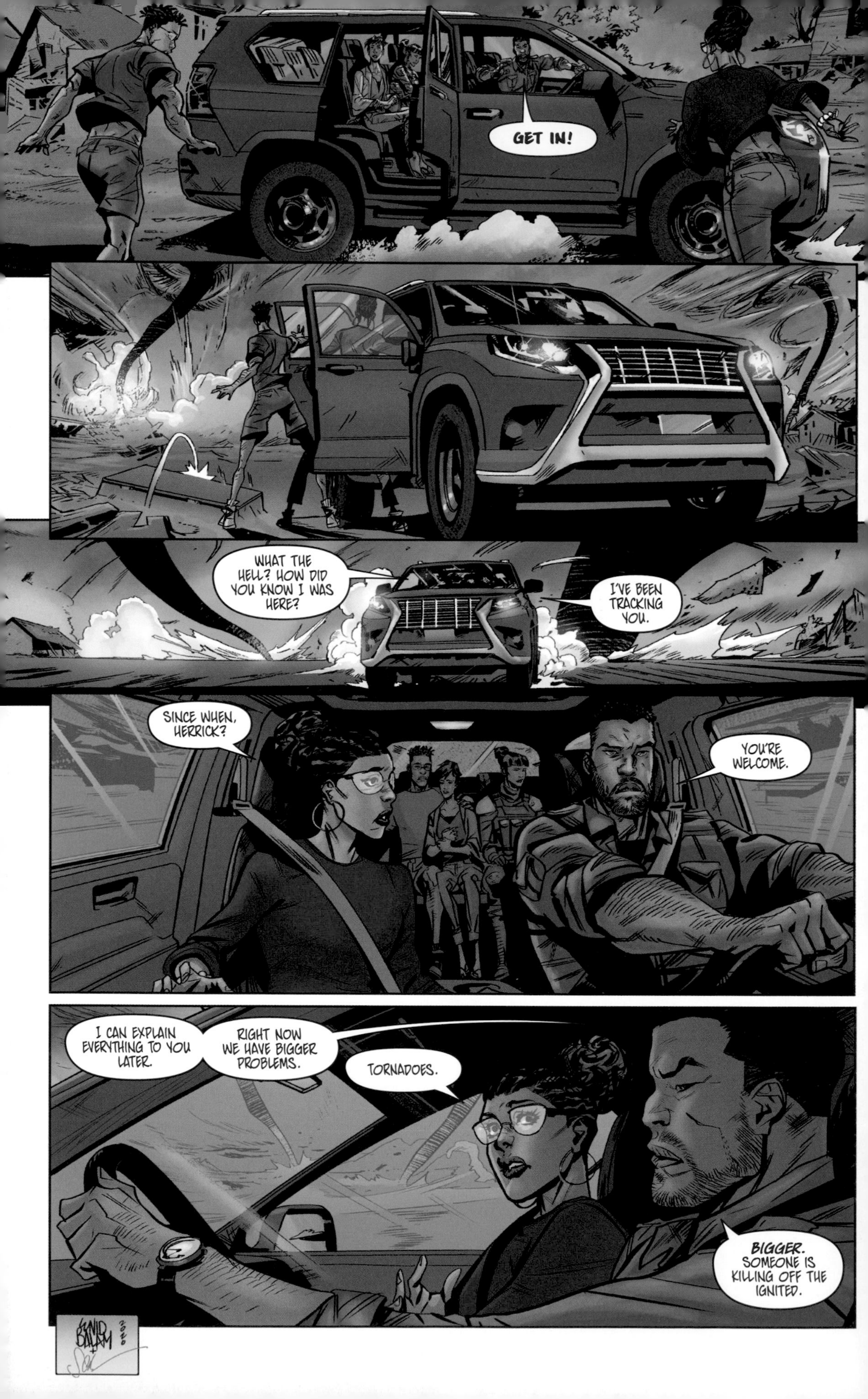
GET IN!
WHAT THE HELL? HOW DID YOU KNOW I WAS HERE?
I'VE BEEN TRACKING YOU.
SINCE WHEN, HERRICK?
YOU'RE WELCOME.
I CAN EXPLAIN EVERYTHING TO YOU LATER.
RIGHT NOW WE HAVE BIGGER PROBLEMS.
TORNADOES.
BIGGER. SOMEONE IS KILLING OFF THE IGNITED.

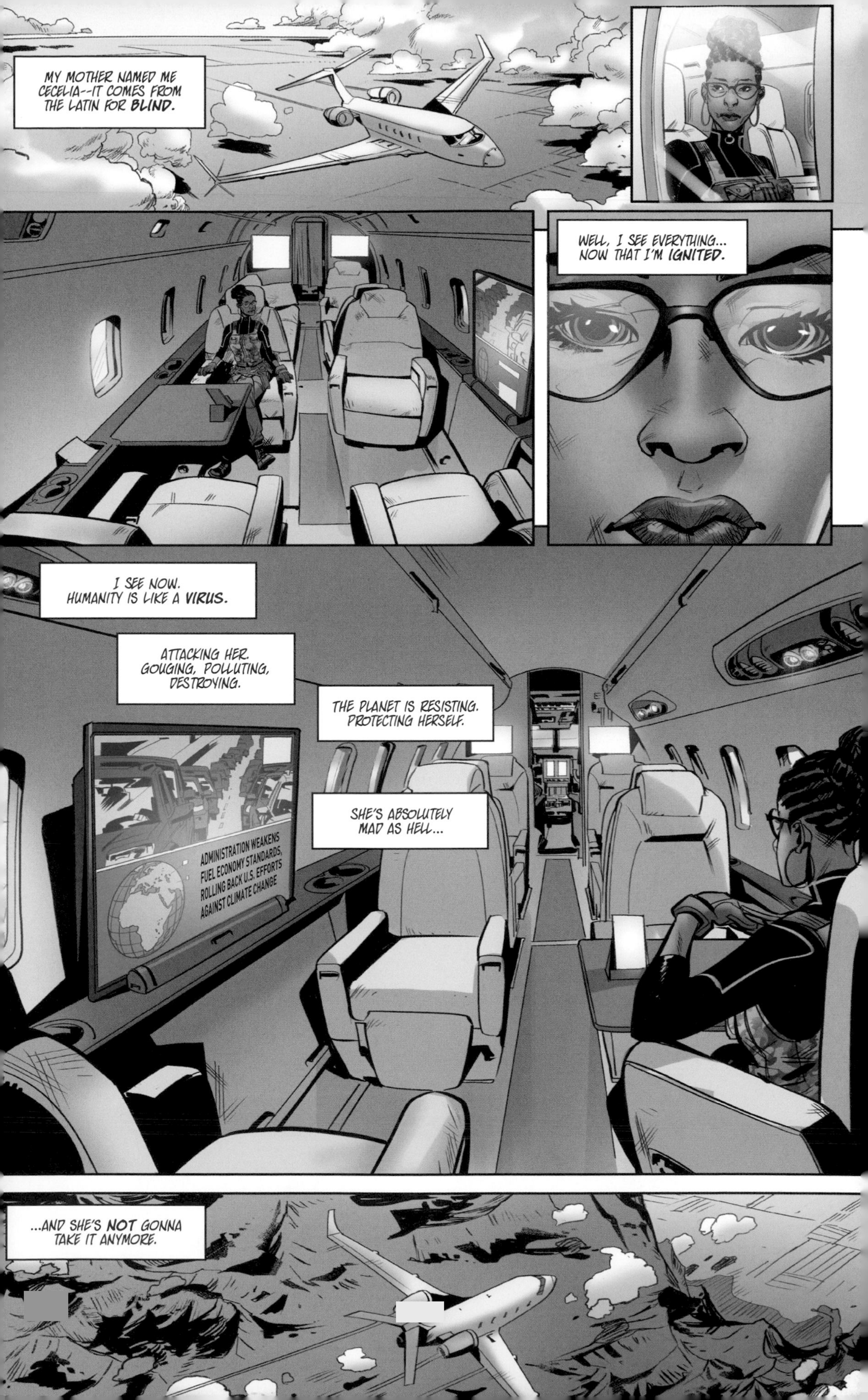
MY MOTHER NAMED ME CECELIA--IT COMES FROM THE LATIN FOR BLIND.
WELL, I SEE EVERYTHING... NOW THAT I'M IGNITED.
I SEE NOW. HUMANITY IS LIKE A VIRUS.
ATTACKING HER. GOUGING, POLLUTING, DESTROYING.
THE PLANET IS RESISTING. PROTECTING HERSELF.
ADMINISTRATION WEAKENS FUEL ECONOMY STANDARDS, ROLLING BACK U.S. EFFORTS AGAINST CLIMATE CHANGE
SHE'S ABSOLUTELY MAD AS HELL...
...AND SHE'S NOT GONNA TAKE IT ANYMORE.

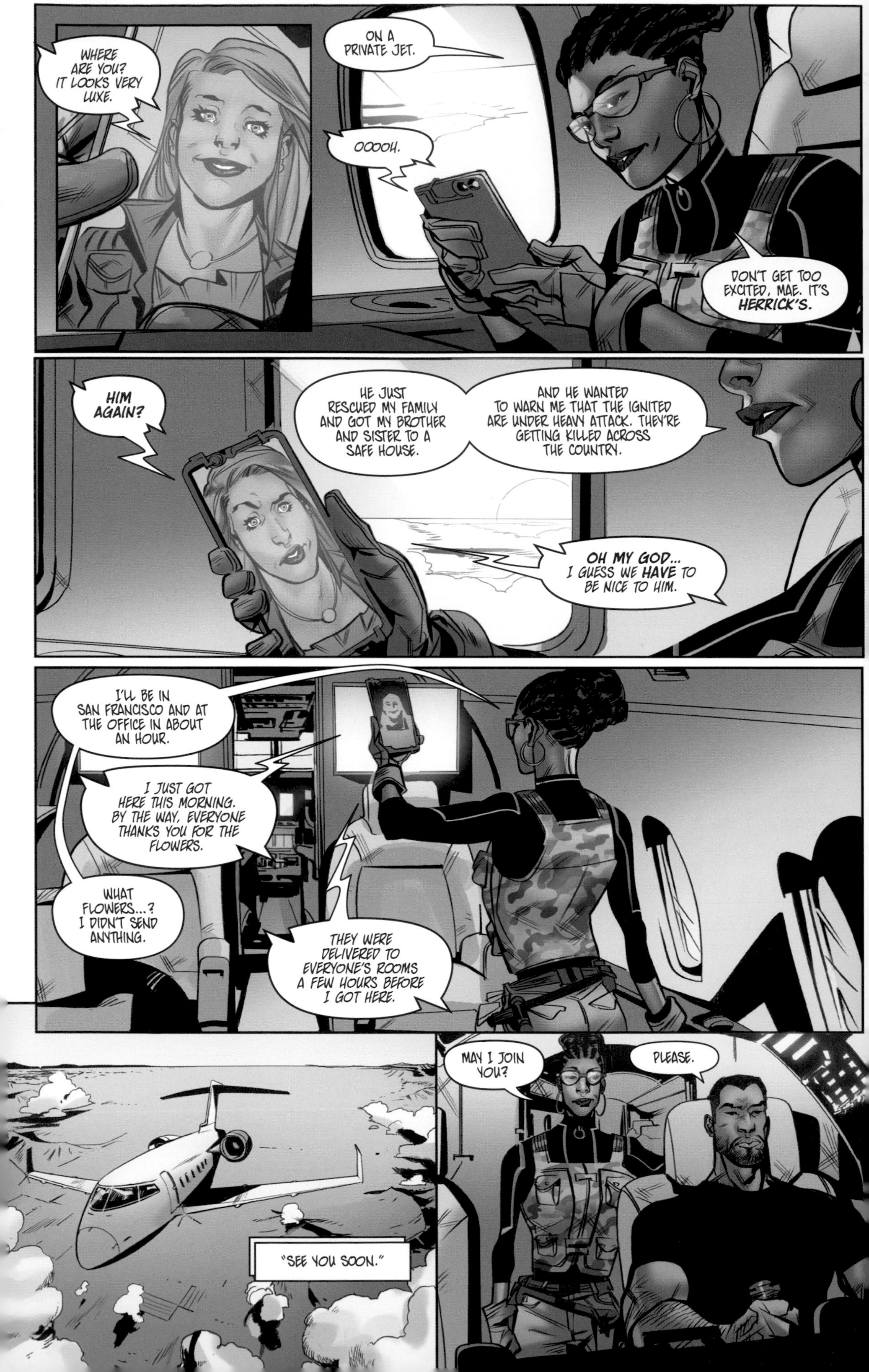
WHERE ARE YOU? IT LOOKS VERY LUXE.
ON A PRIVATE JET.
OOOOH.
DON'T GET TOO EXCITED, MAE. IT'S **HERRICK'S.**
HIM AGAIN?
HE JUST RESCUED MY FAMILY AND GOT MY BROTHER AND SISTER TO A SAFE HOUSE.
AND HE WANTED TO WARN ME THAT THE IGNITED ARE UNDER HEAVY ATTACK. THEY'RE GETTING KILLED ACROSS THE COUNTRY.
OH MY GOD... I GUESS WE **HAVE** TO BE NICE TO HIM.
I'LL BE IN SAN FRANCISCO AND AT THE OFFICE IN ABOUT AN HOUR.
I JUST GOT HERE THIS MORNING. BY THE WAY, EVERYONE THANKS YOU FOR THE FLOWERS.
WHAT FLOWERS...? I DIDN'T SEND ANYTHING.
THEY WERE DELIVERED TO EVERYONE'S ROOMS A FEW HOURS BEFORE I GOT HERE.
"SEE YOU SOON."
MAY I JOIN YOU?
PLEASE.

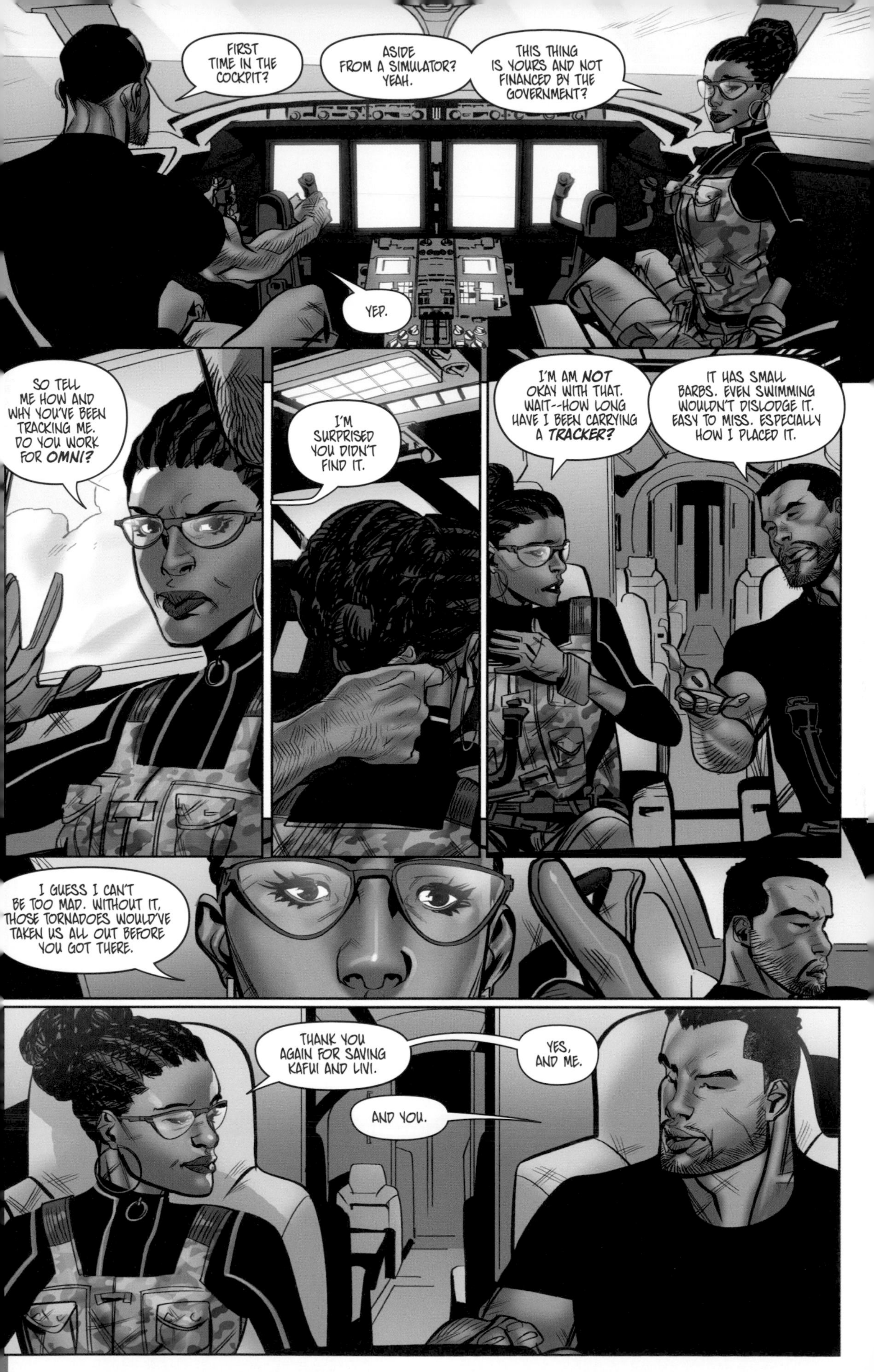
FIRST TIME IN THE COCKPIT?
ASIDE FROM A SIMULATOR? YEAH.
THIS THING IS YOURS AND NOT FINANCED BY THE GOVERNMENT?
YEP.
SO TELL ME HOW AND WHY YOU'VE BEEN TRACKING ME. DO YOU WORK FOR OMNI?
I'M SURPRISED YOU DIDN'T FIND IT.
I'M AM NOT OKAY WITH THAT. WAIT--HOW LONG HAVE I BEEN CARRYING A TRACKER?
IT HAS SMALL BARBS. EVEN SWIMMING WOULDN'T DISLODGE IT. EASY TO MISS. ESPECIALLY HOW I PLACED IT.
I GUESS I CAN'T BE TOO MAD. WITHOUT IT, THOSE TORNADOES WOULD'VE TAKEN US ALL OUT BEFORE YOU GOT THERE.
THANK YOU AGAIN FOR SAVING KAFUI AND LIVI.
YES, AND ME.
AND YOU.

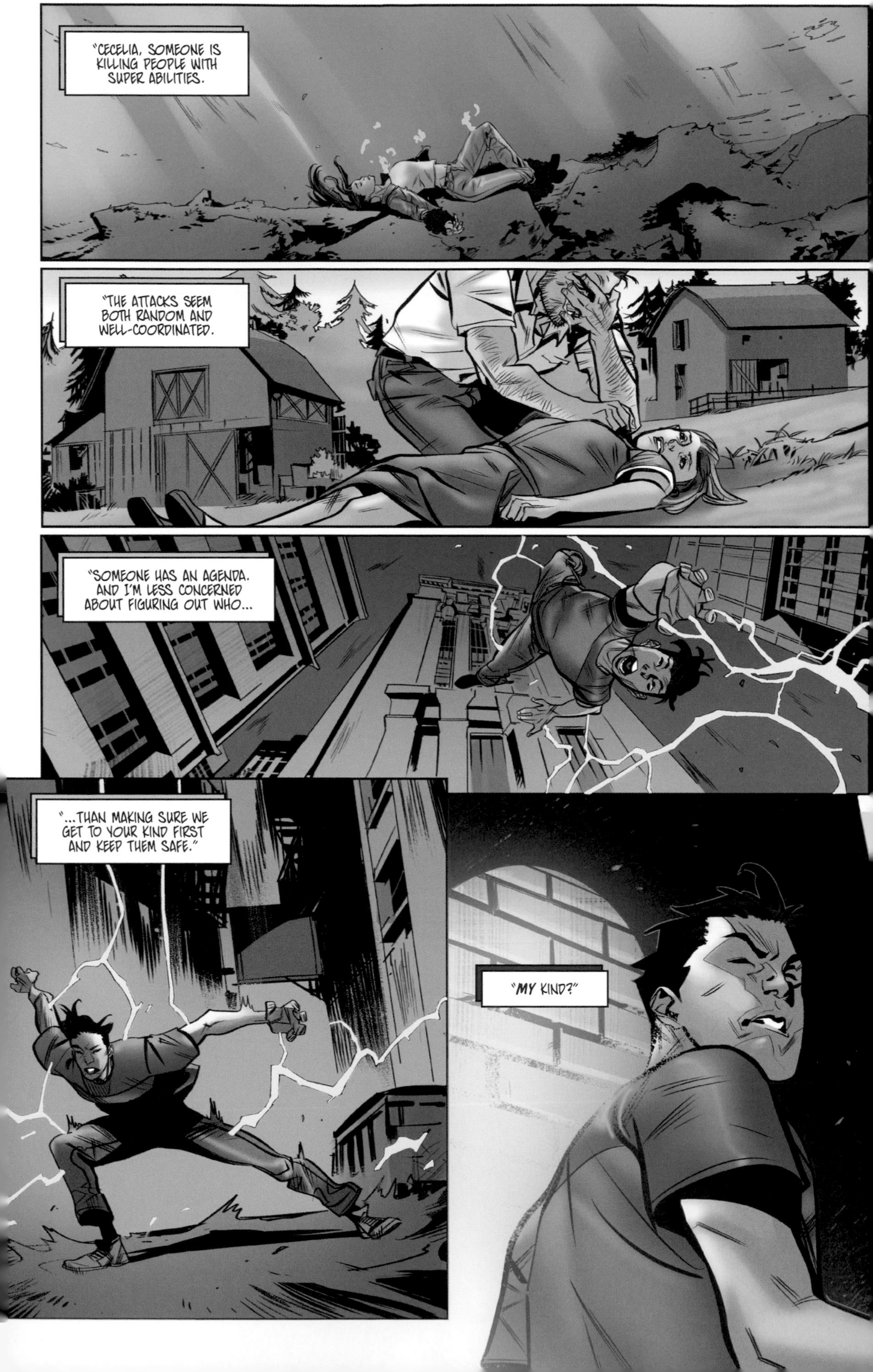
"CECELIA, SOMEONE IS KILLING PEOPLE WITH SUPER ABILITIES.
"THE ATTACKS SEEM BOTH RANDOM AND WELL-COORDINATED.
"SOMEONE HAS AN AGENDA. AND I'M LESS CONCERNED ABOUT FIGURING OUT WHO...
"...THAN MAKING SURE WE GET TO YOUR KIND FIRST AND KEEP THEM SAFE."
"MY KIND?"

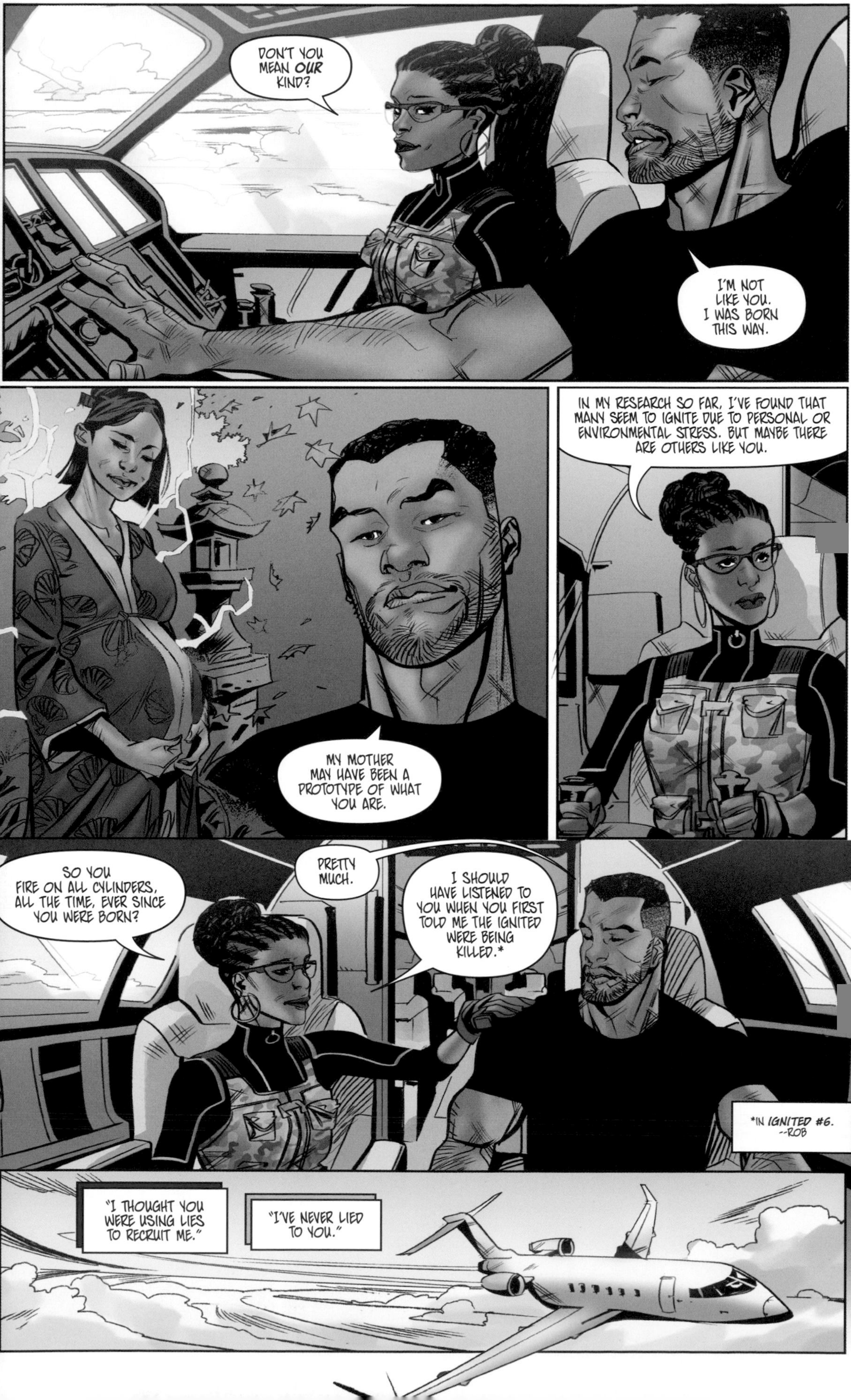
DON'T YOU MEAN OUR KIND?
I'M NOT LIKE YOU. I WAS BORN THIS WAY.
IN MY RESEARCH SO FAR, I'VE FOUND THAT MANY SEEM TO IGNITE DUE TO PERSONAL OR ENVIRONMENTAL STRESS. BUT MAYBE THERE ARE OTHERS LIKE YOU.
MY MOTHER MAY HAVE BEEN A PROTOTYPE OF WHAT YOU ARE.
SO YOU FIRE ON ALL CYLINDERS, ALL THE TIME, EVER SINCE YOU WERE BORN?
PRETTY MUCH.
I SHOULD HAVE LISTENED TO YOU WHEN YOU FIRST TOLD ME THE IGNITED WERE BEING KILLED.*
*IN IGNITED #6. --ROB
"I THOUGHT YOU WERE USING LIES TO RECRUIT ME."
"I'VE NEVER LIED TO YOU."

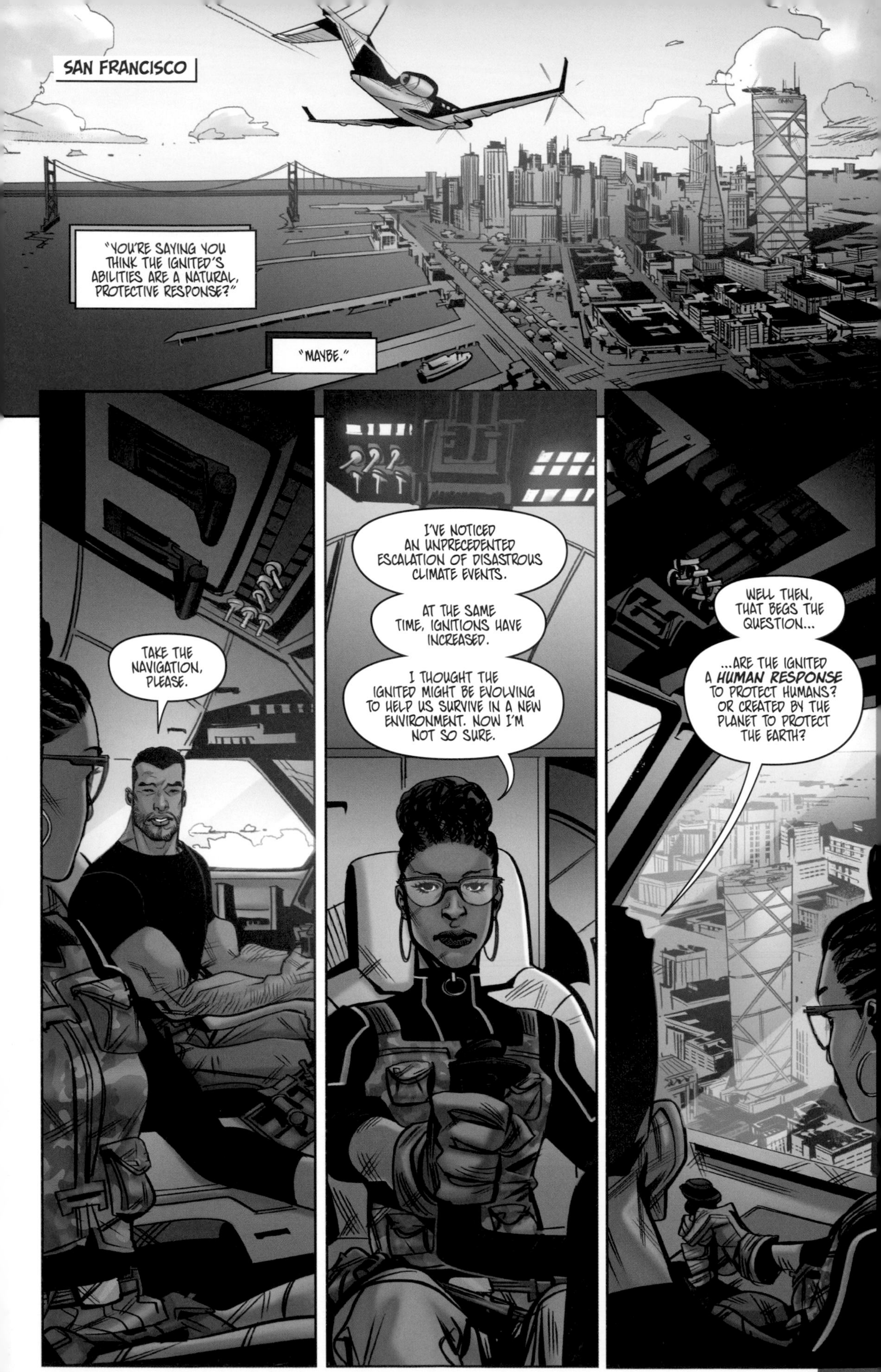
SAN FRANCISCO
"YOU'RE SAYING YOU THINK THE IGNITED'S ABILITIES ARE A NATURAL, PROTECTIVE RESPONSE?"
"MAYBE."
TAKE THE NAVIGATION, PLEASE.
I'VE NOTICED AN UNPRECEDENTED ESCALATION OF DISASTROUS CLIMATE EVENTS.
AT THE SAME TIME, IGNITIONS HAVE INCREASED.
I THOUGHT THE IGNITED MIGHT BE EVOLVING TO HELP US SURVIVE IN A NEW ENVIRONMENT. NOW I'M NOT SO SURE.
WELL THEN, THAT BEGS THE QUESTION...
...ARE THE IGNITED A **HUMAN RESPONSE** TO PROTECT HUMANS? OR CREATED BY THE PLANET TO PROTECT THE EARTH?

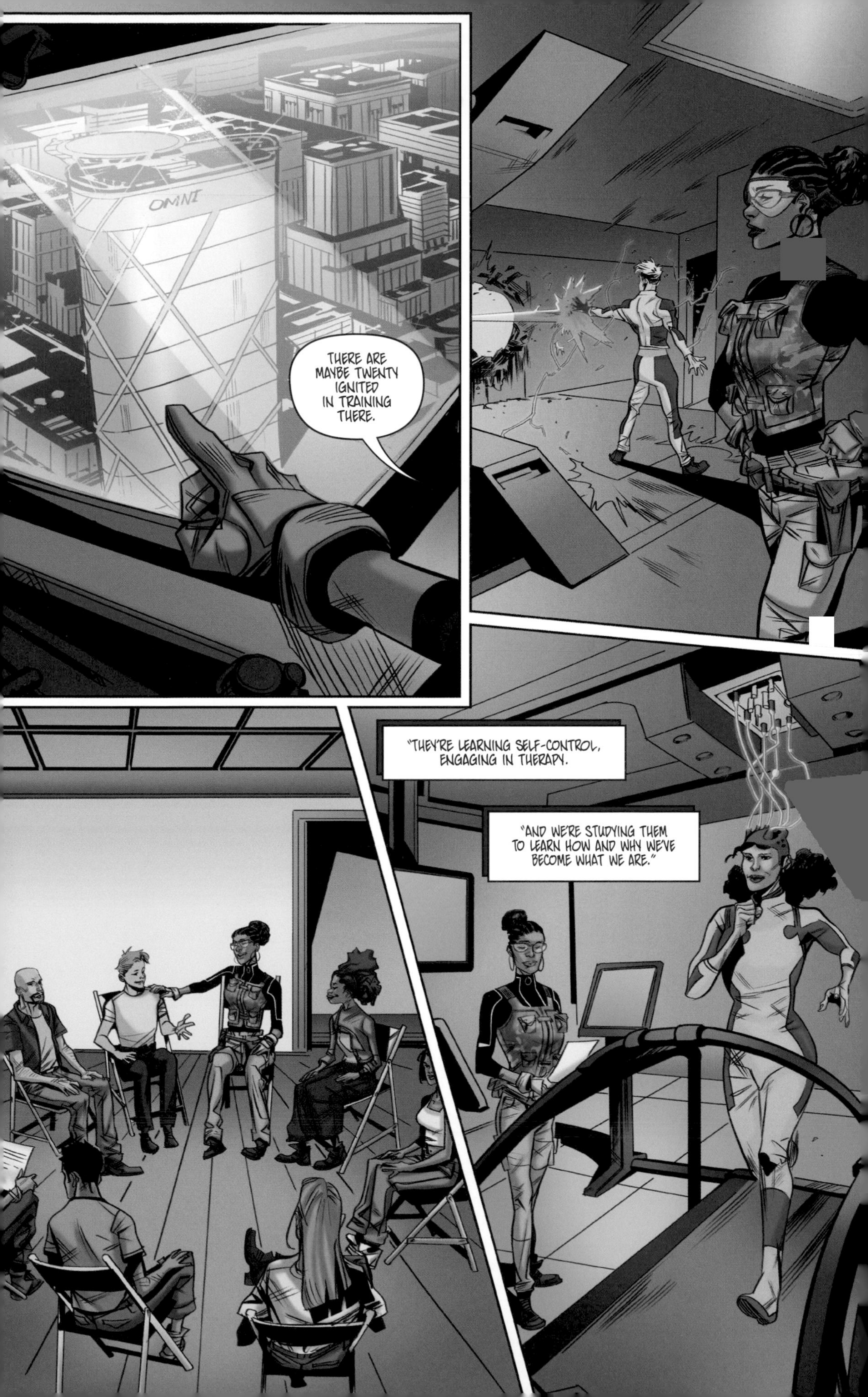
OMNI
THERE ARE MAYBE TWENTY IGNITED IN TRAINING THERE.
"THEY'RE LEARNING SELF-CONTROL, ENGAGING IN THERAPY.
"AND WE'RE STUDYING THEM TO LEARN HOW AND WHY WE'VE BECOME WHAT WE ARE."

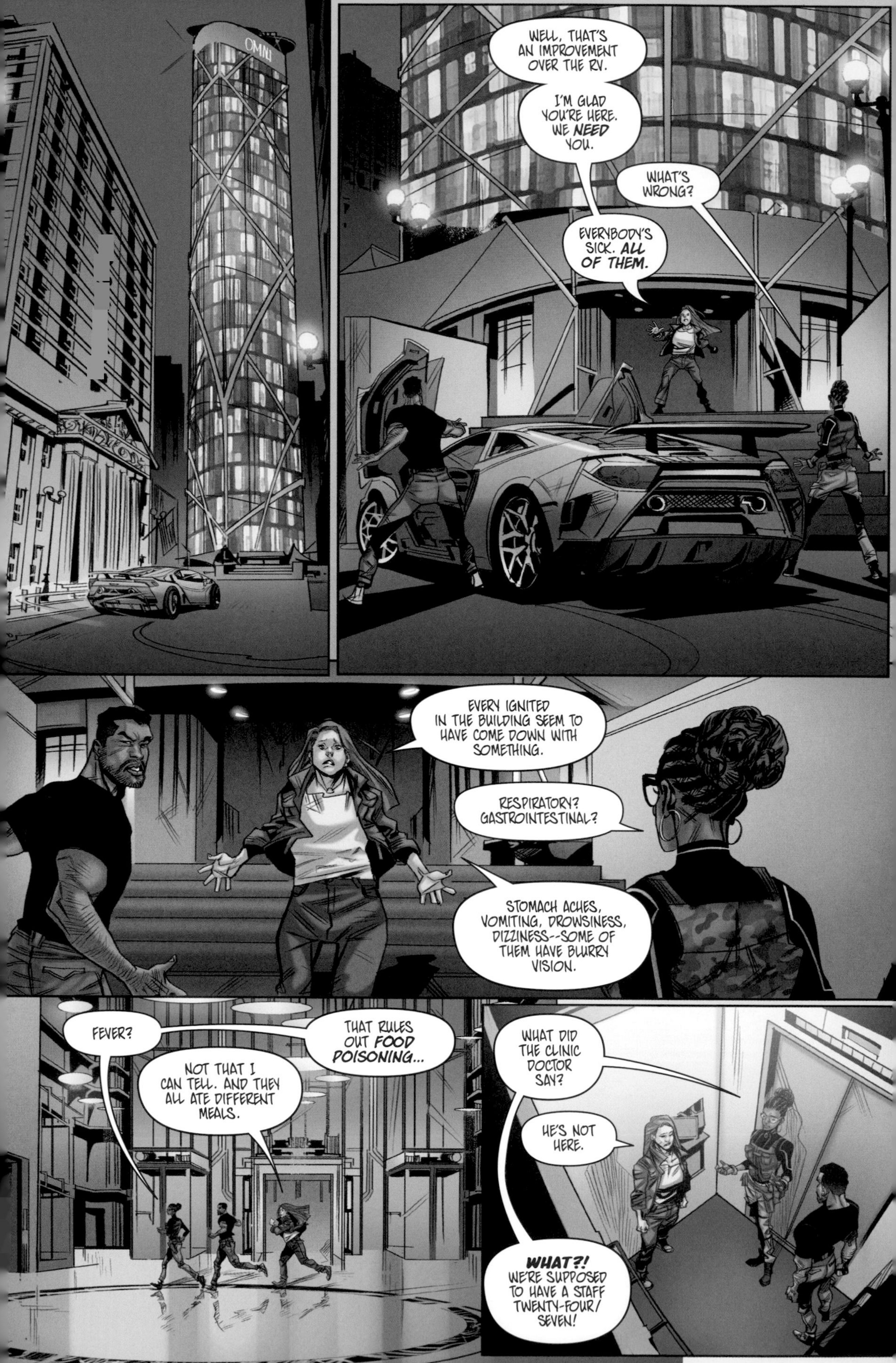
OMNI
WELL, THAT'S AN IMPROVEMENT OVER THE RV.
I'M GLAD YOU'RE HERE. WE NEED YOU.
WHAT'S WRONG?
EVERYBODY'S SICK. ALL OF THEM.
EVERY IGNITED IN THE BUILDING SEEM TO HAVE COME DOWN WITH SOMETHING.
RESPIRATORY? GASTROINTESTINAL?
STOMACH ACHES, VOMITING, DROWSINESS, DIZZINESS--SOME OF THEM HAVE BLURRY VISION.
FEVER?
THAT RULES OUT FOOD POISONING...
NOT THAT I CAN TELL. AND THEY ALL ATE DIFFERENT MEALS.
WHAT DID THE CLINIC DOCTOR SAY?
HE'S NOT HERE.
WHAT?! WE'RE SUPPOSED TO HAVE A STAFF TWENTY-FOUR/SEVEN!

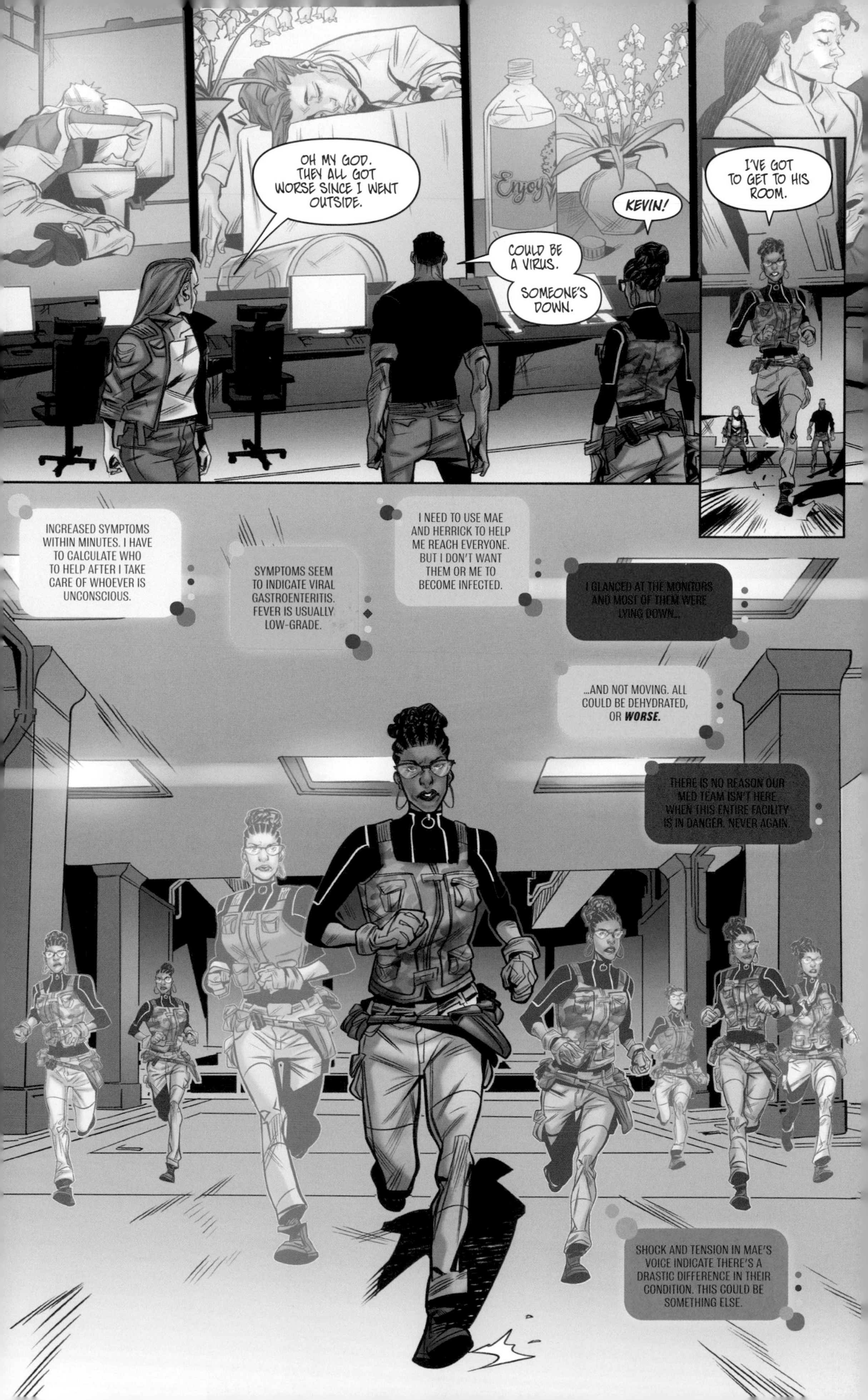
OH MY GOD. THEY ALL GOT WORSE SINCE I WENT OUTSIDE.
COULD BE A VIRUS.
SOMEONE'S DOWN.
KEVIN!
I'VE GOT TO GET TO HIS ROOM.
INCREASED SYMPTOMS WITHIN MINUTES. I HAVE TO CALCULATE WHO TO HELP AFTER I TAKE CARE OF WHOEVER IS UNCONSCIOUS.
SYMPTOMS SEEM TO INDICATE VIRAL GASTROENTERITIS. FEVER IS USUALLY LOW-GRADE.
I NEED TO USE MAE AND HERRICK TO HELP ME REACH EVERYONE. BUT I DON'T WANT THEM OR ME TO BECOME INFECTED.
I GLANCED AT THE MONITORS AND MOST OF THEM WERE LYING DOWN...
...AND NOT MOVING. ALL COULD BE DEHYDRATED, OR **WORSE.**
THERE IS NO REASON OUR MED TEAM ISN'T HERE, WHEN THIS ENTIRE FACILITY IS IN DANGER. NEVER AGAIN.
SHOCK AND TENSION IN MAE'S VOICE INDICATE THERE'S A DRASTIC DIFFERENCE IN THEIR CONDITION. THIS COULD BE SOMETHING ELSE.

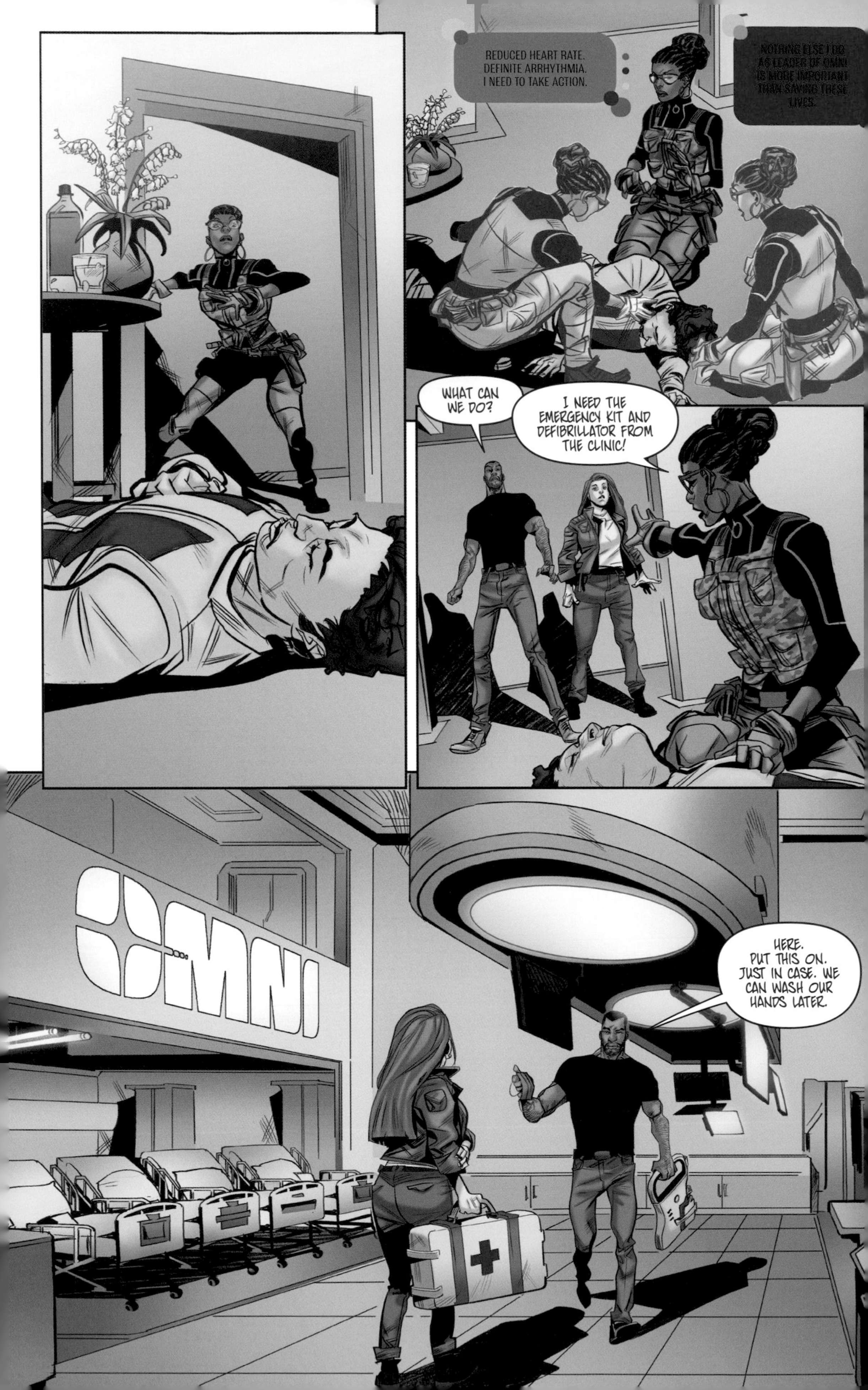
REDUCED HEART RATE. DEFINITE ARRHYTHMIA. I NEED TO TAKE ACTION.
NOTHING ELSE I DO AS LEADER OF OMNI IS MORE IMPORTANT THAN SAVING THESE LIVES.
WHAT CAN WE DO?
I NEED THE EMERGENCY KIT AND DEFIBRILLATOR FROM THE CLINIC!
OMNI
HERE. PUT THIS ON. JUST IN CASE. WE CAN WASH OUR HANDS LATER.

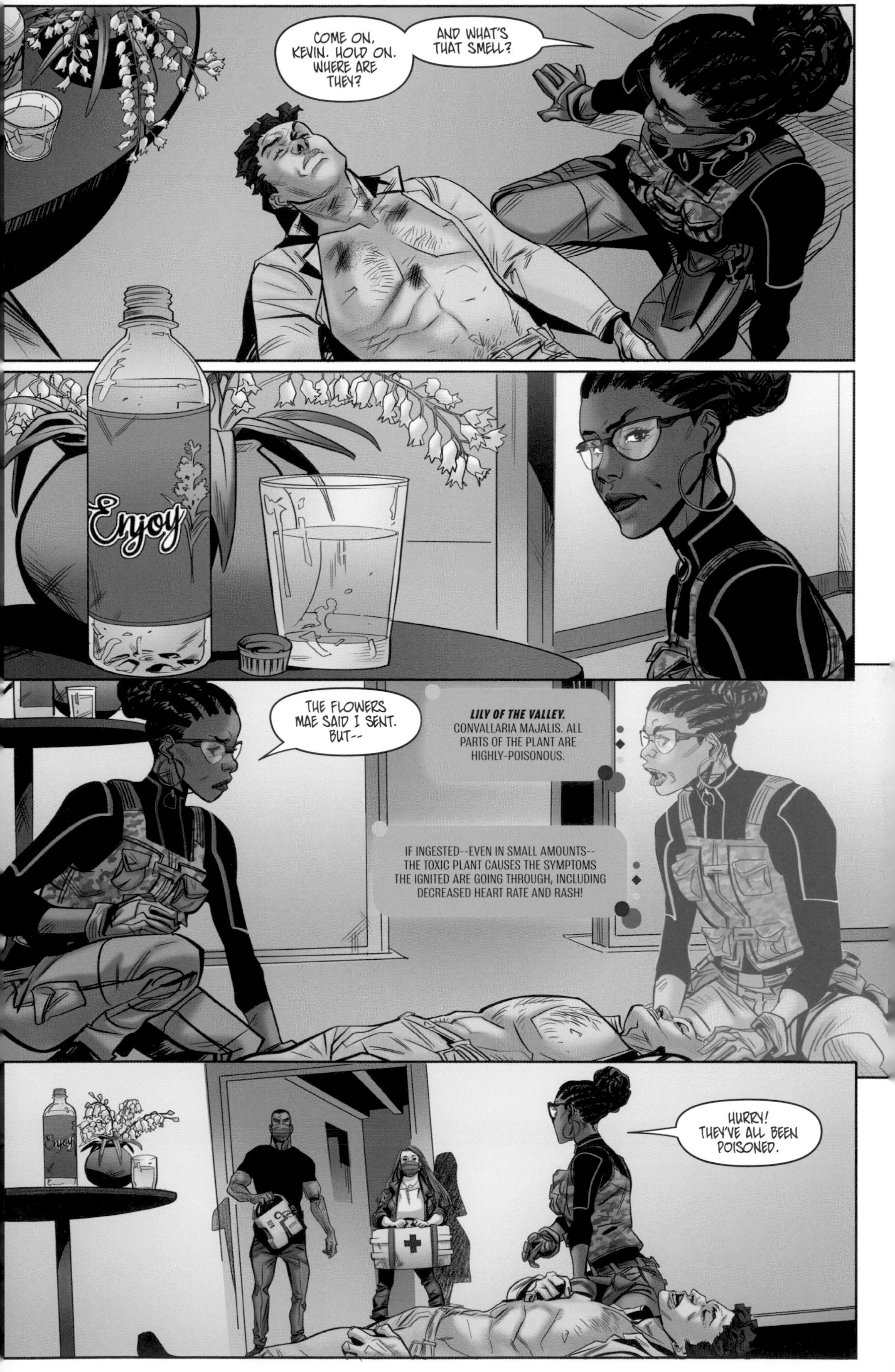
COME ON, KEVIN. HOLD ON. WHERE ARE THEY?
AND WHAT'S THAT SMELL?
Enjoy
THE FLOWERS MAE SAID I SENT. BUT--
LILY OF THE VALLEY. CONVALLARIA MAJALIS. ALL PARTS OF THE PLANT ARE HIGHLY-POISONOUS.
IF INGESTED--EVEN IN SMALL AMOUNTS--THE TOXIC PLANT CAUSES THE SYMPTOMS THE IGNITED ARE GOING THROUGH, INCLUDING DECREASED HEART RATE AND RASH!
Enjoy
HURRY! THEY'VE ALL BEEN POISONED.

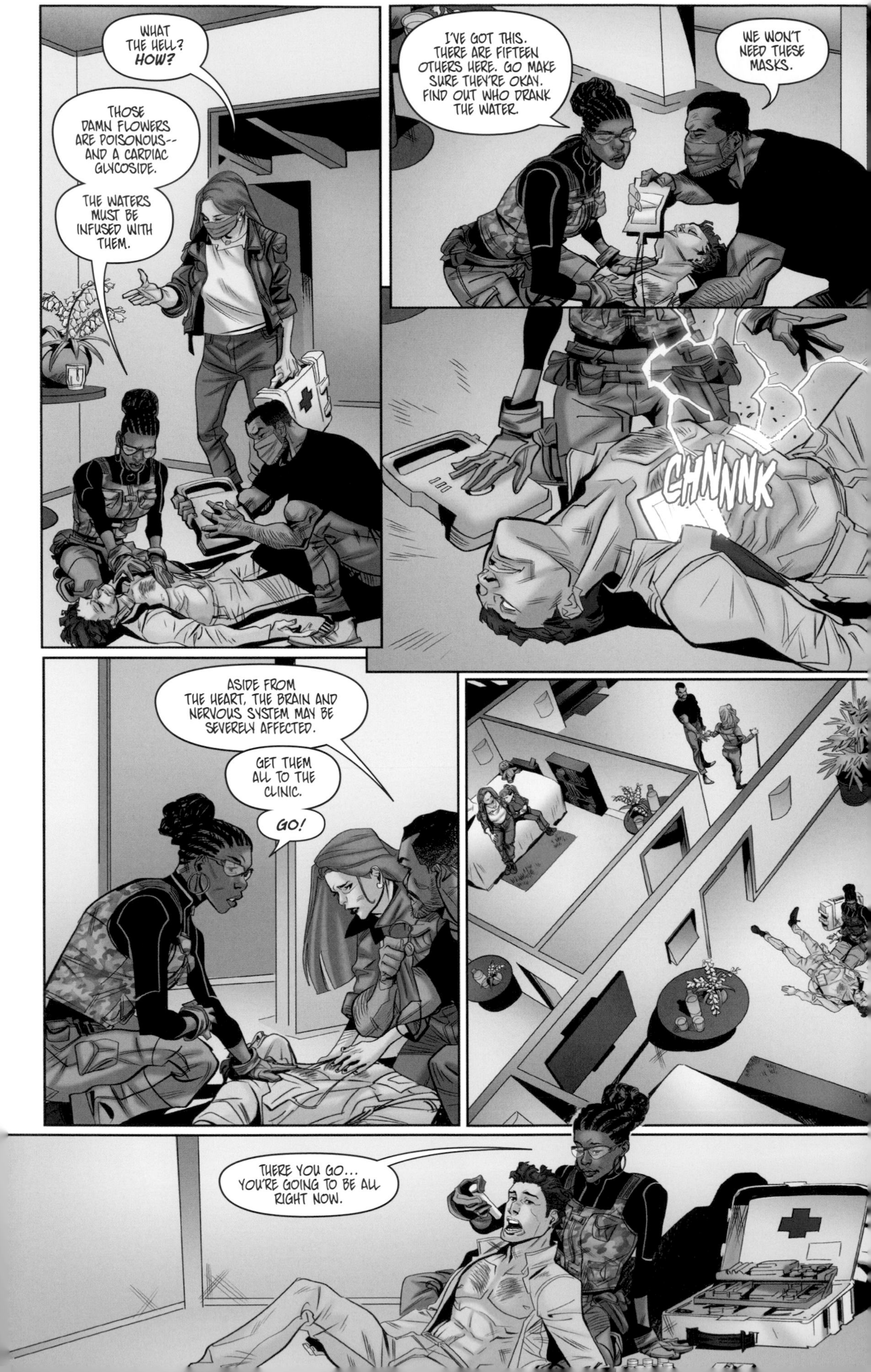
WHAT THE HELL? **HOW?**
THOSE DAMN FLOWERS ARE POISONOUS-- AND A CARDIAC GLYCOSIDE.
THE WATERS MUST BE INFUSED WITH THEM.
I'VE GOT THIS. THERE ARE FIFTEEN OTHERS HERE. GO MAKE SURE THEY'RE OKAY. FIND OUT WHO DRANK THE WATER.
WE WON'T NEED THESE MASKS.
CHNNNK
ASIDE FROM THE HEART, THE BRAIN AND NERVOUS SYSTEM MAY BE SEVERELY AFFECTED.
GET THEM ALL TO THE CLINIC.
GO!
THERE YOU GO... YOU'RE GOING TO BE ALL RIGHT NOW.

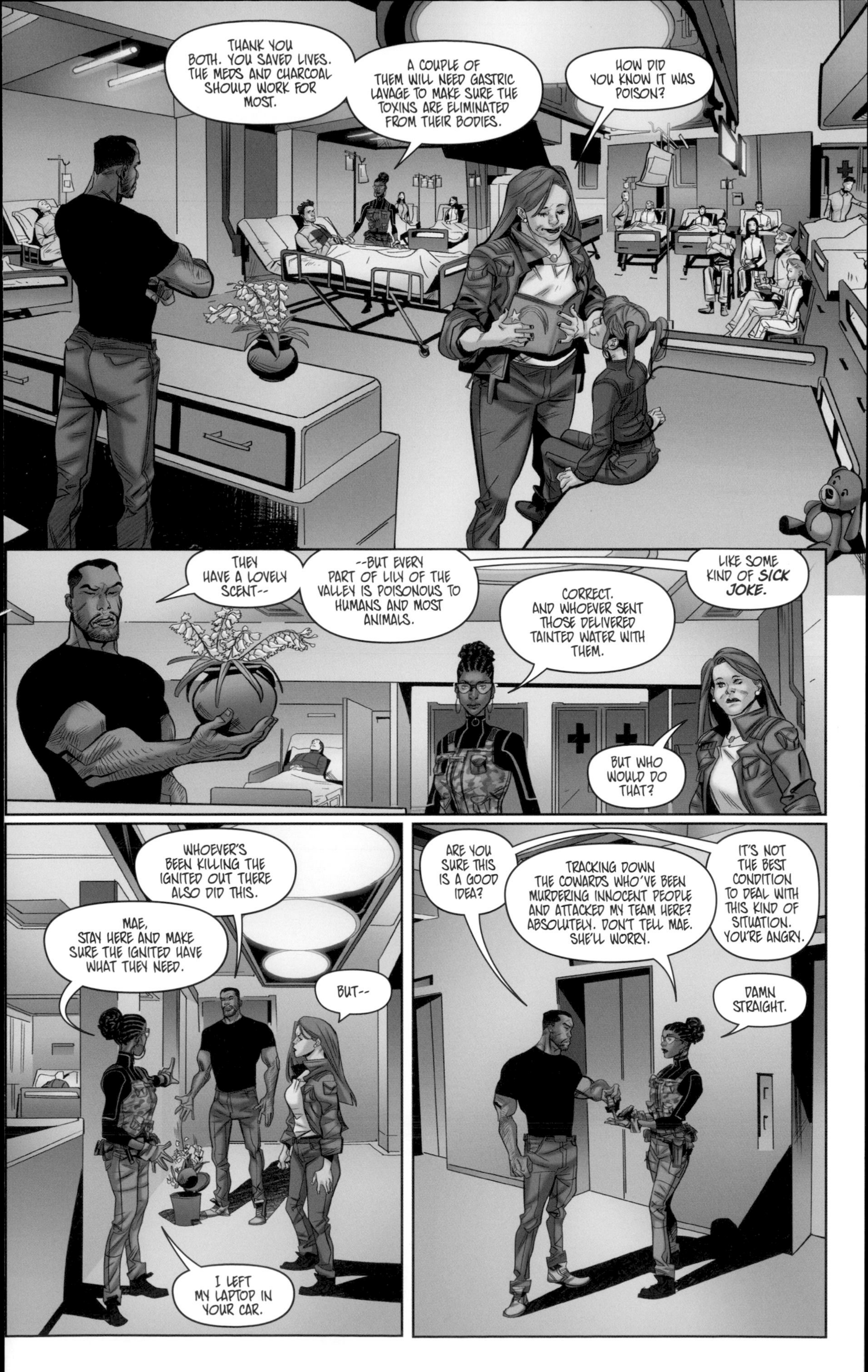
THANK YOU BOTH. YOU SAVED LIVES. THE MEDS AND CHARCOAL SHOULD WORK FOR MOST.
A COUPLE OF THEM WILL NEED GASTRIC LAVAGE TO MAKE SURE THE TOXINS ARE ELIMINATED FROM THEIR BODIES.
HOW DID YOU KNOW IT WAS POISON?
THEY HAVE A LOVELY SCENT--
--BUT EVERY PART OF LILY OF THE VALLEY IS POISONOUS TO HUMANS AND MOST ANIMALS.
LIKE SOME KIND OF SICK JOKE.
CORRECT. AND WHOEVER SENT THOSE DELIVERED TAINTED WATER WITH THEM.
BUT WHO WOULD DO THAT?
WHOEVER'S BEEN KILLING THE IGNITED OUT THERE ALSO DID THIS.
MAE, STAY HERE AND MAKE SURE THE IGNITED HAVE WHAT THEY NEED.
BUT--
I LEFT MY LAPTOP IN YOUR CAR.
ARE YOU SURE THIS IS A GOOD IDEA?
IT'S NOT THE BEST CONDITION TO DEAL WITH THIS KIND OF SITUATION. YOU'RE ANGRY.
TRACKING DOWN THE COWARDS WHO'VE BEEN MURDERING INNOCENT PEOPLE AND ATTACKED MY TEAM HERE? ABSOLUTELY. DON'T TELL MAE. SHE'LL WORRY.
DAMN STRAIGHT.

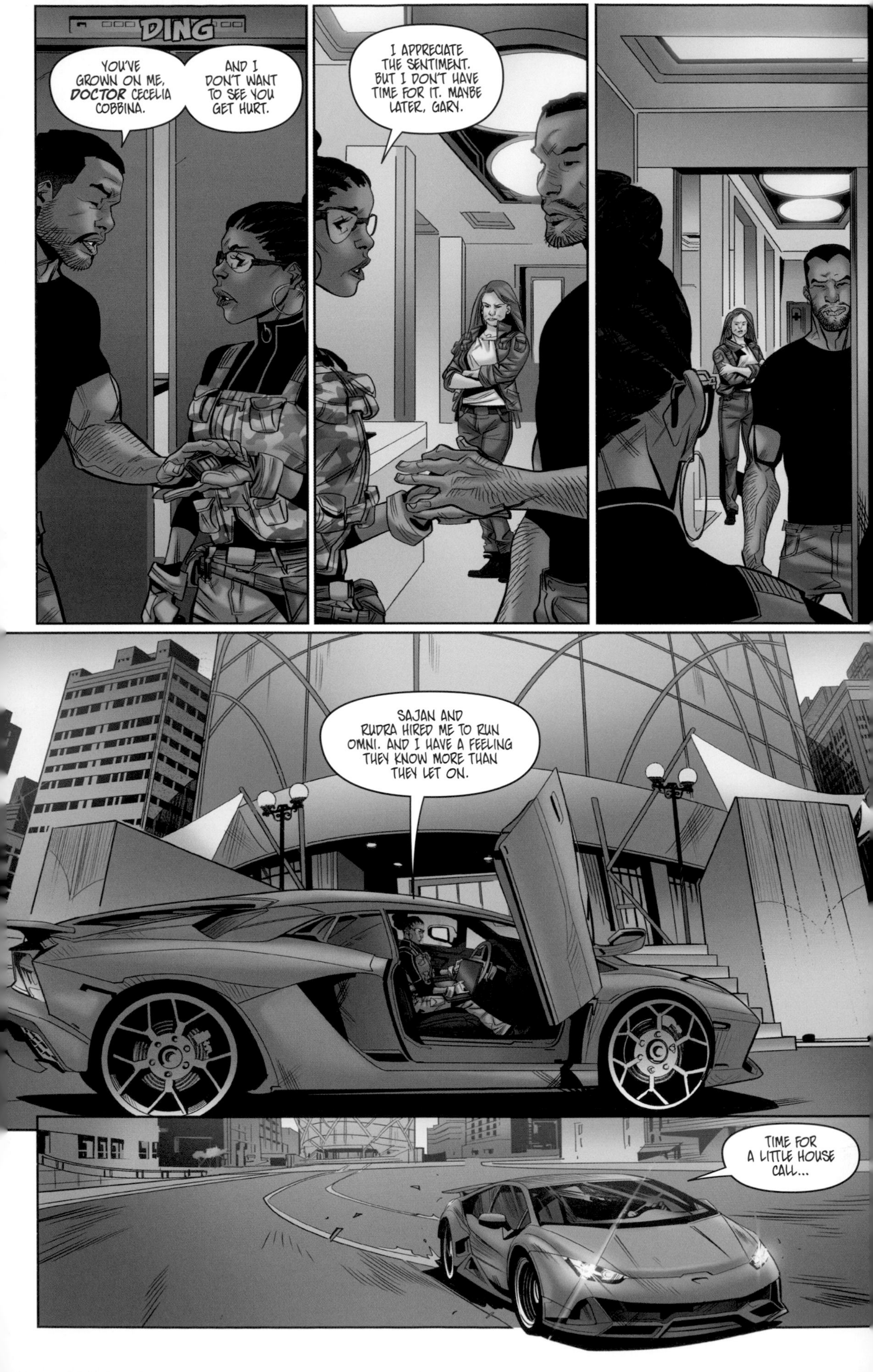
DING
YOU'VE GROWN ON ME, **DOCTOR** CECELIA COBBINA.
AND I DON'T WANT TO SEE YOU GET HURT.
I APPRECIATE THE SENTIMENT. BUT I DON'T HAVE TIME FOR IT. MAYBE LATER, GARY.
SAJAN AND RUDRA HIRED ME TO RUN OMNI. AND I HAVE A FEELING THEY KNOW MORE THAN THEY LET ON.
TIME FOR A LITTLE HOUSE CALL...

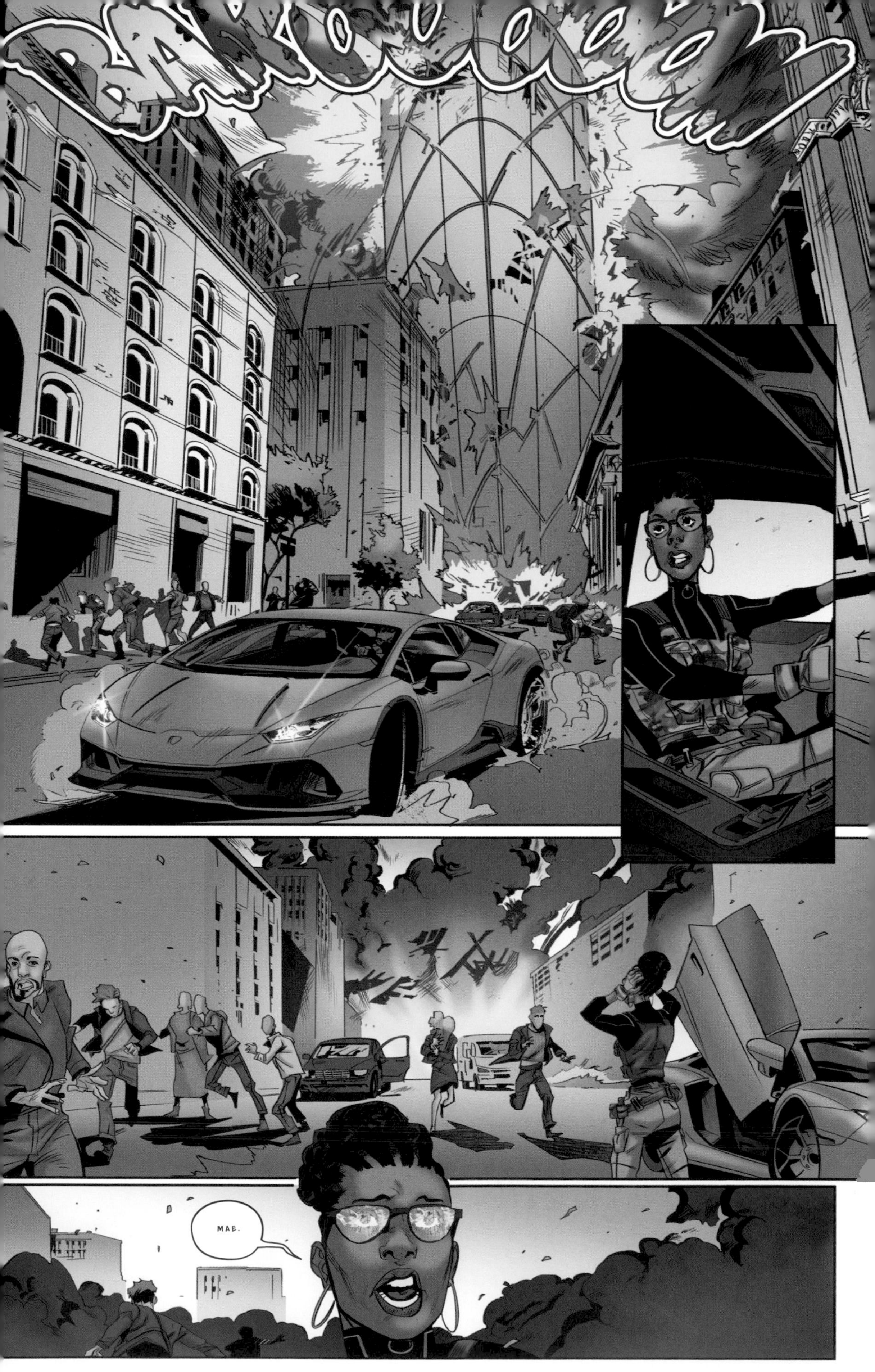
MAE.

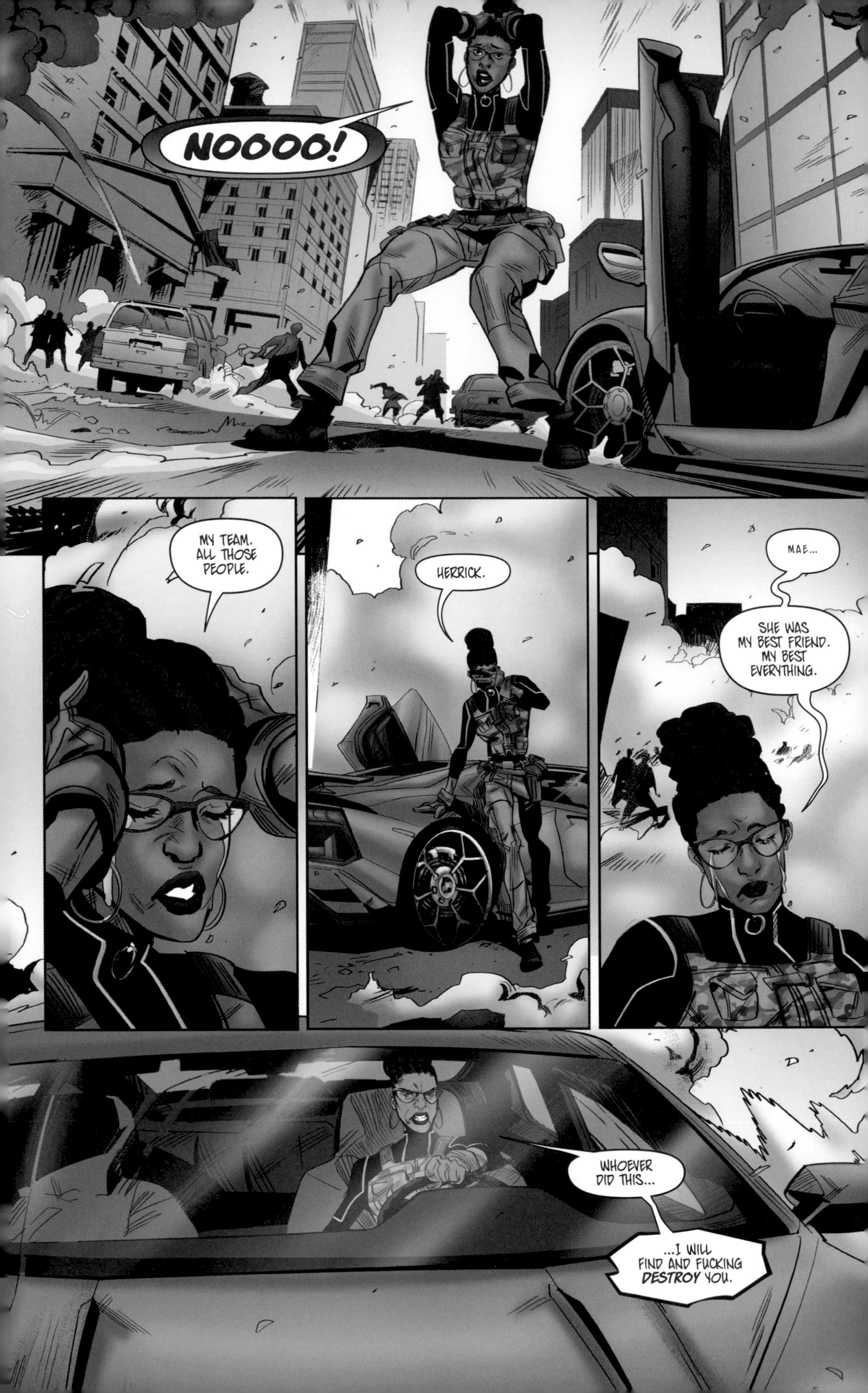
NOOOO!
MY TEAM. ALL THOSE PEOPLE.
HERRICK.
MAE...
SHE WAS MY BEST FRIEND. MY BEST EVERYTHING.
WHOEVER DID THIS...
...I WILL FIND AND FUCKING DESTROY YOU.

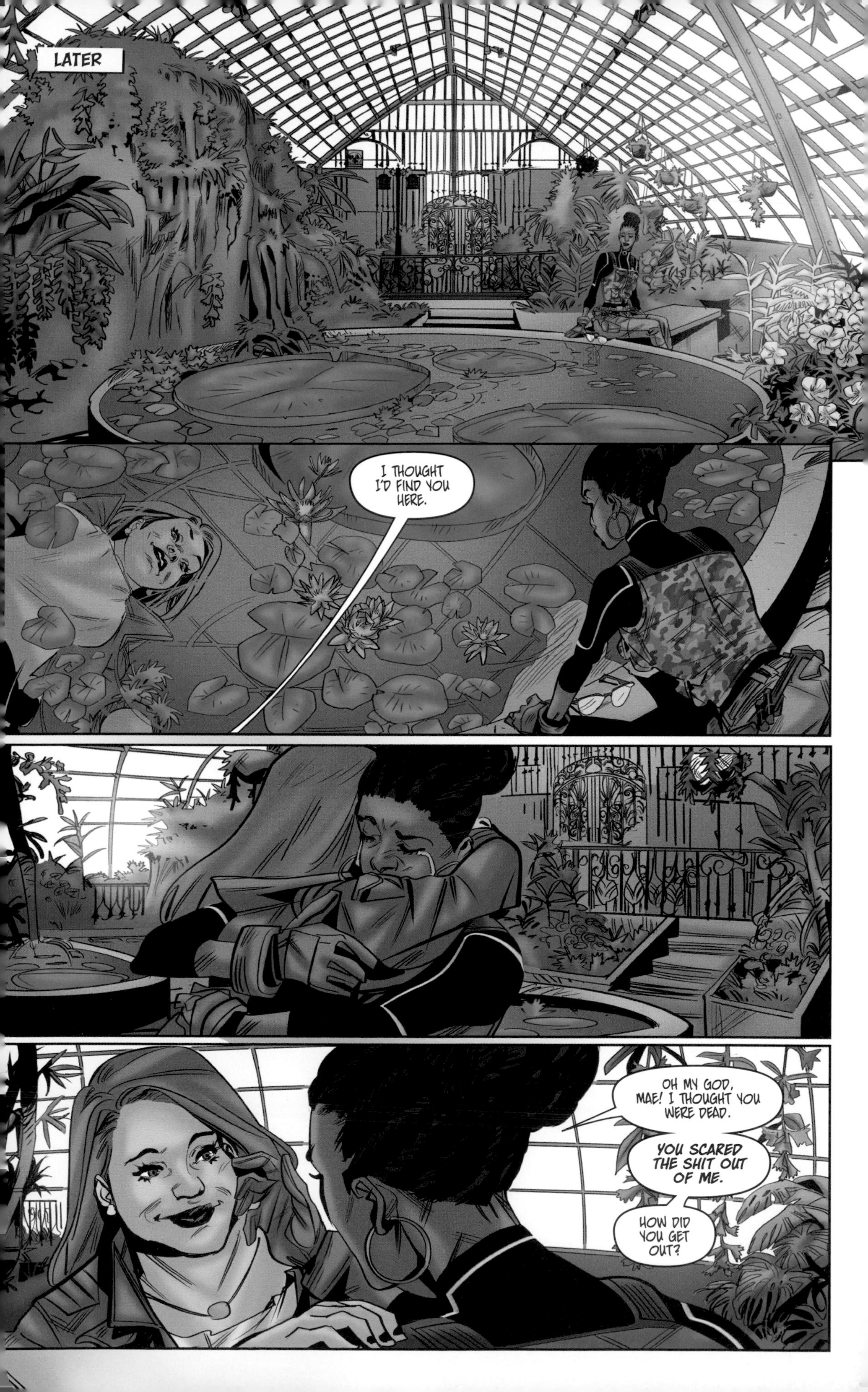
LATER
I THOUGHT I'D FIND YOU HERE.
OH MY GOD, MAE! I THOUGHT YOU WERE DEAD.
YOU SCARED THE SHIT OUT OF ME.
HOW DID YOU GET OUT?

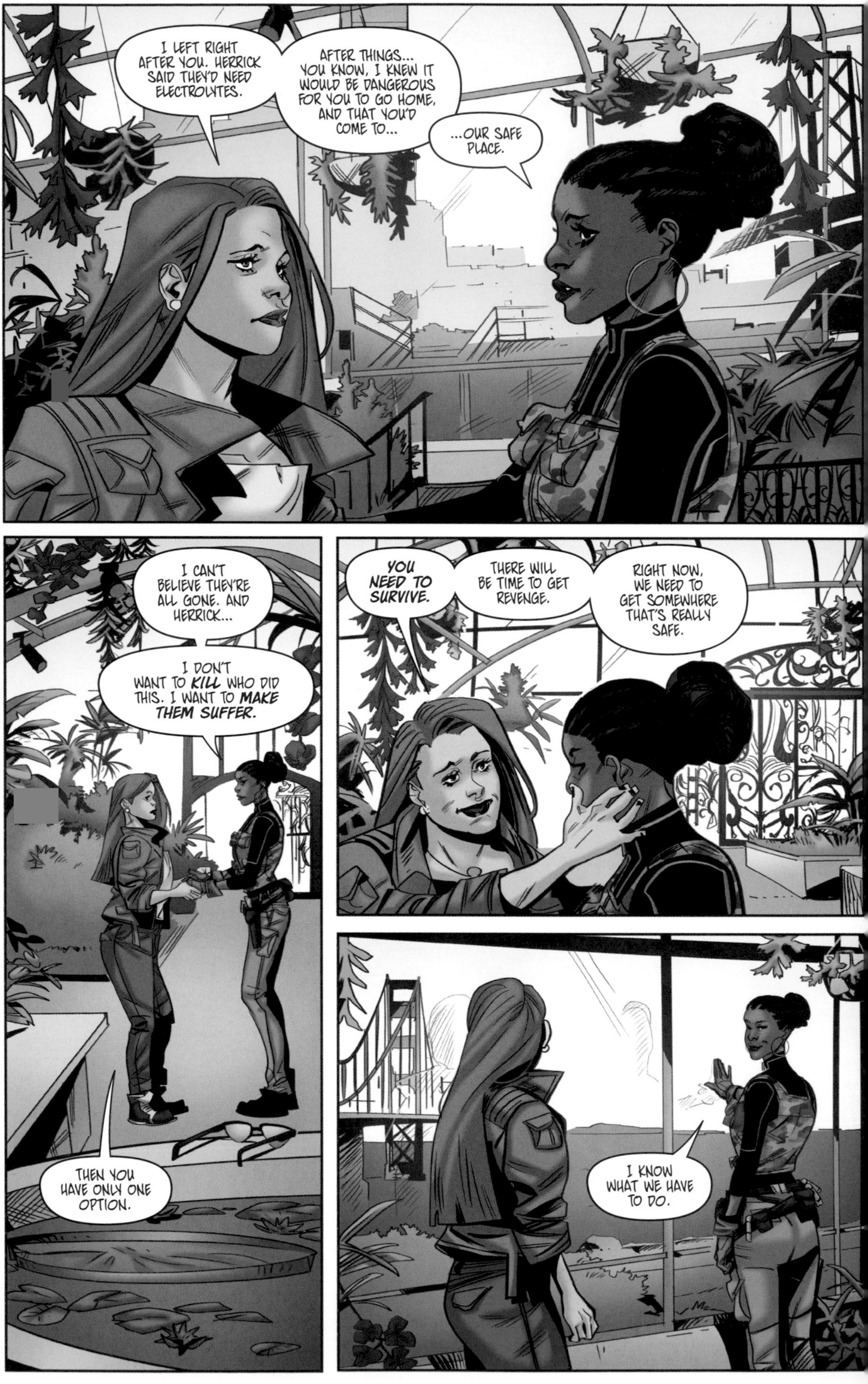
I LEFT RIGHT AFTER YOU. HERRICK SAID THEY'D NEED ELECTROLYTES.
AFTER THINGS... YOU KNOW, I KNEW IT WOULD BE DANGEROUS FOR YOU TO GO HOME, AND THAT YOU'D COME TO...
...OUR SAFE PLACE.
I CAN'T BELIEVE THEY'RE ALL GONE. AND HERRICK...
I DON'T WANT TO **KILL** WHO DID THIS. I WANT TO **MAKE THEM SUFFER.**
THEN YOU HAVE ONLY ONE OPTION.
YOU NEED TO SURVIVE.
THERE WILL BE TIME TO GET REVENGE.
RIGHT NOW, WE NEED TO GET SOMEWHERE THAT'S REALLY SAFE.
I KNOW WHAT WE HAVE TO DO.

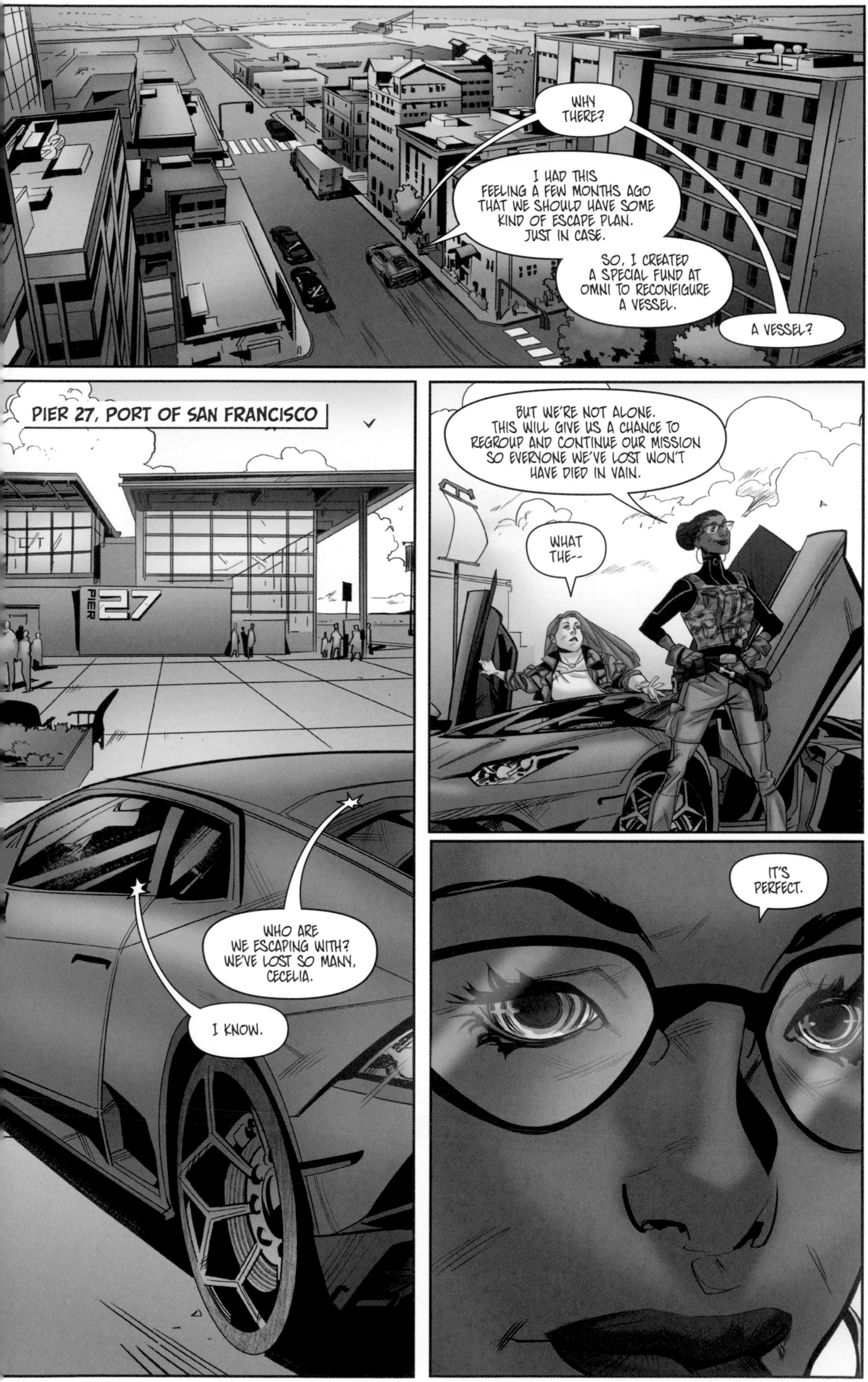
WHY THERE?
I HAD THIS FEELING A FEW MONTHS AGO THAT WE SHOULD HAVE SOME KIND OF ESCAPE PLAN. JUST IN CASE.
SO, I CREATED A SPECIAL FUND AT OMNI TO RECONFIGURE A VESSEL.
A VESSEL?
PIER 27, PORT OF SAN FRANCISCO
PIER 27
WHO ARE WE ESCAPING WITH? WE'VE LOST SO MANY, CECELIA.
I KNOW.
BUT WE'RE NOT ALONE. THIS WILL GIVE US A CHANCE TO REGROUP AND CONTINUE OUR MISSION SO EVERYONE WE'VE LOST WON'T HAVE DIED IN VAIN.
WHAT THE--
IT'S PERFECT.

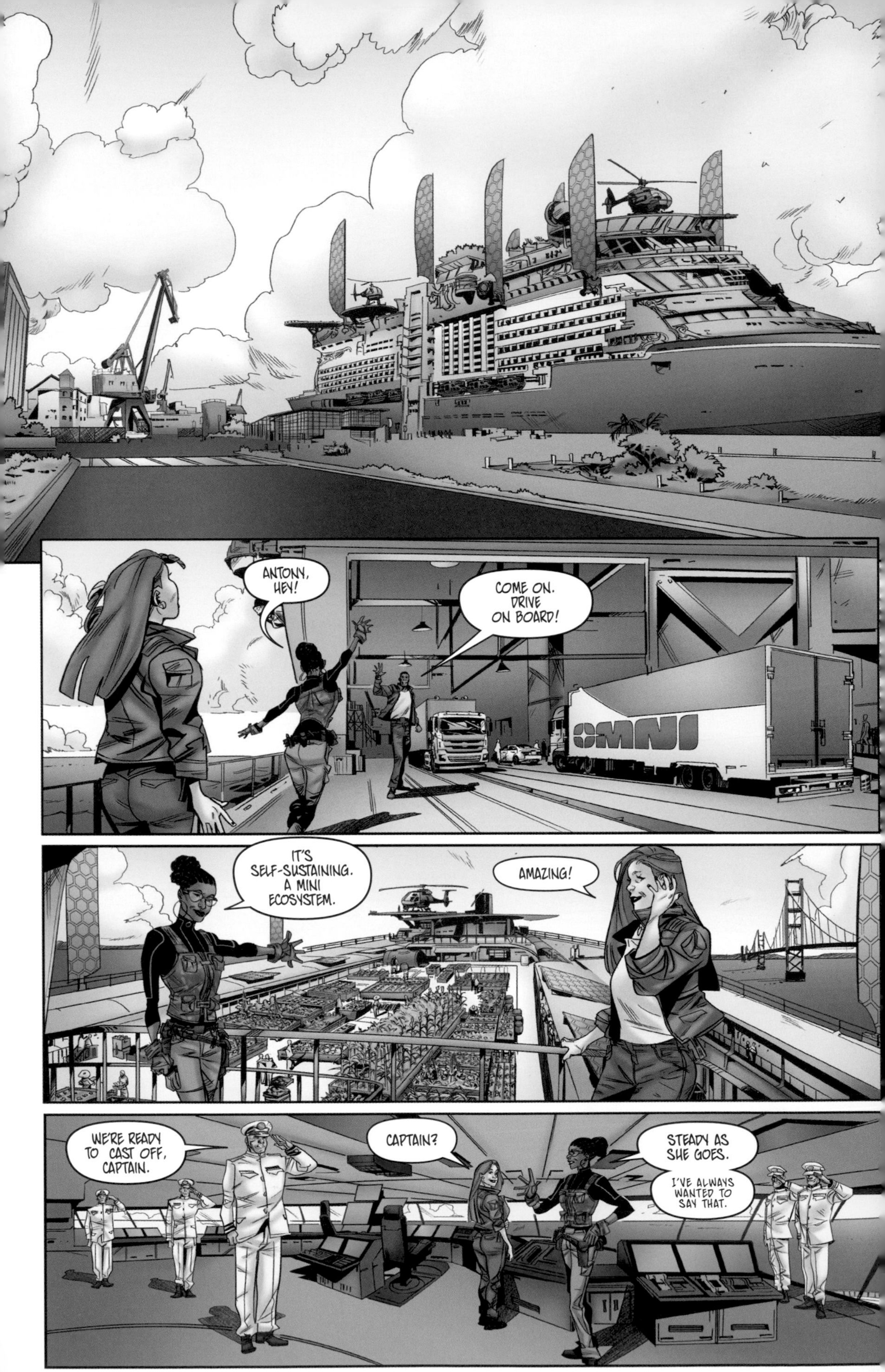
ANTONY, HEY!
COME ON. DRIVE ON BOARD!
OMNI
IT'S SELF-SUSTAINING. A MINI ECOSYSTEM.
AMAZING!
WE'RE READY TO CAST OFF, CAPTAIN.
CAPTAIN?
STEADY AS SHE GOES.
I'VE ALWAYS WANTED TO SAY THAT.

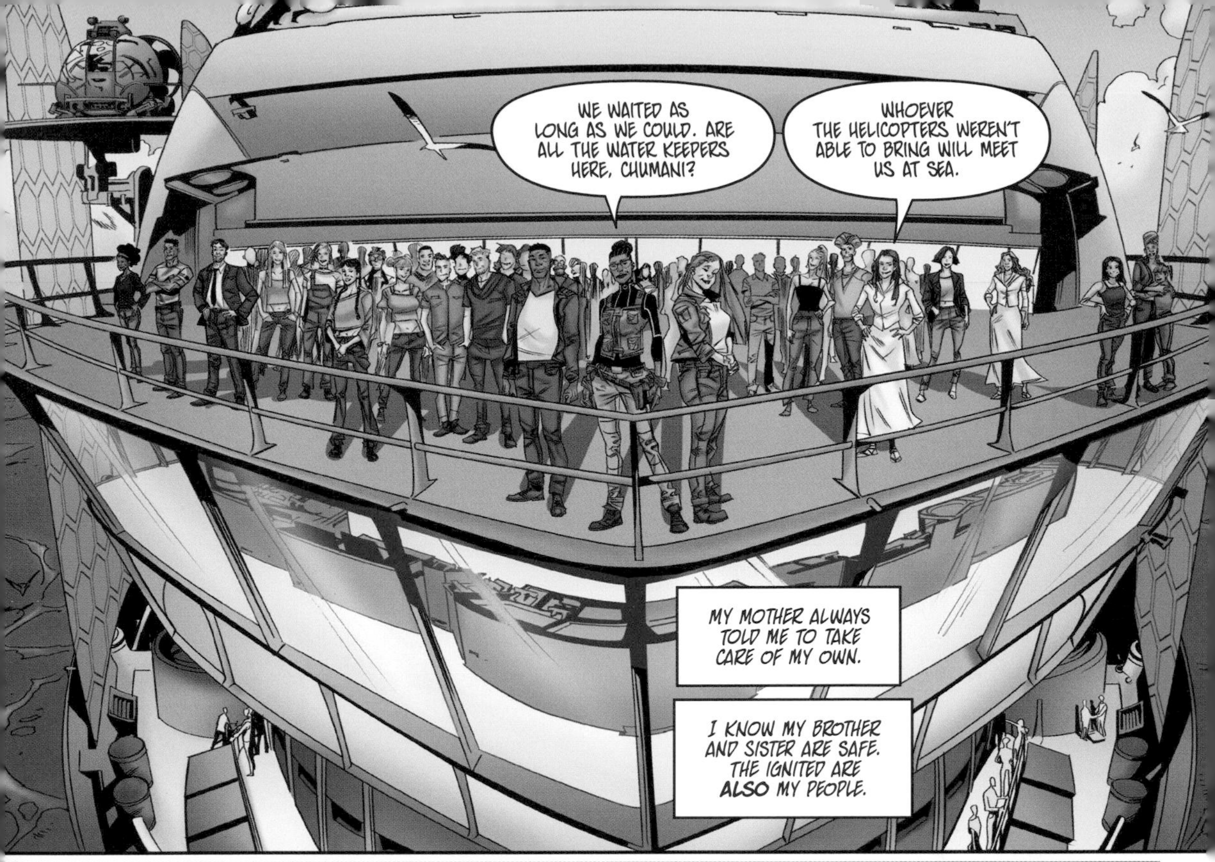
WE WAITED AS LONG AS WE COULD. ARE ALL THE WATER KEEPERS HERE, CHUMANI?
WHOEVER THE HELICOPTERS WEREN'T ABLE TO BRING WILL MEET US AT SEA.
MY MOTHER ALWAYS TOLD ME TO TAKE CARE OF MY OWN.
I KNOW MY BROTHER AND SISTER ARE SAFE. THE IGNITED ARE **ALSO** MY PEOPLE.
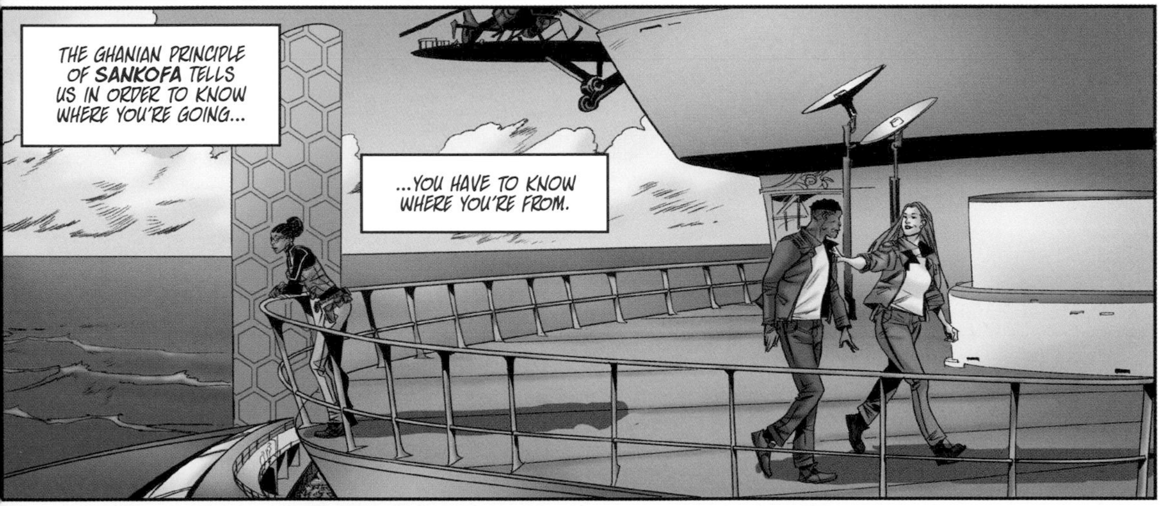
THE GHANIAN PRINCIPLE OF **SANKOFA** TELLS US IN ORDER TO KNOW WHERE YOU'RE GOING...
...YOU HAVE TO KNOW WHERE YOU'RE FROM.
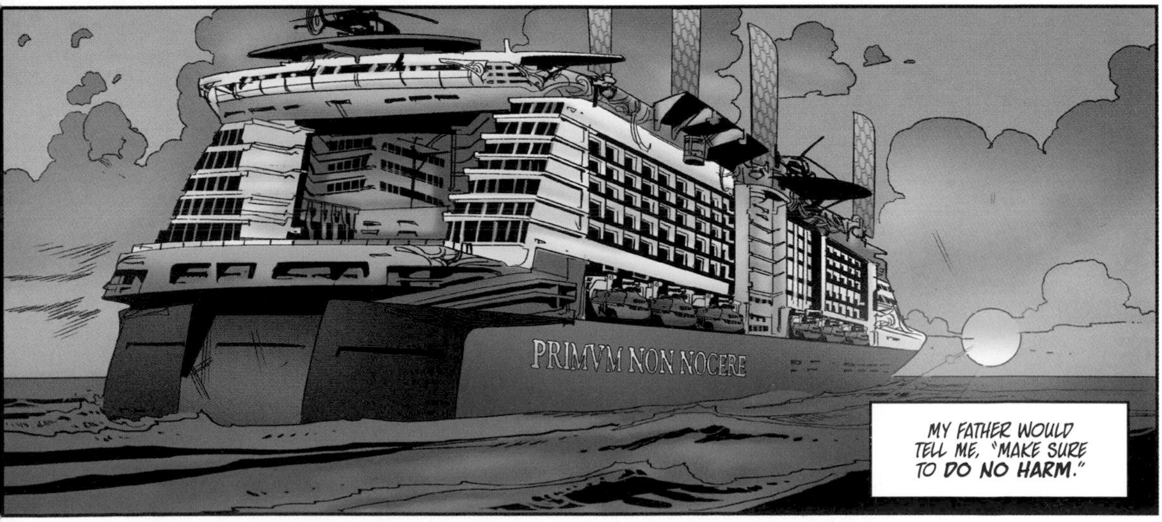
PRIMVM NON NOCERE
MY FATHER WOULD TELL ME, "MAKE SURE TO **DO NO HARM**."

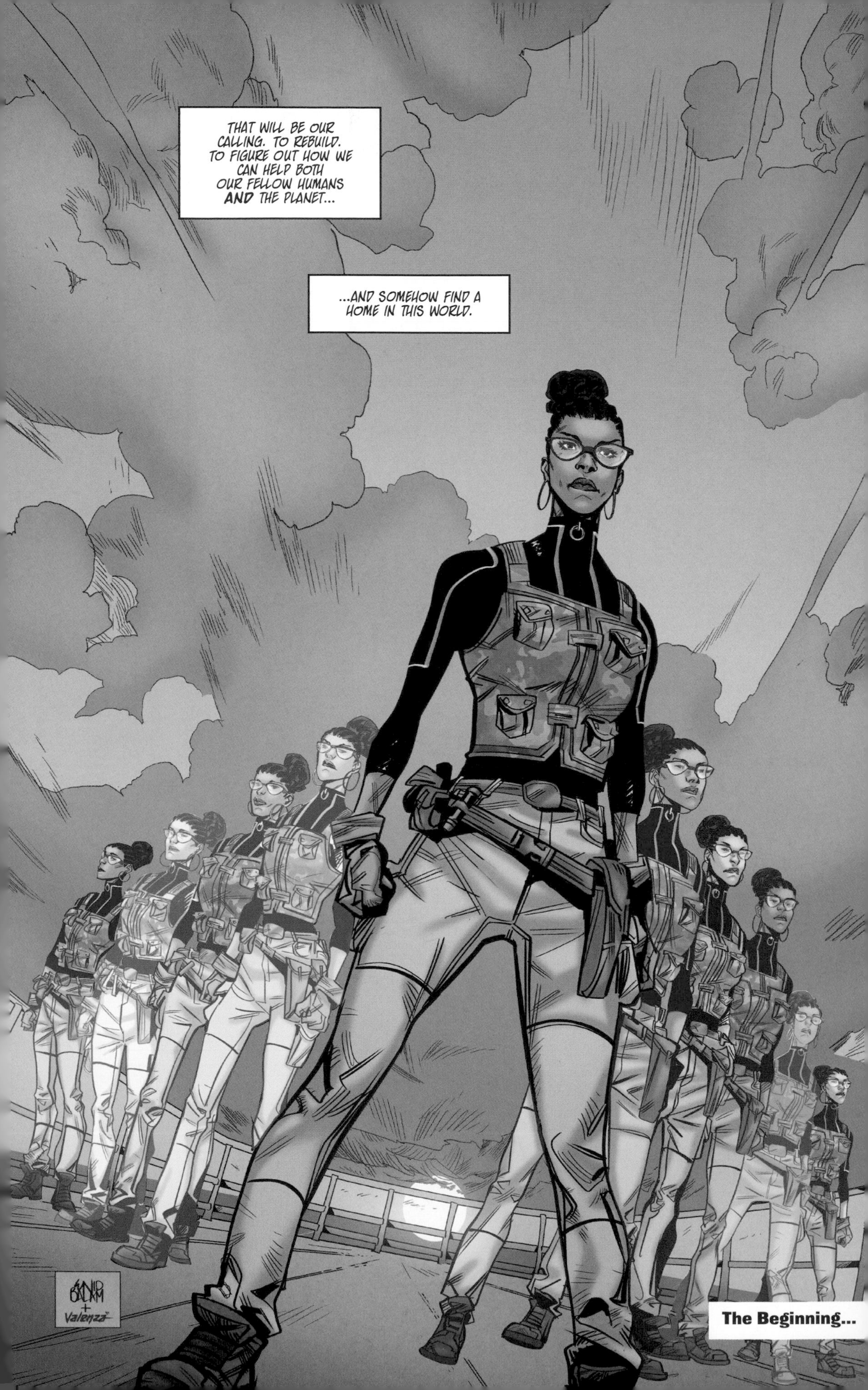
THAT WILL BE OUR CALLING. TO REBUILD. TO FIGURE OUT HOW WE CAN HELP BOTH OUR FELLOW HUMANS **AND** THE PLANET...
...AND SOMEHOW FIND A HOME IN THIS WORLD.
The Beginning...

OMNI PRESCRIPTIONS

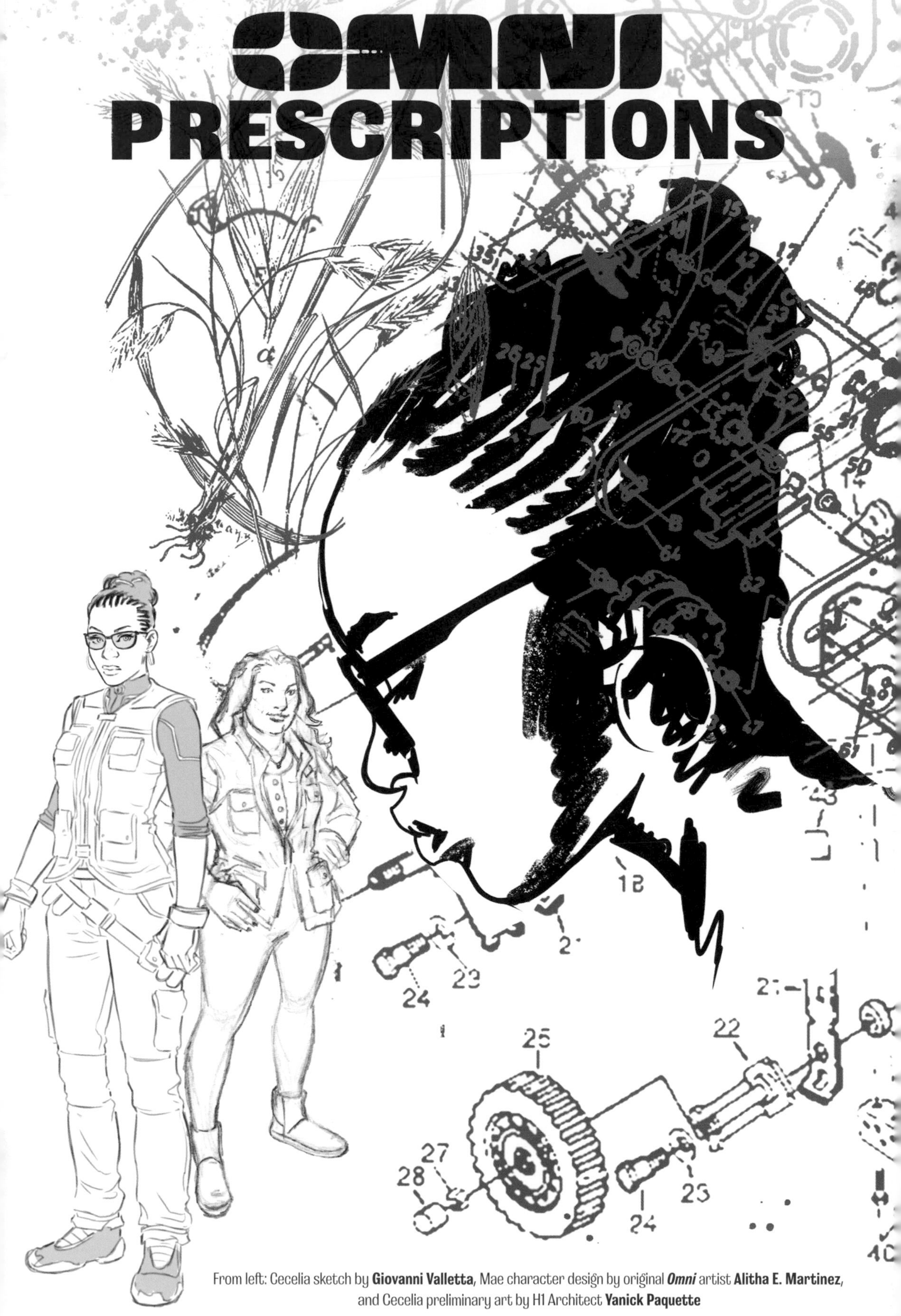

From left: Cecelia sketch by **Giovanni Valletta**, Mae character design by original ***Omni*** artist **Alitha E. Martinez**, and Cecelia preliminary art by H1 Architect **Yanick Paquette**

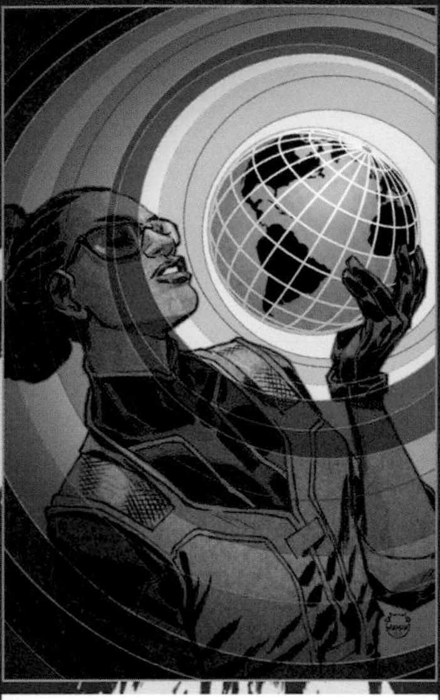

OMNI # 5 cover by Dave Johnson

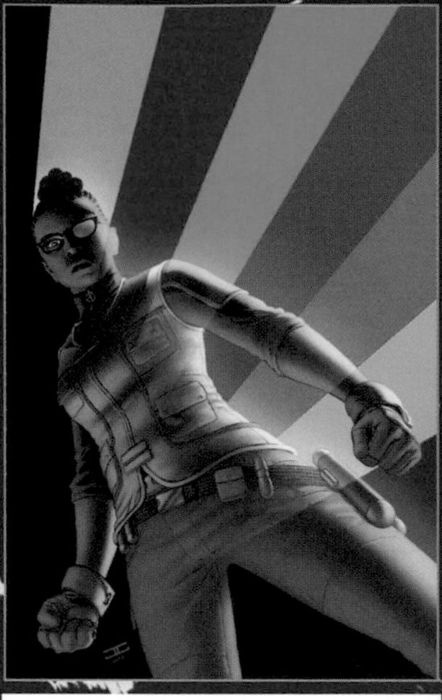

OMNI #6 cover by John Cassaday & Laura Martin

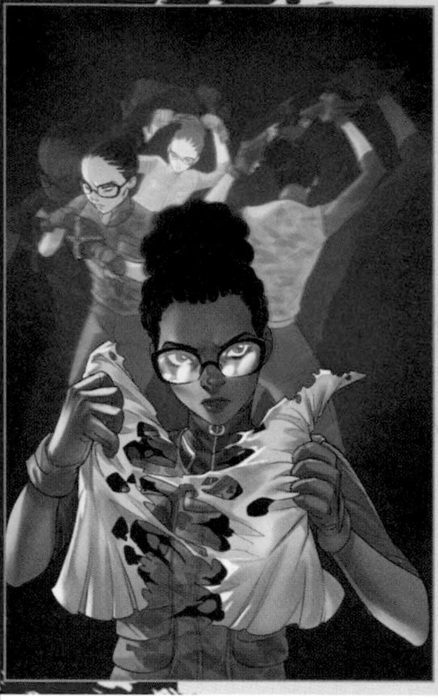

OMNI #7 cover by Mirka Andolfo

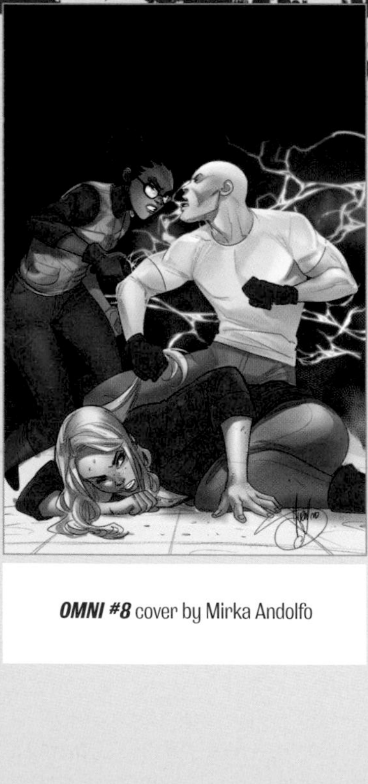

OMNI #8 cover by Mirka Andolfo

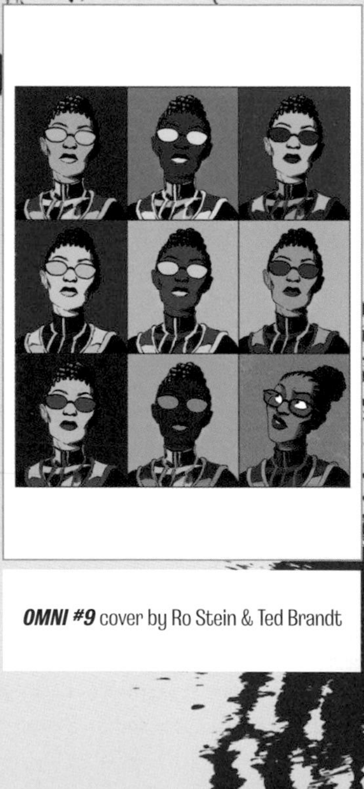

OMNI #9 cover by Ro Stein & Ted Brandt

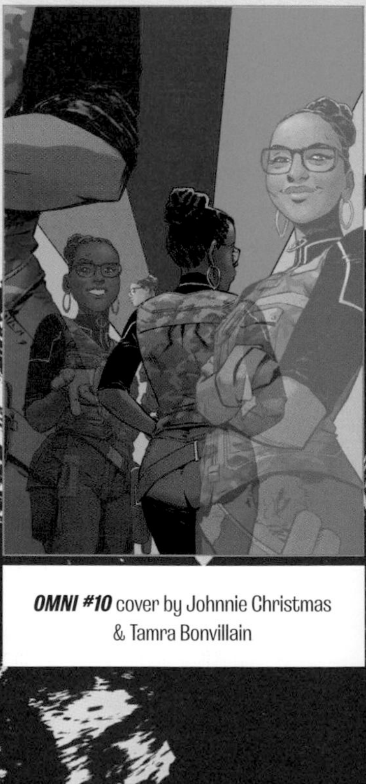

OMNI #10 cover by Johnnie Christmas & Tamra Bonvillain

VIRAGO AND THE POWER OF ONE

A virago is a woman who demonstrates exemplary and heroic qualities. The word comes from the Latin word virāgō, meaning a female warrior, heroine.

Since the beginning of humanity, women have been warriors and heroines. We've hunted and gathered, braved excruciating childbirth, led armies and countries, run for president and vice president, spied behind enemy lines, freed slaves, piloted night gliders over Nazi Germany, administered medicine on battlefields, sat on the highest courts, organized and marched against racism, nurtured children, ambushed sex traffickers, founded charities, made major scientific discoveries, pioneered in a vast array of industries, achieved heights in the arts. The list goes on and on. And yet, throughout most of the world, we are still treated as second-class citizens and are unheralded, underpaid, underestimated. However, we soldier on and rise up despite the challenges.

A momentous time is before all of us, regardless of gender and orientation, that tasks us to rise up against our own cowardice and ignorance, our hatred and lack of compassion, our fear, and irrationality. Women are as prone to these negative characteristics as anyone. And so, while I start from a point of my own origin as a cisgender female, I appeal to all of you to become warriors, not for one political party or religion or gender, but for humanity. We are quite literally on the brink of life ending as we've come to know it.

The signs, both enviromental and social, have been there for decades, and we've ignored them at our own peril. We see it happening on the West Coast, threatened by climate fires the extent of which was predicted by speculative writer Octavia Butler. To date, her extraordinary work has surprisingly not found its way to the forms of media that would have spread her urgent message more widely to the general public. We see it in how there is nothing good in the increasingly brutal and militarized police on the rise around the world. We have generations of old and young squeezed by the limitations of the coming years and a dark horizon of our own making that tells them their last days will be supremely difficult or their future as young adults will be terrifying and unpredictably dangerous.

And yet, because I am a realist with an optimistic streak, I believe there is hope. I have always tried to focus on the here and now. And in that sense, how we meet where we are can be as important as agonizing over where we have been and will be. With the current facts, it can be debilitating and defeatist to not focus on what is right before us. Here is an uncompromising fact: We all die. Sooner or later, no matter how smart, rich, connected, healthy, lucky, protected, or powerful you are, you die. It is part of the natural order of things. Accepting this fact gives us an opportunity, regardless of how dire the worldwide circumstances, to live as well as we can, as compassionately and bravely as we can right now, today. It gives us a chance to act in love toward each other and our planet, to give our all and not give up. To make the most of every moment we have. Because we should always live that way. It provides us with the fire to fiercely fight for justice because there is no time like the present to uplift human rights and civil rights for as many as possible.

In 1957, Benton Resnick, Alfred Hassler, and Sy Barry wrote and illustrated a comic book of the moment called "Martin Luther King and The Montgomery Story." It inspired and gave strength to 18-year-old John Lewis. A simple thing—words, pen, ink, and color to paper—had the power to help transform our world. I hear my father's voice echoing in my memory, singing the Civil Rights Movement anthem "We shall overcome someday." And I know that someday is now. Don't wait for more innocents to die. No more Georges, Breonnas, Ahmauds, Dijons, or Sandras. No more avoidance of the plight of our indigenous brothers and sisters who suffer most. Don't stand by as another transgender death is reported. Don't stay silent as immigrants are villainized and the mentally ill victimized. Don't shut your eyes as the land and water are threatened. You don't have to wait for a leader or organized action. You yourself are the change, the power to transform. Be proactive and speak out in any and every way at your disposal: Voting, protesting, posting, writing, discussing, boycotting, teaching, praying, meditating, filming, drawing, hiring, confronting. Don't give up and don't stop.

One voice, one action, one step, gathered with others makes a mighty tide. Like Cecelia Cobbina in OMNI and the gathered Ignited, and like the Water Keepers acting as one to save lives, each person can be a beacon for others, reflecting their courage, compassion, and strength to their neighbors, friends, co-workers, families. We can stand as individuals, but we cannot fight the darkness alone. It will swallow us up. Together, we can send it fleeing from the expanse of brightness that is released by our bold words put into action. This is our legacy. A legacy of Light that combats fear, hatred, violence, cowardice, greed. It uplifts us and joins us with the greatest and most loving deeds of our ancestors. The darkness cannot be allowed to divide us and write the narrative of our lives and convince us it has won. It cannot be allowed to gain that much power and hold sway over our imagination so much that it is all we see and seems undefeatable. It thinks it can act with impunity. Only if we let it. It thinks it can keep killing us. We can stop it in its tracks. It cannot take what we do not give it. It is desperate and fears one thing most of all... that we will all see it for what it is and stand unerringly against it and march forward together to show it doesn't belong here and has no place.

This will not be easy. It might mean facing your dark side when it's uncomfortable or fighting when you'd rather sit it out or take the high road. It could mean embracing others in love when it's the last thing you want to do and you're not sure they deserve it. It will require consistency and stamina but also self-forgiveness and self-love, which is difficult for many of us. If we cannot find a way to love ourselves, we have no hope of helping anyone, let alone the world.

It gives me hope to know that you read these words and maybe, even in your frustration, anger, and sadness, you find a small ray of encouragement to make you stronger and help you make your stand. Know that you are not alone. Your bravery already moves me, and I stand with you in the power of all standing as one, and one standing for all.

—Melody Cooper
September 2020